Vocabulary Practice and Tests

GRADE 8

Vocabulary Practice

- Words in Context
- Analogies
- Multiple Meanings
- Synonyms, Antonyms
- Prefixes, Suffixes, Roots
- Word Origins

Vocabulary Tests

- Standardized Test Formats for Lesson Tests, Synonyms and Antonyms, Word Analysis, Multiple Meaning Words
- Sentence Completions

HOLT McDOUGAL
a division of Houghton Mifflin Harcourt

Consultant

Norbert Elliot, general editor of *Vocabulary Practice,* has a Ph.D. in English from The University of Tennessee. He is a professor of English at New Jersey Institute of Technology. A former site director for the National Writing Project, he has directed summer language arts institutes for kindergarten through twelfth-grade teachers in the public schools. A specialist in test development and evaluation of writing, Norbert Elliot has written books and articles on writing assessment, communication, and critical thinking. Dr. Elliot is the father of five children and is married to Lorna Jean Elliot, under whose care, he says, "everything thrives."

CONNECTING NEW WORDS AND PATTERNS **155**

SKILLS AND STRATEGIES
- Understanding Analogies
- Types of Analogies
- Solving Analogies

READING NEW WORDS IN CONTEXT **173**

SKILLS AND STRATEGIES
- Reading Longer Passages
- Reading Strategically

CONTEXT: The First Americans

CONTEXT: Coming to the United States

CONTEXT: Voices of the United States

Vocabulary Tests

COMMON ROOTS, PREFIXES, AND SUFFIXES

The following tables list some common roots, prefixes, and suffixes. Use these tables to help you determine the meaning of a word by examining its structure.

ROOTS		
BASE	**MEANING**	**EXAMPLES**
act	to do, drive	**act**ion, **act**or, re**act**, trans**act**, en**act**
alt	high	**alt**itude, **alt**imeter
ann, enn	year	**ann**ual, per**enn**ial, bicent**enn**ial
aqua	water	**aqua**rium, **aqua**marine, **aqua**naut
aster, astro	star	**astro**nomy, **astro**nomical, **aster**isk
aud	to hear	**aud**ience, **aud**itorium, **aud**ible
biblio, bibli	book	**biblio**grapher, **biblio**mania, **bibli**cal
bio	life	**bio**logy, **bio**chemistry, **bio**degradable
cede	to go; to yield	inter**cede**, super**cede**, con**cede**
cent	one hundred	per**cent**, bi**cent**ennial, **cent**ennial
chrono	time	**chrono**logy, **chrono**meter, **chrono**scope
circ, circum	around	**circum**ference, **circ**le, **circ**ular
cred	to believe, trust	**cred**ibility, in**cred**ible, **cred**it, **cred**ential
dem	people	**dem**ocracy, **dem**agogue, epi**dem**ic
dent	tooth	**dent**ist, **dent**al, **dent**ifrice
dic, dict	to say, to speak; to assert	**dict**ion, **dict**ionary, **dict**ate
dur	hard, lasting	**dur**ation, **dur**able, en**dur**e
fin	end, limit	**fin**ish, **fin**ite, in**fin**ite, **fin**al
gen	race, family, kind	**gen**ealogy, **gen**eral, **gen**eration
geo	earth	**geo**logy, **geo**centric, **geo**dynamics
graph, gram	to write, draw, record	auto**graph**, tele**gram**, para**graph**
hab	to have, hold; to dwell	**hab**it, **hab**itat, in**hab**it
hydro	water	**hydro**gen, **hydro**dynamics, **hydro**plane
hypo	under, below	**hypo**dermic, **hypo**tension, **hypo**thermia
jur, jus, judic	law, right, judgment	**jur**ist, **jus**tify, **judic**ial
leg	law	**leg**al, **leg**islator, **leg**itimate
loc	place	**loc**al, **loc**alize, re**loc**ate, dis**loc**ate

ROOTS *(continued)*

BASE	MEANING	EXAMPLES
logue, logo	idea, word, speech, reason	dialogue, monologue, epilogue, logical
manu	hand	manual, manufacture
med, medi	middle	mediate, medieval, mediocre
meter, metr	measure	diameter, metric, millimeter
morph	form	pseudomorph, mesomorph, metamorphosis
micro	small	microscope, microorganism
mono	one	monologue, monogamy, monograph
mov, mob, mot	to move	mob, mobile, remove, motion
noc, nox	night	equinox, nocturnal, nocturne
ped	foot	pedestal, pedestrian, pedal
peri	around	perimeter, periscope, periphery
petr	rock	petrify, petroleum, petroglyph
phon	sound, voice	phonetics, phonics, telephone
photo	light	photography, photoflash, photogenic
port	to carry	import, export, portable
pyr	fire	pyromania, pyrotechnic
sci	to know	conscience, science, scientist
scope	to see	kaleidoscope, telescope, microscope
scrib, script	to write	inscribe, subscription, script
sign	mark	signal, signature, insignia
spec, spect, spic	to see, look at, behold	inspect, respect, spectacle, species
syn, sym	together	symphony, synthesize
techn	art, skill	technical, technology, technique
temp	time	temporary, temper
therm	heat	thermometer, thermonuclear
tract	to pull, draw	attract, retract, traction
vis, vid	to see, look	revision, video, visible
volve	roll	involve, revolve, revolution

PREFIXES

PREFIX	MEANING	EXAMPLES
ab–	from; away from	**ab**normal, **ab**duct, **ab**sent, **ab**hor
ad–	to; motion toward; addition to	**ad**apt, **ad**dict, **ad**here, **ad**mit
aero–	air	**aero**bic, **aero**biology, **aero**space
amphi–	both, around	**amphi**bian, **amphi**theater
an–	not	**an**archy, **an**esthesia, **an**onymous
ante–	before	**ante**bellum, **ante**cede, **ante**date
anti–	against; opposite; reverse	**anti**aircraft, **anti**freeze, **anti**biotics
ap–	to; nearness to	**ap**proximate, **ap**point, **ap**proach
auto–	self	**auto**matic, **auto**graph, **auto**biography
bene–	good	**bene**diction, **bene**factor, **bene**volent
bi–	two	**bi**facial, **bi**focal, **bi**ennial
circum–	around	**circum**navigate, **circum**ference
co–, con–	together	**co**author, **co**operate, **con**front, **con**found
contra–	against	**contra**dict, **contra**distinguish, **contra**ry
de–	opposite of; away from; undo	**de**activate, **de**form, **de**grade, **de**plete, **de**scend
dis–	opposite	**dis**agree, **dis**arm, **dis**continue, **dis**honest
ex–	out; beyond; away from; former	**ex**cel, **ex**clude, **ex**hale, **ex**ile
extra–	outside; beyond; besides	**extra**ordinary, **extra**curricular
for–	not	**for**bid, **for**get, **for**go
fore–	before	**fore**cast, **fore**word, **fore**stall, **fore**thought
hyper–	more than normal; too much	**hyper**active, **hyper**critical, **hyper**tension
il–	not	**il**legal, **il**legible, **il**literate, **il**logical
im–	into	**im**mediate, **im**merse, **im**migrate, **im**port
im–	not	**im**balance, **im**mature, **im**mobilize
in–	not; go into	**in**accurate, **in**active, **in**habit
inter–	among; between	**inter**action, **inter**cede, **inter**change
intra–	within	**intra**mural, **intra**state, **intra**venous
ir–	not	**ir**redeemable, **ir**regular, **ir**responsible
mal–	wrong; bad	**mal**adjusted, **mal**function, **mal**ice
mis–	wrong; bad; no; not	**mis**fire, **mis**behave, **mis**conduct
non–	not; opposite of	**non**committal, **non**conductor, **non**partisan
ob–	against	**ob**stacle, **ob**stinate, **ob**struct, **ob**ject

PREFIXES (continued)

PREFIX	MEANING	EXAMPLES
per–	through	**per**colate, **per**ceive
post–	after	**post**glacial, **post**graduate, **post**erior
pre–	before	**pre**amble, **pre**arrange, **pre**caution
pro–	before; for; in support of	**pro**gnosis, **pro**gram, **pro**logue, **pro**phet
pro–	forward	**pro**ceed, **pro**duce, **pro**ficient, **pro**gress
re–	back; again	**re**call, **re**cede, **re**flect, **re**pay
retro–	backward	**retro**active, **retro**spect, **retro**cede
se–	apart	**se**cure, **se**cede, **se**cession
self–	of the self	**self**-taught, **self**-worth, **self**-respect, **self**ish
semi–	half; partly	**semi**circle, **semi**formal, **semi**trailer
sub–	under; beneath	**sub**contract, **sub**ject, **sub**marine, **sub**merge
super–	over	**super**abound, **super**abundant, **super**human
sur–	over; above	**sur**charge, **sur**face, **sur**mount, **sur**pass
trans–	across; over	**trans**atlantic, **trans**cend, **trans**cribe, **trans**fer
ultra–	extremely	**ultra**liberal, **ultra**modern, **ultra**sonic
un–	not	**un**able, **un**comfortable, **un**certain, **un**happy

© Houghton Mifflin Harcourt Publishing Company

SUFFIXES

SUFFIX	MEANING	EXAMPLES
–able, ible	able to be; capable of being	intelligible, probable, inevitable
–ade	action or process	blockade, escapade, parade
–age	action or process	marriage, pilgrimage, voyage
–al, –ial	of; like; relating to; suitable for	potential, musical, national
–ance	act; process; quality; state of being	tolerance, alliance, acceptance
–ant	one who	assistant, immigrant, merchant
–ary	of; like; relating to	customary, honorary, obituary
–ate	characteristic of; to become	officiate, consecrate, activate
–cle, –icle	small	corpuscle, cubicle, particle
–cy	fact or state of being	diplomacy, privacy, relevancy
–dom	state or quality of	boredom, freedom, martyrdom
–ence	act or state of being	occurrence, conference
–ent	doing; having; showing	fraudulent, dependent, negligent
–er	one who; that which	boxer, rancher, employer
–ery	place for; act, practice of	surgery, robbery, nursery
–esque	like	picturesque, statuesque
–ess	female	goddess, heiress, princess
–ful	full of	careful, fearful, joyful, thoughtful
–ible	capable of being	collectible, legible, divisible
–ic	relating to; characteristic of	comic, historic, poetic, public
–ify	to make; to cause to be	modify, glorify, beautify, pacify
–ion	act, condition, or result of	calculation, action, confederation
–ish	of or belonging to; characterized by	tallish, amateurish, selfish
–ism	act, practice, or result of; example	barbarism, heroism, cyncism
–ity	condition; state of being	integrity, sincerity, calamity, purity
–ive	of; relating to; belonging to; tending to	inquisitive, active, creative
–ize	make; cause to be; subject to	jeopardize, standardize, computerize
–less	without	ageless, careless, thoughtless, tireless
–let	small	islet, leaflet, owlet, rivulet, starlet
–like	like; characteristic of	childlike, waiflike
–logy	study or theory of	biology, ecology, geology

SUFFIXES (continued)

SUFFIX	MEANING	EXAMPLES
–ly	every	daily, weekly, monthly, yearly
–ly	like; characteristic of	fatherly, queenly, deadly
–ly	resembling	officially, sincerely, kindly
–ment	action or process	development, government
–ment	state or quality of	amusement, amazement, predicament
–ment	product or thing	fragment, instrument, ornament
–ness	state or quality of being	kindness, abruptness, happiness
–or	one who	actor, auditor, doctor, donor
–ous	having; full of; characterized by	riotous, courageous, advantageous
–ship	state or quality of being	censorship, ownership, governorship
–some	like; tending to be	meddlesome, bothersome, noisome
–tude	state or quality of being	solitude, multitude, aptitude
–y	characterized by	thrifty, jealousy, frequency, sticky

CONTEXT

The words, phrases, or sentences around an unfamiliar word often provide clues about the word's meaning. In some cases, **signal words** can act as clues. See pp. 173–174 for further discussion of context clues.

Restatement Clues

Look for words and phrases that define an unfamiliar word or restate its meaning in familiar terms.

EXAMPLE   The dried rose was as *fragile* as a butterfly's wing. **In other words,** its delicate petals can be damaged easily.

From the context, readers can tell that *fragile* means "damaged easily." The phrase *in other words* signals that the words *easily damaged* restate the meaning of the word *fragile*.

Restatement Signal Words		
in other words	that is	these

Example Clues

Examples sometimes give us hints to a word's meaning. If an unfamiliar word means a certain type of thing, action, or characteristic, examples of the type can be excellent clues to the word's meaning.

EXAMPLE   When our neighbors travel, they always look for comfortable *accommodations,* **such as** a beach cottage, hotel suite, or mountain cabin.

From the context, readers can tell that the word *accommodations* means "a place to stay." The words *such as* signal that the list of places to stay provides examples of *accommodations.*

Example Signal Words		
for example	such as	in that
likewise	especially	

Contrast/Antonym Clues

Look for words or phrases that are the opposite of a word's meaning.

EXAMPLE   Knowledge is a *remedy* for many environmental problems, **but** knowledge without action cannot cure the ills.

From the context, readers can tell that *remedy* means "cure." The word ***but*** signals that *remedy* contrasts with the phrase "cannot cure."

Contrast/Antonym Signal Words			
but	not	in contrast	on the other hand
however	still	although	some . . . but others

Keyword Clues

Look for words or phrases that modify or are related to the unfamiliar word.

EXAMPLE   The two characters in my story believe it is their *destiny* to be enemies. Their elders have taught them that this is **meant to be.**

From the context, readers can tell that *destiny* means "something that necessarily happens to a person." The words *meant to be* signal the meaning of the word.

Definition/Explanation Clues

A sentence may actually define or explain an unfamiliar word.

EXAMPLE   Alan will help the woman once she **escapes** and becomes a *fugitive* from her troubled country.

From the context, readers can tell that *fugitive* means "runaway." The word *escapes* signals the meaning of the word.

How We Make New Words Our Own

Use the **Context Structure Sound Dictionary (CSSD)** strategy to improve your vocabulary, to make new words your own. Use one or more of the strategies to determine the meanings of each word you do not know. The exercises that follow will show you how to go about making new words your own.

HOW TO DO EXERCISE 1 *Wordbusting*

In these exercises, you will read the Vocabulary Word in a sentence. You will figure out the word's meaning by looking at its **context,** its **structure,** and its **sound.** Then you will look up the word in a **dictionary** and write its meaning *as it is used in the sentence.*

Here is an example of the Wordbusting strategy, using the word *manuscript.*

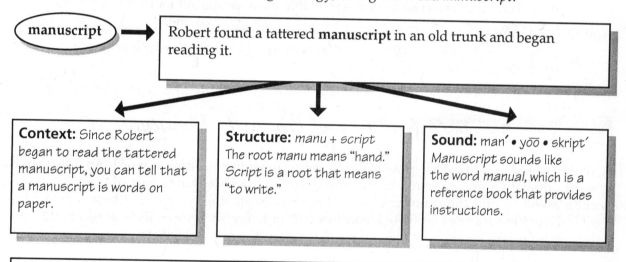

manuscript → Robert found a tattered **manuscript** in an old trunk and began reading it.

Context: Since Robert began to read the tattered manuscript, you can tell that a manuscript is words on paper.

Structure: *manu + script* The root *manu* means "hand." *Script* is a root that means "to write."

Sound: man' • yo͞o • skript' *Manuscript* sounds like the word *manual,* which is a reference book that provides instructions.

Dictionary: "a handwritten or typewritten document or paper, especially a copy of an author's work"

Hint #1 **Context:** Look for clues to the meaning of the word in the sentence. For example, "reading" is a keyword that helps reveal the meaning of *manuscript.*

Hint #2 **Structure:** Examine the word parts for roots, prefixes, and suffixes that you know. Consult the word-part tables on pages ix–xiv for meanings of parts you do not know.

Hint #3 **Sound:** Say the word aloud and listen for any word parts you know.

Hint #4 **Dictionary:** If you cannot determine a word's meaning from applying context, structure, and sound strategies, look up the unfamiliar word in a dictionary. Read all the definitions, and choose one that best fits the given sentence.

Context Clues ☞

In this exercise, you will again see the new word used in a sentence. This exercise gives you the word's definition, and you must match the word in the sentence with its meaning. The word may be used in the same way as it was used in Wordbusting, or it may be used in a new way.

Here's an example of a Context Clues exercise:

COLUMN A	COLUMN B
_D_ **1.** word: _____decrease_____ *v.* to become smaller; to lessen; *n.* a lessening	(D) Recent years have seen a steady rise in the number of cat owners. On the other hand, there has been a **decrease** in the number of dog owners.

Hint #1 First, scan the definitions in Column A. Then, read Column B and look for clues to the meaning of the word. Here, the words "on the other hand" tell us that the sentence containing the word **decrease** contrasts with the sentence containing the words "a steady rise." Thus, the correct definition is probably the opposite of "a steady rise."

Hint #2 Read column A and look for a likely definition of the word. In the example, the student chose the definition that contained the meaning "a lessening," which is most nearly the opposite of "a rise."

Hint #3 Write the word in the blank so that later you can find its definition at a glance.

HOW TO DO EXERCISE 3 *Like and Opposite Meanings* ☞

A synonym is a word that has practically the same meaning as another word. An antonym is a word opposite in meaning to another word. In the Like Meanings part of Exercise 3, you will be asked to find the synonym for (or, in some cases, the phrase that best defines) the Vocabulary Word. In the Opposite Meanings part of Exercise 3, you will be asked to find the antonym for (or, in some cases, the phrase that means the opposite of) the Vocabulary Word.

Here is an example of a Like Meanings item:

21. decrease the shedding of fur
  (A) remove
  (B) make comfortable
  (C) add to
  (D) lessen

Hint #1 Don't be fooled by choices that are closely related to the Vocabulary Word. Choice A may be tempting, but the removal of shedding is more extreme than a **decrease** in shedding.

Hint #2 Don't be fooled by distantly related choices. An animal may be more comfortable when it sheds, but there is no direct link between **decrease** and Choice B.

Hint #3 Don't be fooled by the opposite of the Vocabulary Word. Choice C would be the correct choice if this were an Opposite Meanings exercise, but here you are looking for a similar meaning.

MAKING NEW WORDS YOUR OWN

Lesson 11 CONTEXT: Coming to the United States
My Great-Great-Grandparents' Story

People have come to the United States for a variety of reasons. Many have come in search of religious or political freedom. Others have come seeking economic opportunity. All have come with high hopes of building a new life in a new land. For those immigrants who come to the United States through New York Harbor, the first glimpse of the Statue of Liberty is an unforgettable moment of promise.

In the following exercises, you will have the opportunity to expand your vocabulary by reading about the arrival of two immigrants. These ten Vocabulary Words will be used.

aristocrat	decade	emigrate	malnutrition	optimism
censorship	deport	famine	morale	refuge

EXERCISE 1 *Wordbusting* ✍

Directions. Follow these instructions for this word and the nine words on the next page.
- Figure out the word's meaning by looking at its **context,** its **structure,** and its **sound.** Fill in at least one of the three **CSS** boxes.
- Then, look up the word in a dictionary, read all of its meanings, and write the meaning of the word as it is used in the sentence.
- Follow this same process for each of the Vocabulary Words on the next page. You will need to draw your own map for each word. Use a separate sheet of paper.

1.

(aristocrat) → When my great-great-grandmother met my great-great-grandfather on board the ship to the United States, she did not know that he was an **aristocrat** because he was dressed in peasant's clothing.

Context:	Structure:	Sound:

Dictionary:

2.
censorship → He was leaving Russia because of **censorship**. The government did not approve of his ideas and had forbidden him to operate his newspaper.

3.
decade → He had struggled to publish his thoughts for a **decade**. After ten years of fighting, however, he was exhausted.

4.
deport → He didn't think the government would **deport** him, but there was always a possibility that he might be forced to leave Russia.

5.
emigrate → He decided to **emigrate** from Russia to begin a new life in the United States.

6.
famine → My great-great-grandmother was leaving Russia because of a **famine** in her part of the country. Many members of her family had died from lack of food.

7.
malnutrition → She was suffering from **malnutrition;** she had had nothing but bread and water to eat for several months.

8.
morale → She was sick and depressed when she got on the ship, but soon her health and her **morale** began to improve.

9.
optimism → One source of her new **optimism** was her love for my great-great-grandfather. She felt in her heart that their love story would have a happy ending.

10.
refuge → They were holding hands on the deck of the ship when they sailed past the Statue of Liberty. At last they had reached a place of safety, a place of **refuge**.

EXERCISE 2 *Context Clues*

Directions. Scan the definitions in Column A. Then, think about how the boldface words are used in the sentences in Column B. To complete the exercise, match each definition in Column A with the correct Vocabulary Word from Column B. Write the letter of your choice on the line provided. Finally, write the Vocabulary Word on the line before the definition.

COLUMN A

_____ **11.** word: _____

v. to move from one region or country to settle in another

_____ **12.** word: _____

n. inadequate nutrition; poor health caused by undernourishment

_____ **13.** word: _____

n. a member of the nobility; person with tastes of the upper class

_____ **14.** word: _____

n. shelter or protection from danger or distress; any place or thing that provides relief, help, or sanctuary; a haven

_____ **15.** word: _____

n. the act of or a system of making objections to and removing parts of books, letters, news, and so on

_____ **16.** word: _____

n. a tendency to expect the best possible outcome or to look on the bright side

_____ **17.** word: _____

n. a state of mind of an individual or group, especially when confident, cheerful, and willing to perform

_____ **18.** word: _____

v. to remove, especially to send out of the country; to behave in a specific manner

_____ **19.** word: _____

n. a widespread and drastic shortage, usually of food

_____ **20.** word: _____

n. a period of ten years

COLUMN B

(A) My great-great-grandfather had trouble adjusting to life in the United States because, as an **aristocrat,** he was not used to being treated like a common person.

(B) For my great-great-grandmother, adjustment was easier. After her experience with **famine,** she was happy to be in a place where food was plentiful.

(C) She would **deport** herself in the most graceful manner. My great-great-grandfather was impressed with her and how she conducted herself.

(D) Even though he had some money, they had financial difficulties during the first **decade** of their marriage. After ten years, however, they were living comfortably.

(E) During those ten years, he sometimes wondered whether it had been a mistake to **emigrate** from Russia.

(F) Her **optimism,** on the other hand, always amazed him. She never doubted for a minute that they would succeed in the new land.

(G) He often took **refuge** in her positive approach to life. Her cheerful outlook sheltered him from distress.

(H) He was also grateful to work for a newspaper that was free from **censorship.** In the United States, he could print his opinions without government interference.

(I) With the encouragement of his wife, he was usually able to maintain high **morale.**

(J) She always grew a small garden for her family. She wanted them to have plenty of vegetables so that they would never suffer from **malnutrition** as she had.

EXERCISE 3 *Like Meanings and Opposite Meanings* ☞

Directions. For each item below, circle the letter of the choice that means the same, or about the same, as the boldface word.

21. an act of **censorship**
    - (A) examining and removing
    - (B) borrowing from another source
    - (C) approving wholeheartedly
    - (D) believing wholeheartedly

22. after a **decade**
    - (A) ten weeks
    - (B) ten months
    - (C) ten days
    - (D) ten years

23. to **deport** the leader
    - (A) send away
    - (B) execute
    - (C) put on trial
    - (D) hold

24. to boost **morale**
    - (A) good deeds
    - (B) spirits
    - (C) food supply
    - (D) choice

25. to suffer from **malnutrition**
    - (A) the study of food
    - (B) nourishing food
    - (C) overeating
    - (D) inadequate food

Directions. For each item below, circle the letter of the choice that means the opposite, or about the opposite, of the boldface word.

26. in a spirit of **optimism**
    - (A) kindness
    - (B) anger
    - (C) joy
    - (D) despair

27. a place of **refuge**
    - (A) emptiness
    - (B) danger
    - (C) honesty
    - (D) safety

28. a young **aristocrat**
    - (A) peasant
    - (B) noble
    - (C) animal
    - (D) human

29. a decision to **emigrate**
    - (A) eat
    - (B) leave
    - (C) remain
    - (D) starve

30. a time of **famine**
    - (A) hunger
    - (B) plenty
    - (C) being famous
    - (D) being unknown

MAKING NEW WORDS YOUR OWN

Lesson 15 | CONTEXT: Coming to the United States
Southeast Asians in Houston, Texas

Houston, Texas, has been the final destination for many immigrants, including thousands who have arrived from the southeast Asian nations of Vietnam, Laos, and Cambodia. Houston is very different from southeast Asia, but the immigrants have worked hard to make a new life in a new land.

In the following exercises, you will have the opportunity to expand your vocabulary by reading about one family that escaped from Vietnam in the 1970s and now lives in Houston. Below are ten Vocabulary Words that will be used in these exercises.

dedicate	dispense	exertion	humidity	restrain
depose	dissect	haven	memento	tumult

EXERCISE 1 *Wordbusting*

Directions. Follow these instructions for this word and the nine words on the next page.
- Figure out the word's meaning by looking at its **context,** its **structure,** and its **sound.** Fill in at least one of the three **CSS** boxes. Alternate which boxes you complete.
- Then, look up the word in a dictionary, read all of its meanings, and write the meaning of the word as it is used in the sentence.
- Follow this same process for each of the Vocabulary Words on the next page. You will need to draw your own map for each word. Use a separate sheet of paper.

1.

(dedicate) ⟶ Nguyen Truong had intended to **dedicate** his life to farming, but as it turned out, he had to devote his life to something else. He became involved in the civil war that raged in his country, Vietnam.

Context:

Structure:

Sound:

Dictionary:

2.

depose ➡️ If he had been able to **depose** the leader in his village, his story might be different, but Nguyen Truong was unable to remove him from office.

3.

dispense ➡️ He had to **dispense** with his plan to become a farmer, but he never gave up his dream of a better life for his children.

4.

dissect ➡️ He made a pla~~n~~ ~~e~~scape from Vietnam with his family. He shared the plan with ~~h~~ ~~i~~e so that she could **dissect** it thoroughly. They wanted to be s~~ur~~ ~~t~~hat every single part had been carefully thought out.

5.

exertion ➡️ The escape would require all of their mental energy. It would also call for a great deal of physical **exertion**.

haven ➡️ On the first night of the journey, the family found a safe **haven** in a cave in the jungle.

7.

humidity ➡️ They traveled by night so they could avoid the heat and **humidity**. The high temperature and the dampness would tax their strength.

8.

memento ➡️ They could not bring much with them, but each family member carried a **memento,** or keepsake.

9.

restrain ➡️ They spent many days on a small boat at sea. Even though they **re-strained** their appetites and managed their supplies carefully, they almost ran out of food and water before they were rescued.

10.

tumult ➡️ When they reached shore, they were happy to escape the **tumult** and the noise of the large waves crashing into the small boat.

EXERCISE 2 Context Clues ✍

Directions. Scan the definitions in Column A. Then, think about how the boldface words are used in the sentences in Column B. To complete the exercise, match each definition in Column A with the correct Vocabulary Word from Column B. Write the letter of your choice on the line provided. Finally, write the Vocabulary Word on the line before the definition.

COLUMN A	COLUMN B

COLUMN A

_____ **11.** word: _____

n. moisture; dampness; the amount of moisture in the air

_____ **12.** word: _____

v. to devote to a sacred or special purpose; to inscribe a work of art to someone out of affection or respect

_____ **13.** word: _____

n. a souvenir; a keepsake; anything kept or given to remind one of the past

_____ **14.** word: _____

v. to remove from office or high position; to testify or state under oath but out of court.

_____ **15.** word: _____

v. to hold back from action; to control; to limit or restrict

_____ **16.** word: _____

v. to cut apart; to analyze closely

_____ **17.** word: _____

n. a violent or noisy commotion of a crowd; a disorderly disturbance; a disturbance of mind or feeling

_____ **18.** word: _____

v. to distribute or administer; to do without; to do away with something

_____ **19.** word: _____

n. a harbor or port; a place of safe shelter

_____ **20.** word: _____

n. a strong effort; the act of using

COLUMN B

(A) Eventually the family settled in Houston, where the heat and **humidity** reminded them of the muggy climate of Vietnam.

(B) Sometimes the noise and commotion of the city was disturbing, especially the **tumult** of the traffic.

(C) However, after the hard trip at sea and the months in the refugee camp, the city seemed like a safe **haven**.

(D) Nguyen Truong was pleased that they had escaped before the leader of the village tried to force him to **depose,** or swear under oath, that his neighbors had been disloyal.

(E) The family's **mementos** were very dear to them. The keepsakes reminded them of their old home far away.

(F) Sometimes he had to **restrain** himself from weeping. He held back his tears because he didn't want to upset his grandchildren.

(G) He felt especially sad on Tet, the Vietnamese New Year, when the Vietnamese people traditionally **dedicate** themselves to remembering their past.

(H) During the New Year celebration, neighbors made wonderful treats for one another and **dispensed,** or handed out, gifts of money to the children of the community.

(I) Preparation for Tet required hours of hard work, but no one minded the **exertion**. It was an opportunity to share time with family.

(J) During New Year celebrations, the family members paused to **dissect** their emotions. They found themselves analyzing and evaluating their old lives and their new ones.

EXERCISE 3 *Like Meanings and Opposite Meanings* 👈

Directions. For each item below, circle the letter of the choice that means the same, or about the same, as the boldface word.

21. very low **humidity**

(A) moisture content
(B) heat index
(C) percentages
(D) score

22. in a quiet **haven**

(A) hospital
(B) palace
(C) shelter
(D) heritage

23. a small **memento**

(A) loss
(B) ghost
(C) memory
(D) keepsake

24. to **dedicate** some money

(A) save secretly
(B) borrow
(C) write
(D) set aside

25. to **dissect** his motives

(A) believe
(B) analyze
(C) ignore
(D) understand

Directions. For each item below, circle the letter of the choice that means the opposite, or about the opposite, of the boldface word.

26. to **restrain** strong emotion

(A) train
(B) let go
(C) feel deeply
(D) struggle with

27. the distant **tumult**

(A) memories
(B) friends
(C) calm
(D) noise

28. to **depose** the king

(A) crown
(B) get rid of
(C) argue against
(D) remember

29. a period of **exertion**

(A) work
(B) rest
(C) time
(D) loss

30. to **dispense** with the idea

(A) eliminate
(B) forget
(C) share
(D) keep

MAKING NEW WORDS YOUR OWN

Lesson 16 | CONTEXT: Coming to the United States

Remembering the Past

Making the decision to leave home and begin life in a new country was a very difficult one for many immigrants. However, it was just the first in a series of difficult steps. The journey to the United States may have been long and dangerous. And, once there, immigrants faced the gigantic task of adjusting to life in a new country.

In the following exercises, you will have the opportunity to expand your vocabulary by reading about the problems some immigrants faced upon arrival in the United States. Below are ten Vocabulary Words that will be used in these exercises.

hamper	impose	intercept	negligent	recuperate
imperative	inconsiderate	liable	presume	spacious

EXERCISE 1 Wordbusting ✍

Directions. Follow these instructions for this word and the nine words on the next page.
- Figure out the word's meaning by looking at its **context,** its **structure,** and its **sound.** Fill in at least one of the three **CSS** boxes. Alternate which boxes you complete.
- Then, look up the word in a dictionary, read all of its meanings, and write the meaning of the word as it is used in the sentence.
- Follow this same process for each of the Vocabulary Words on the next page. You will need to draw your own map for each word. Use a separate sheet of paper.

1.

(hamper) → Many problems might arise in their homelands that could **hamper** immigrants' efforts to come to the United States. Fortunately, these problems didn't hold everyone back.

Context:	Structure:	Sound:

Dictionary:

Name _____ Date _____ Class _____

2.

(imperative) ➔ It was **imperative** that some people flee to freedom, for their lives were at stake.

3.

(impose) ➔ Many immigrants still come for the same reason that the first European immigrants came. Their governments **impose** unfair restrictions on them, and they can't live under such forced limitations.

4.

(inconsiderate) ➔ Immigrants who came in the late 1800s and early 1900s often encountered **inconsiderate** immigration officials who treated them rudely.

5.

(intercept) ➔ Immigration officials were supposed to **intercept** new arrivals who were ill and send them back to their homelands.

6.

(liable) ➔ These officials were **liable,** or responsible, for preventing the spread of diseases such as tuberculosis.

7.

(negligent) ➔ If they were **negligent** in their duty, they could get in trouble. Perhaps that is what made some of them overly cautious.

8.

(presume) ➔ Unfortunately, sometimes an official would **presume** that an immigrant was seriously ill when in reality he or she was simply exhausted from a difficult voyage.

9.

(recuperate) ➔ Sometimes an immigrant would be given time to **recuperate** from an illness. When well, the immigrant would be admitted into the country.

10.

(spacious) ➔ Immigrants were overjoyed to be admitted to the United States. They were sure that this new **spacious** nation would offer them plenty of room to carve out a new life.

EXERCISE 2 *Context Clues* ✍

Directions. Scan the definitions in Column A. Then, think about how the boldface words are used in the sentences in Column B. To complete the exercise, match each definition in Column A with the correct Vocabulary Word from Column B. Write the letter of your choice on the line provided. Finally, write the Vocabulary Word on the line before the definition.

COLUMN A	COLUMN B

COLUMN A

_____ **11.** word: _____
n. a large covered basket or container; *v.* to hold back or hinder

_____ **12.** word: _____
adj. absolutely necessary, urgent; commanding; describing a verb that expresses a command; *n.* a command

_____ **13.** word: _____
adj. lacking concern for the needs of others; thoughtless; selfish

_____ **14.** word: _____
v. to take or seize en route; to block

_____ **15.** word: _____
adj. containing much space; vast; roomy

_____ **16.** word: _____
v. to return to health and strength; to recover from financial losses

_____ **17.** word: _____
v. to take for granted; to suppose to be true; to take upon oneself with authority

_____ **18.** word: _____
adj. guilty of neglect; failing to show proper care or caution

_____ **19.** word: _____
adj. likely; subject or susceptible; legally responsible

_____ **20.** word: _____
v. to place or set on with authority; to inflict by force; to pass off deceptively; (with *on* or *upon*) to take advantage of

COLUMN B

(A) I went with my great-grandfather to visit the museum at Ellis Island. Today, the building is open and **spacious,** but when he arrived there as a boy, its halls were crowded with people.

(B) He thinks it is **imperative** that the whole family remember their heritage; that's why he felt it was necessary to take me to Ellis Island.

(C) He worries that he has been **negligent** in keeping us in touch with our past, but he has really done a good job of it.

(D) Things went smoothly for him at Ellis Island except for one **inconsiderate** official who changed the spelling of his name from Wdzieczak to Wechik. The official didn't even ask whether he minded the change.

(E) Although he didn't say so, I **presume** he will be taking my cousins to the museum next summer. He takes some of his great-grandchildren every summer.

(F) He has been ill lately, but he is beginning to **recuperate**.

(G) I do want him to tell me more stories about the family history, but I don't want to **impose** on him. Having someone ask you lots of questions can be tiring after a while.

(H) Until recently, he was **liable** to fall asleep in the middle of a tale, but I don't think that will be likely once he is feeling better.

(I) Once we went on a picnic. I will never forget how his eyes twinkled as he pulled the food from the picnic **hamper** and told me stories of crossing the Atlantic.

(J) "As we left Gdansk," he began, "we were **intercepted** by my Aunt Eva, who stopped us and begged to go with us to the United States."

EXERCISE 3 *Like Meanings and Opposite Meanings* ✍

Directions. For each item below, circle the letter of the choice that means the same, or about the same, as the boldface word.

21. to **recuperate** his losses
(A) count
(B) understand
(C) lose
(D) regain

22. to **presume** to challenge the official
(A) win over
(B) dare
(C) refuse to count on
(D) rely heavily on

23. to **intercept** the message
(A) send
(B) stop
(C) hear
(D) believe

24. to **impose** her views
(A) get
(B) force on others
(C) design
(D) carefully explain

25. to be **liable** for the mistake
(A) forgiven
(B) concerned
(C) sorry
(D) responsible

Directions. For each item below, circle the letter of the choice that means the opposite, or about the opposite, of the boldface word.

26. in **spacious** quarters
(A) roomy
(B) ugly
(C) cramped
(D) beautiful

27. to be **negligent**
(A) stupid
(B) intelligent
(C) careless
(D) careful

28. an **inconsiderate** host
(A) thoughtful
(B) thoughtless
(C) well-dressed
(D) sloppily dressed

29. an **imperative** consideration
(A) essential
(B) minor
(C) rude
(D) polite

30. to **hamper** the efforts
(A) throw out
(B) box
(C) hinder
(D) encourage

MAKING NEW WORDS YOUR OWN

Lesson 17 | **CONTEXT: Coming to the United States**

The Ballad of Mary Margaret Murphy

Each person who has immigrated to the United States has a special story to tell. Some are stories of triumph, and some are stories of tragedy. Most are stories of ordinary people. All of them, however, are stories of hope for a good life in a new country.

In the following exercises, you will have the opportunity to expand your vocabulary by reading about two immigrants. Below are ten Vocabulary Words that will be used in these exercises.

aroma	elegant	gracious	manageable	occupant
capital	frequency	haughty	monopoly	probation

EXERCISE 1 *Wordbusting*

Directions. Follow these instructions for this word and the nine words on the next page.
- Figure out the word's meaning by looking at its **context,** its **structure,** and its **sound.** Fill in at least one of the three **CSS** boxes. Alternate which boxes you complete.
- Then, look up the word in a dictionary, read all of its meanings, and write the meaning of the word as it is used in the sentence.
- Follow this same process for each of the Vocabulary Words on the next page. You will need to draw your own map for each word. Use a separate sheet of paper.

1.

aroma → Every time I smell the fragrant **aroma** of a rich stew bubbling on the stove, I think of my great-grandmother, Mary Margaret Murphy.

Context:

Structure:

Sound:

Dictionary:

2.

(capital) → She emigrated from County Cork in Ireland and settled in Boston, the **capital** of Massachusetts. She dreamed that someday one of her children would live in the governor's mansion.

3.

(elegant) → She found work as a maid in one of those **elegant** townhouses on Beacon Hill, the fancy section of town.

4.

(frequency) → The kitchen had to be scrubbed with such **frequency** that she felt that was all she ever did.

5.

(gracious) → Sometimes she felt sad when she compared her hard life to the **gracious** lifestyle of her employers.

6.

(haughty) → Her employers could be **haughty** and sometimes treated her as if they were better than she was.

7.

(manageable) → Although the work was difficult and her schedule was demanding, she found a way to make it **manageable**.

8.

(monopoly) → Her employers did not have a **monopoly** on all her time. She had some days off, and on those days she rested and dreamed of her future.

9.

(occupant) → She had fallen in love with another **occupant** of the boardinghouse where she lived.

10.

(probation) → In her heart, she had put him on **probation**. She thought he was handsome and charming, but was he worthy of her love?

EXERCISE 2 Context Clues ✍

Directions. Scan the definitions in Column A. Then, think about how the boldface words are used in the sentences in Column B. To complete the exercise, match each definition in Column A with the correct Vocabulary Word from Column B. Write the letter of your choice on the line provided. Finally, write the Vocabulary Word on the line before the definition.

COLUMN A

_____ **11.** word: _____

n. the official seat of government; the total wealth of a business; wealth available for investment; *adj.* first, foremost; excellent; punishable by death

_____ **12.** word: _____

adj. proud and vain to the point of being conceited; scornful of others

_____ **13.** word: _____

adj. showing kindness and courtesy; elegant and refined

_____ **14.** word: _____

adj. capable of being controlled, directed, or accomplished

_____ **15.** word: _____

n. the exclusive control of anything; a company with such control

_____ **16.** word: _____

adj. tasteful, beautiful, and luxurious; refined in manner, taste, and style

_____ **17.** word: _____

n. one who resides in or occupies a house, land, or a position

_____ **18.** word: _____

n. a fragrant or appetizing smell

_____ **19.** word: _____

n. a trial period

_____ **20.** word: _____

n. the rate or number of times a thing recurs within a given time or group

COLUMN B

(A) Timothy O'Malley was in love with Mary Margaret, but he didn't want to tell her until he had enough **capital** to start his own business. He scrimped and saved to make that dream come true.

(B) He thought Mary Margaret was the most **elegant** woman he had ever seen, despite her lack of education and her hands, which were red and raw from hard work.

(C) Mary Margaret was a warm and **gracious** person, with a quick smile and a loving heart.

(D) The **frequency** with which Timothy looked at her across the supper table had already given her a good clue to his feelings.

(E) He did not know that he had a **monopoly** on her heart; she was interested in no one else.

(F) Other men were also interested in Mary Margaret, including the **occupant** of the small house behind the mansion where she worked.

(G) Another woman might have become conceited, even **haughty,** knowing she had so many admirers, but not Mary Margaret.

(H) She made the situation **manageable** by ignoring most of her would-be boyfriends. She never let the admiration go to her head.

(I) One day Timothy O'Malley finished his period of **probation** at the bank and became a full-time employee. That night, he splashed on his lilac aftershave, dressed in his best clothes, and went to ask Mary Margaret to marry him.

(J) When I smell the **aroma** of lilac aftershave, I always imagine Mary Margaret saying, "I thought you'd never ask!"

EXERCISE 3 *Like Meanings and Opposite Meanings* ✍

Directions. For each item below, circle the letter of the choice that means the same, or about the same, as the boldface word.

21. the **aroma** of stew
    (A) flavor
    (B) love
    (C) smell
    (D) price

22. with some **frequency**
    (A) hurry
    (B) regularity
    (C) hesitation
    (D) friendliness

23. a **monopoly** of the business
    (A) increase
    (B) loss
    (C) game
    (D) control

24. the **occupant** of the palace
    (A) person who lives in
    (B) person who believes in
    (C) person who relies on
    (D) person who loses

25. the end of **probation**
    (A) guesswork
    (B) a month
    (C) a year
    (D) trial period

Directions. For each item below, circle the letter of the choice that means the opposite, or about the opposite, of the boldface word.

26. an **elegant** dress
    (A) beautiful
    (B) shabby
    (C) expensive
    (D) small

27. a **manageable** amount
    (A) easy
    (B) large
    (C) uncontrollable
    (D) questionable

28. a **haughty** manner
    (A) friendly
    (B) cruel
    (C) disorganized
    (D) quick

29. a **capital** idea
    (A) serious
    (B) bad
    (C) excellent
    (D) interesting

30. a **gracious** host
    (A) courteous
    (B) rude
    (C) remarkable
    (D) rich

MAKING NEW WORDS YOUR OWN

Lesson 18 | CONTEXT: Coming to the United States
Discovering New Holidays

Adjusting to a new culture means adjusting to its holidays. Of course, many cultures share holidays. Many immigrants to the United States probably already celebrated Christmas, Hanukkah, or Ramadan, as well as the New Year. Most immigrants, however, encounter strictly American holidays—such as Thanksgiving—for the first time.

In the following exercises, you will have the opportunity to expand your vocabulary by reading about Thanksgiving celebrations. Below are ten Vocabulary Words that will be used in these exercises.

baste	dismantle	populate	remote	saturate
diminish	embarrass	prearrange	rigid	sedate

EXERCISE 1 *Wordbusting*

Directions. Follow these instructions for this word and the nine words on the next page.
- Figure out the word's meaning by looking at its **context,** its **structure,** and its **sound.** Fill in at least one of the three **CSS** boxes. Alternate which boxes you complete.
- Then, look up the word in a dictionary, read all of its meanings, and write the meaning of the word as it is used in the sentence.
- Follow this same process for each of the Vocabulary Words on the next page. You will need to draw your own map for each word. Use a separate sheet of paper.

1.

(baste) → As the students in Ms. Smith's family-living class at Xavier High learn to stuff a Thanksgiving turkey and **baste** it with its own juices, they are discussing family celebrations.

Context:	Structure:	Sound:

Dictionary:

2.

Cooking all week has not **diminished** their enthusiasm for the holiday. In fact, they are as excited as ever.

3.

At one table, students have started to **dismantle** the complicated centerpiece that Ms. Smith made. She wants to take it apart and put it away before the final bell rings for holiday break.

4.

Ms. Smith is talking to a new student, Ezekiel, who recently arrived from Nigeria. "I don't want to **embarrass** you," she says because she is afraid her question might make him feel foolish, "but are you familiar with our Thanksgiving holiday?"

5.

"Yes," says Ezekiel, "I believe its origins are from the time that Europeans first began to settle and **populate** this continent."

6.

"That's right," says Lynda. "It was the Pilgrims who held the first Thanksgiving feast. Ms. Smith, did the Pilgrims **prearrange** the first feast, or did it just sort of happen, without planning?"

7.

"I think William Bradford, the governor of the Pilgrim's settlement in Plymouth, planned it in advance," Alfonso offers. "I have a **remote** memory of discussing all of this in Mr. Dawson's history class, but the class was so long ago that I'm not sure."

8.

"Here's what I think you should know, Ezekiel," says Amber. "In this country, we aren't **rigid** about how we celebrate the holiday. You can do it in any way you see fit."

9.

"I like to **saturate** cheese cloth with melted butter and drape it over the turkey while it roasts," says Elsbeth.

10.

sedate

"It's fun to discuss our family celebrations," says Ms. Smith. "Some dinners are formal, quiet, and **sedate**, but my family's is always casual, noisy, and rowdy."

EXERCISE 2   *Context Clues* ✍

Directions. Scan the definitions in Column A. Then, think about how the boldface words are used in the sentences in Column B. To complete the exercise, match each definition in Column A with the correct Vocabulary Word from Column B. Write the letter of your choice on the line provided. Finally, write the Vocabulary Word on the line before the definition.

COLUMN A

_____ **11.** word: _____
v. to prepare in advance or beforehand; to plan ahead

_____ **12.** word: _____
v. to tear down; to take apart; to strip of furnishing or equipment

_____ **13.** word: _____
adj. distant; isolated or out of the way; not obvious; slight; cool and aloof

_____ **14.** word: _____
v. to furnish with inhabitants; to inhabit

_____ **15.** word: _____
adj. stiff; firmly fixed; very strict

_____ **16.** word: _____
v. to soak thoroughly; to fill completely; to drench

_____ **17.** word: _____
adj. serious and unemotional; quiet; composed; *v.* to administer a tranquilizer

_____ **18.** word: _____
v. to cause someone to feel ill at ease and self-conscious

_____ **19.** word: _____
v. to sew together with loose, temporary stitches; to moisten food with liquid or oil as it roasts or bakes; to attack verbally

_____ **20.** word: _____
v. to make or become smaller; to decrease; to detract from the authority of

COLUMN B

(A) "Learning about the different ways people celebrate Thanksgiving has not **diminished** my enthusiasm for the holiday," says Heather.

(B) Eleni says, "In my family, we **prearrange** our holiday. In fact, we plan weeks in advance."

(C) "In October, my mother was **basting** scraps of material together for a huge holiday quilt. She is still sewing on it," Eleni adds.

(D) "One year my family went to a cabin in a **remote** part of the mountains for Thanksgiving. We wanted to get away from the hustle and bustle of civilization," Karen remarks.

(E) "It was kind of funny because my dad, who is the cook in the family, had to **dismantle** almost our whole kitchen and pack it in the van."

(F) "Personally, I was a little **embarrassed** to be taking a microwave to the wilderness, but Dad isn't self-conscious about anything!"

(G) "At least we didn't take the radio or the television. For once, we were able to avoid all the noise that usually **saturates** the air so that you can't even hear yourself think!"

(H) "My family is like Karen's," Joe remarks. "We're not at all **rigid** about Thanksgiving— except for one strict rule. My mother always makes mashed potatoes."

(I) "At my grandmother's house, the adults sit down to a quiet, **sedate** meal. We kids, however, are anything but well behaved."

(J) "You know," says Ms. Smith, "there may be as many ways to celebrate Thanksgiving as there are families who live in this country, who **populate** our cities and towns."

EXERCISE 3   *Like Meanings and Opposite Meanings* 👈

Directions. For each item below, circle the letter of the choice that means the same, or about the same, as the boldface word.

21. to **baste** your opponent
(A) attack
(B) review
(C) abuse
(D) thank

22. to **embarrass** the child
(A) encourage
(B) ignore
(C) shame
(D) talk to

23. to **populate** the city
(A) leave
(B) approve of
(C) live in
(D) avoid

24. to **prearrange** the trip
(A) travel
(B) forget
(C) plan
(D) reschedule

25. to **saturate** the sponge
(A) locate
(B) wash
(C) throw out
(D) soak

Directions. For each item below, circle the letter of the choice that means the opposite, or about the opposite, of the boldface word.

26. to **diminish** the supply
(A) increase
(B) make smaller
(C) hide from
(D) find

27. to **dismantle** the equipment
(A) take apart
(B) put together
(C) buy
(D) sell

28. a **remote** spot
(A) dirty
(B) unusual
(C) close
(D) distant

29. a **rigid** attitude
(A) good
(B) terrible
(C) strict
(D) flexible

30. to **sedate** the patient
(A) put to sleep
(B) wake up
(C) quiet
(D) alarm

MAKING NEW WORDS YOUR OWN

Lesson 19 | **CONTEXT: Coming to the United States**
Tracing a Heritage

When and how did your family come to the United States? Were they here to greet the Europeans who first landed? Did they arrive with the French in Louisiana? Were they forced to come here in slavery? Did they enter Hawaii from Korea in the late 1800s? Perhaps they fled Vietnam in 1975? Or perhaps they arrived from another place, at another time. Finding out when and how your family first arrived can be a rewarding experience.

In the following exercises, you will have the opportunity to expand your vocabulary by reading about the heritages of several different students. Below are ten Vocabulary Words that will be used in these exercises.

access	circumnavigate	liberate	pleasantry	regime
accommodations	evacuate	notify	provision	remorse

EXERCISE 1 *Wordbusting* ✍

Directions. Follow these instructions for this word and the nine words on the next page.
- Figure out the word's meaning by looking at its **context**, its **structure**, and its **sound**. Fill in at least one of the three **CSS** boxes. Alternate which boxes you complete.
- Then, look up the word in a dictionary, read all of its meanings, and write the meaning of the word as it is used in the sentence.
- Follow this same process for each of the Vocabulary Words on the next page. You will need to draw your own map for each word. Use a separate sheet of paper.

1.

(access) → "I don't know if you will have **access** to all the information you need to complete this assignment, but I want you to do your best to discover where your family came from and why," says Mr. Whitley.

Context:	Structure:	Sound:

Dictionary:

2.

"We may have to make some **accommodations,** or adjustments, to the assignment if you can't find the information," he adds.

3.

Mr. Whitley briefly reminds his class of the history of people coming to the Americas, including the Europeans' desire to **circumnavigate** the globe—to set out heading west and return from the east. These explorers didn't realize that North America would get in their way.

4.

"My parents left Cambodia when they were ordered to leave, or **evacuate,** Phnom Penh," remarks Lo.

5.

"My family came when Hitler invaded Czechoslovakia. They knew he did not want to **liberate** them but that they would go to prison or die," says April.

6.

"I wish you had decided to **notify** us earlier about this project," says Danny. "My grandparents were here last week, and I could have talked with them if you had told us about it sooner."

7.

"My grandmother came from Japan, and she learned English gradually. For many years all she could do was exchange a few **pleasantries,** such as 'How are you?' and 'Nice weather,'" says Rita.

8.

"Perhaps I should make **provision** to visit my great-aunt this weekend," says Jimmy. "She knows more than anyone else about my dad's family history. I'll call the retirement home."

9.

"My family came to the United States to escape the **regime** that was in power in Guatemala," says Luiz. "That government mistreated members of my family."

10.

remorse

"When my mother left Laos, she had to leave her family behind. That decision filled her with **remorse** because she was very close to them," says Jenny.

© Houghton Mifflin Harcourt Publishing Company

EXERCISE 2 *Context Clues* ✍️

Directions. Scan the definitions in Column A. Then, think about how the boldface words are used in the sentences in Column B. To complete the exercise, match each definition in Column A with the correct Vocabulary Word from Column B. Write the letter of your choice on the line provided. Finally, write the Vocabulary Word on the line before the definition.

<table>
<tr><td>COLUMN A</td><td>COLUMN B</td></tr>
</table>

_____ **11.** word: _____

v. to set free; to release from bondage or enemy occupation

_____ **12.** word: _____

v. to give notice; to inform

_____ **13.** word: _____

n. the right to enter, make use of, or communicate with; a passage or means of entering, approaching, or using; a sudden outburst; *v.* to gain entrance

_____ **14.** word: _____

n. a good-natured joke; a polite remark

_____ **15.** word: _____

n. the act of providing; a preparation made for the future; a requirement; [*pl.*] food or supplies for the future

_____ **16.** word: _____

v. to travel completely around a thing

_____ **17.** word: _____

n. a system or form of government or rule; a political or social system

_____ **18.** word: _____

n. adjustment; convenience; compromise; room and board; lodgings; seating on a public vehicle

_____ **19.** word: _____

n. bitter regret; a sense of guilt

_____ **20.** word: _____

v. to empty; to withdraw; to remove for reasons of safety; to vacate

(A) "Later my mother made **provision** for them to come to the United States. Those preparations were difficult to make," Jenny adds.

(B) "Although their **accommodations** here were simple, the new housing was an improvement over the way they had lived in Laos."

(C) "My grandparents just made their first trip back to Russia since the Communist **regime** fell from power. The change in government made them feel safe there," Nadia comments.

(D) "My great-grandfather came to the United States after World War II because he admired the U.S. soldiers who **liberated** him from the prison camp," remarks Hayley.

(E) "For a long time, we could not **access** information about our relatives in Argentina," Trina says, "but now we can communicate with them by phone or e-mail."

(F) "One of my aunts was able to **notify** us that my cousin Roberto was alive and well."

(G) "My grandparents decided to flee from Cuba after Fidel Castro came to power. They **evacuated** the country in 1961," said Ignacio.

(H) "My parents risked their lives to get here. If I complain about my life, I usually feel **remorse** later. I feel guilty when I remember what they have been through."

(I) "Yes," says Jenny. "Some of our ancestors practically **circumnavigated** the globe to get here. So I feel kind of silly for complaining about having to walk to school."

(J) "I love my grandparents, but we can exchange only a few **pleasantries** since I don't know much German," says Karl.

EXERCISE 3 *Like Meanings and Opposite Meanings* ☞

Directions. For each item below, circle the letter of the choice that means the same, or about the same, as the boldface word.

21. to have **access** to the files
    (A) brought things
    (B) avoided using
    (C) the right to use
    (D) forgotten

22. pleasant **accommodations**
    (A) friends
    (B) living quarters
    (C) plans for the future
    (D) thoughts

23. to **circumnavigate** the park
    (A) donate money to
    (B) investigate
    (C) visit
    (D) travel around

24. to make **provision** for
    (A) plans
    (B) friends
    (C) housing
    (D) peace

25. a friendly **regime**
    (A) game
    (B) government
    (C) animal
    (D) boss

Directions. For each item below, circle the letter of the choice that means the opposite, or about the opposite, of the boldface word.

26. to **liberate** the animals
    (A) free
    (B) cage
    (C) purchase
    (D) sell

27. to feel **remorse**
    (A) pride and joy
    (B) bitter regret
    (C) tired
    (D) rested

28. to **notify** the authorities
    (A) recognize
    (B) identify with
    (C) refuse to tell
    (D) inform

29. to **evacuate** the building
    (A) destroy
    (B) rebuild
    (C) empty
    (D) fill up

30. to offer a **pleasantry**
    (A) friendly remark
    (B) rude comment
    (C) snack
    (D) invitation

MAKING NEW WORDS YOUR OWN

Lesson 20 | CONTEXT: Coming to the United States
Coming Soon to a Theater Near You

The immigrant experience has been the subject of many interesting films. Two of the best are *Hester Street* and *Avalon,* but there are many other good ones. Since we are a nation of immigrants, it should come as no surprise that films about immigrants are continually popular.

In the following exercises, you will have the opportunity to expand your vocabulary by reading about two students' plan to make a film about immigrants. Below are ten Vocabulary Words that will be used in these exercises.

adept	disagreeable	jeopardize	persistent	titanic
dingy	humiliate	maroon	thrifty	verify

EXERCISE 1 *Wordbusting*

Directions. Follow these instructions for this word and the nine words on the next page.
- Figure out the word's meaning by looking at its **context,** its **structure,** and its **sound.** Fill in at least one of the three **CSS** boxes. Alternate which boxes you complete.
- Then, look up the word in a dictionary, read all of its meanings, and write the meaning of the word as it is used in the sentence.
- Follow this same process for each of the Vocabulary Words on the next page. You will need to draw your own map for each word. Use a separate sheet of paper.

1.

(adept) → "I'm **adept** with words, and you're good with cameras, so why don't we make a film?" Carlo asked Eric. "We can use the script I wrote in my drama class as a basis."

Context:	Structure:	Sound:

Dictionary:

2.

dingy → "We could use that **dingy** old warehouse down at the end of Main Street for our studio. It's so shabby that it would make a great, creepy set," Carlo continued.

3.

maroon → "I agree. We can make the **maroon** walls look like the red brick exterior of the apartment building."

4.

disagreeable → "We could get Anthony to play the mean old **disagreeable** landlord. You know how good he can be at whining and complaining, don't you, Eric?"

5.

humiliate → "Do you think it would **humiliate** Anna if we asked her to play the mother?" Carlo asked. "She's certain to want to play the beautiful young daughter, and I don't want to embarrass her."

6.

jeopardize → "I don't want to **jeopardize** our friendship. You know how touchy Anna can be. If she gets upset about our casting decisions, our entire relationship could be threatened," he went on.

7.

persistent → "But," Carlo continued, "if I go about it right, if I'm **persistent** and don't give up, I'll bet I can get her to play the part."

8.

thrifty → "It's lucky that my mother is **thrifty**. She saves absolutely everything, so we can get a lot of our props from the trunks in our attic."

9.

titanic → "She has one **titanic** trunk that must hold a million things. That huge trunk may have all the props we could possibly use."

10.

verify → "Before we start, though, I want to **verify** with Ms. Jenkins that we will get as much credit for this project as we could for a research paper. I think we will, but I want to make sure," Carlo concluded.

EXERCISE 2 *Context Clues* ✍

Directions. Scan the definitions in Column A. Then, think about how the boldface words are used in the sentences in Column B. To complete the exercise, match each definition in Column A with the correct Vocabulary Word from Column B. Write the letter of your choice on the line provided. Finally, write the Vocabulary Word on the line before the definition.

COLUMN A	COLUMN B

COLUMN A

____ **11.** word: _____
adj. unpleasant; offensive; quarrelsome and bad-tempered

____ **12.** word: _____
adj. economical; frugal; careful about expenses

____ **13.** word: _____
v. to offend someone's pride or dignity; to reduce someone in position or in esteem; to embarrass

____ **14.** word: _____
v. to prove to be true; to check the truth of something; to confirm

____ **15.** word: _____
v. to imperil; to risk injury or loss

____ **16.** word: _____
adj. skillful; expert

____ **17.** word: _____
adj. dirty-looking; grimy; shabby

____ **18.** word: _____
adj. continuing; enduring; refusing to give up

____ **19.** word: _____
adj. of great size, strength, or power

____ **20.** word: _____
v. to strand a person on a desolate coast or island; to abandon; *n.* a dark reddish brown or purplish red color

COLUMN B

(A) "You're certainly **adept** at talking, Carlo. You haven't let me get a word in edgewise," Eric said.

(B) "I agree that Anna is the best person to play the mother. She can bring a **titanic** dimension to the role, a force that we need."

(C) "I'll work on getting Zack to play her **disagreeable** boss. It should be easy since he prefers playing nasty people anyway."

(D) "Where do we get furniture that looks old enough and **dingy** enough to be the furniture in the apartment set? I seem to remember a worn-out sofa in the teachers' lounge."

(E) "I want Courtney to play the **thrifty** next-door neighbor who works hard and saves her money to bring her father to the United States."

(F) "I like the idea that she is **persistent** in achieving her dream. Actually, the character reminds me of Courtney—she can be pretty determined herself."

(G) "We'll get Max to play the landlord who tries to **humiliate** the young mother when she needs more time to pay the rent. I love the way you wrote that scene where she refuses to become embarrassed about her money problems."

(H) "I think it really helps the audience to see what it is like to feel **marooned**, to feel alone and abandoned, in a strange city."

(I) "I let my grandmother read the script, and she **verified** that that was the way she felt when she first came to this country. She thought our script was right on target."

(J) "I think we need to do some more research, though. I don't want to **jeopardize** our grade by making mistakes in the script."

EXERCISE 3 *Like Meanings and Opposite Meanings* ✍

Directions. For each item below, circle the letter of the choice that means the same, or about the same, as the boldface word.

21. to become an **adept** artist
    - (A) interesting
    - (B) starving
    - (C) forgotten
    - (D) skillful

22. to **maroon** the boat
    - (A) purchase
    - (B) sell
    - (C) sail
    - (D) abandon

23. a **titanic** mistake
    - (A) large
    - (B) unfortunate
    - (C) small
    - (D) unlucky

24. a **persistent** problem
    - (A) constantly occurring
    - (B) seriously threatening
    - (C) very minor
    - (D) highly unusual

25. a **thrifty** purchase
    - (A) economical
    - (B) expensive
    - (C) unjustified
    - (D) unfortunate

Directions. For each item below, circle the letter of the choice that means the opposite, or about the opposite, of the boldface word.

26. in a **disagreeable** situation
    - (A) unusual
    - (B) uncomfortable
    - (C) pleasant
    - (D) common

27. to **humiliate** the shopkeeper
    - (A) praise
    - (B) shame
    - (C) pay
    - (D) advise

28. to **jeopardize** the plan
    - (A) endanger
    - (B) rescue
    - (C) create
    - (D) destroy

29. to **verify** the story
    - (A) hear
    - (B) tell
    - (C) support
    - (D) deny

30. a **dingy** window
    - (A) clean
    - (B) dirty
    - (C) broken
    - (D) whole

MAKING NEW WORDS YOUR OWN

Lesson 21 | CONTEXT: Voices of the United States
Dreaming of the Future

The United States of America is made up of millions of individuals from hundreds of different heritages. Each of these heritages has its own special voice, just as each individual does. This chorus of many voices is what makes our country unlike any other in the world. For, although each voice is different, together they sing of freedom and possibility.

In the following exercises, you will have the opportunity to expand your vocabulary by reading about the dream of one teenager to be a voice for the United States. Below are ten Vocabulary Words that will be used in these exercises.

aspiration	foreword	premier	sable	satire
diplomat	obituary	pun	salutation	tariff

EXERCISE 1 Wordbusting ✍

Directions. Follow these instructions for this word and the nine words on the next page.
- Figure out the word's meaning by looking at its **context,** its **structure,** and its **sound.** Fill in at least one of the three **CSS** boxes. Alternate which boxes you complete.
- Then, look up the word in a dictionary, read all of its meanings, and write the meaning of the word as it is used in the sentence.
- Follow this same process for each of the Vocabulary Words on the next page. You will need to draw your own map for each word. Use a separate sheet of paper.

1.

(aspiration) → My **aspiration** is to be a voice for the United States overseas. I have had this dream for a long time.

Context:	Structure:	Sound:

Dictionary:

2.

 → I want to be a **diplomat;** I want to represent my country's interests when meeting with representatives from other governments.

3.

 → I want to be the person that publishers ask to write the **foreword,** or introduction, to books about other lands.

4.

 → When I die, I want my **obituary** in the newspaper to say, "She served her country well."

5.

 → I want to meet with presidents, kings, **premiers,** and other heads of state.

6.

 → In other words—to make an awful **pun**—when I collect articles about my career, I want my bulletin board to be "tactful." (Get it? "Tacked full!")

7.

 → I can see myself now, walking up the steps to the White House in my **sable**-colored coat, the dark contrasting with the white pillars.

8.

 → Of course, I'll have to learn all the proper forms of greetings, the **salutations,** for addressing heads of state.

9.

 → I don't want to make myself or my country the object of **satire,** or ridicule.

10.

 → I want to deal with important issues, like **tariff** agreements, which deal with taxes on imports and exports.

EXERCISE 2   *Context Clues* 👈

Directions. Scan the definitions in Column A. Then, think about how the boldface words are used in the sentences in Column B. To complete the exercise, match each definition in Column A with the correct Vocabulary Word from Column B. Write the letter of your choice on the line provided. Finally, write the Vocabulary Word on the line before the definition.

COLUMN A	COLUMN B

COLUMN A

_____ **11.** word: _____

n. a tax or list of taxes on trade goods

_____ **12.** word: _____

n. the use of irony, sarcasm, ridicule, or wit to expose foolishness or vice; a literary work that uses such devices

_____ **13.** word: _____

n. a gesture of greeting; the opening greeting in a letter

_____ **14.** word: _____

n. a small, dark mammal sometimes bred for its fur; *adj.* black or dark brown

_____ **15.** word: _____

n. a play on words; *v.* to play on words

_____ **16.** word: _____

n. a prime minister; a chief executive; *adj.* most important; supreme

_____ **17.** word: _____

n. a published notice of a person's death, usually with a brief biography

_____ **18.** word: _____

n. a book's introduction, a preface

_____ **19.** word: _____

n. a government representative; a person skillful in dealing with others

_____ **20.** word: _____

n. a great ambition; a breathing in; in medicine, the removal of fluids; the act of pronouncing a sound that begins with a puff of breath, such as an *h*

COLUMN B

(A) My older sister is usually the **diplomat** in our family. She smooths out all our disagreements. Last night was different; she went out of her way to annoy me.

(B) Last night she reminded me that my first **aspiration**—that is, my first great ambition—had been to be a big bird.

(C) "Imagine reading your **obituary,** or death notice, in the newspaper if you had succeeded," she joked.

(D) Then she made a terrible **pun:** "The big bird is dead. Her goose is cooked."

(E) I told her that when I became successful, I'd make her use a formal **salutation,** or greeting, when addressing me—maybe something like "the Most Honorable and Admired Lacy Wescott."

(F) She said that if I did become famous, she wanted to write the **foreword** to my autobiography. "Your sister is best suited to introducing you to your readers," she said.

(G) She says that she may just go with me to Washington and New Delhi and Tokyo. The **premier** reason she gives is "to see the world," but she admits that a secondary reason is "just to annoy you."

(H) I can just see myself discussing a **tariff,** or trade-tax, agreement with an important official while my big sister stands around.

(I) She'd say things like "I always said **sable** was a terrible color for you. You just don't look good in black."

(J) My sister can ridicule me all she wants, but being the object of her **satire** will not keep me from my dreams.

EXERCISE 3   *Like Meanings and Opposite Meanings* ✍

Directions. For each item below, circle the letter of the choice that means the same, or about the same, as the boldface word.

21. a high-ranking **diplomat**

    (A) movie star
    (B) writer
    (C) government official
    (D) classical musician

22. a silly **pun**

    (A) play on words
    (B) childish story
    (C) prank
    (D) rabbit

23. a beautiful **sable**

    (A) race horse
    (B) dog with a thick coat
    (C) cat with no tail
    (D) small animal with dark fur

24. the art of **satire**

    (A) diplomacy
    (B) ridicule
    (C) escaping
    (D) conversation

25. a high **tariff**

    (A) tax on imports
    (B) government official
    (C) cost of living
    (D) art form

Directions. For each item below, circle the letter of the choice that means the opposite, or about the opposite, of the boldface word.

26. a **premier** reason

    (A) major
    (B) minor
    (C) clear
    (D) unclear

27. a friendly **salutation**

    (A) military maneuver
    (B) greeting
    (C) farewell
    (D) telephone call

28. the **foreword** to the work

    (A) understanding
    (B) explanation
    (C) introduction
    (D) conclusion

29. to read his **obituary**

    (A) birth notice
    (B) death notice
    (C) last name
    (D) first name

30. her painful **aspiration**

    (A) friendship
    (B) breathing in
    (C) headache
    (D) breathing out

MAKING NEW WORDS YOUR OWN

Lesson 22 CONTEXT: Voices of the United States
The Founders

The United States of America first began to find its voice as a nation when it was still a collection of colonies dependent on England. Many of the people who first spoke of the ideals of freedom and democracy would become the founders of the United States and the authors of its Constitution.

In the following exercises, you will have the opportunity to expand your vocabulary by reading about that early period in U.S. history. These ten Vocabulary Words will be used.

blockade	generate	neutral	pewter	quench
confiscate	indelible	obscure	quaint	urgent

EXERCISE 1 *Wordbusting*

Directions. Follow these instructions for this word and the nine words on the next page.
- Figure out the word's meaning by looking at its **context,** its **structure,** and its **sound.** Fill in at least one of the three **CSS** boxes. Alternate which boxes you complete.
- Then, look up the word in a dictionary, read all of its meanings, and write the meaning of the word as it is used in the sentence.
- Follow this same process for each of the Vocabulary Words on the next page. You will need to draw your own map for each word. Use a separate sheet of paper.

1.

(blockade) ⟶ Some colonists had begun to speak out even before the British dared to **blockade** Boston Harbor. However, after the British forcefully closed the port, the colonists took action. They formed the First Continental Congress, paving the way for armed rebellion.

Context:	Structure:	Sound:

Dictionary:

2.

 confiscate → The act that led to the closing of the port was the Boston Tea Party. On December 16, 1773, to protest a high tax, a group of colonists **confiscated** the tea that was on some ships in the harbor. After they took it, they threw it overboard.

3.

 generate → The colonists were reacting to the British efforts to **generate,** or produce, wealth through unfair taxation.

4.

 indelible → The colonists who protested British taxes made an **indelible** mark on the nation's mind. The phrase "no taxation without representation" is imprinted forever in our minds.

5.

 neutral → Not all the colonists opposed the British. Some actually supported them, while others, remaining **neutral,** joined neither side.

6.

 obscure → We know well the names of the leaders of the American Revolution, but time tends to **obscure** the names of other heroes—the ordinary people who fought the battles and supported the armies.

7.

 pewter → Paul Revere was a metalsmith who put aside his silver trays and **pewter** candlesticks to make his famous ride. His riding partners, however, are not as well remembered as he is.

8.

 quaint → These heroes of the Revolutionary War may seem like **quaint** figures in some old-fashioned story, but they played a real role in history.

9.

 quench → Once the desire for liberty flamed in the hearts of these men and women, it was impossible to **quench** the fire of revolution.

10.

 urgent → They came to see independence as an **urgent** need, something to be demanded immediately.

EXERCISE 2 *Context Clues*

Directions. Scan the definitions in Column A. Then, think about how the boldface words are used in the sentences in Column B. To complete the exercise, match each definition in Column A with the correct Vocabulary Word from Column B. Write the letter of your choice on the line provided. Finally, write the Vocabulary Word on the line before the definition.

COLUMN A

_____ **11.** word: _____
adj. attractively old-fashioned; unusual, curious, fanciful

_____ **12.** word: _____
v. to put out (a fire or light); to end or destroy by satisfying or cooling; to cool hot metal by thrusting into water

_____ **13.** word: _____
adj. calling for haste or immediate action; pressing or insistent

_____ **14.** word: _____
n. the closing off of an area by enemy ships or troops; any obstruction or hindrance; *v.* to obstruct or hinder

_____ **15.** word: _____
adj. taking no sides; belonging to neither extreme in type, kind, etc.; having little color; *n.* a nation that takes no sides; a disengaged position of gears

_____ **16.** word: _____
v. to seize by authority

_____ **17.** word: _____
v. to produce or bring into being

_____ **18.** word: _____
adj. unerasable; permanent

_____ **19.** word: _____
adj. not clear; not well known; hidden; dark; *v.* to make dim; to conceal

_____ **20.** word: _____
n. a dull gray alloy of tin with lead, copper, and other metals

COLUMN B

(A) The American Revolution made an **indelible** impression on the world. Its importance to world history cannot be erased.

(B) Actually, some of the founders' ideas once created debate, but now they **generate** little controversy.

(C) People who feel strongly about democracy often cannot understand how anyone could have remained **neutral** during the conflict.

(D) The motives of those colonists who supported the British now seem **obscure** to many people. To historians, however, those motives are clear.

(E) Today, we may think of the founders as pleasantly old-fashioned people in powdered wigs and knee breeches or flowing gowns. In fact, they were much more than **quaint** historical figures.

(F) Their likenesses appear on china cups and **pewter** plates from souvenir stands, but this does not make them trivial.

(G) They were human beings who felt an **urgent** need for liberty and a pressing desire for justice.

(H) Once they took up the cause of liberty, nothing could **quench** their campaign. The founders were not satisfied until they had established independence.

(I) Early patriots fought bravely against the British, who tried to **confiscate** their private property and take away their freedom.

(J) They would let no **blockade** close their ports, nor would they let any obstacle stand in the way of their freedom.

EXERCISE 3 *Like Meanings and Opposite Meanings* 👉

Directions. For each item below, circle the letter of the choice that means the same, or about the same, as the boldface word.

21. to run through the **blockade**
    (A) line
    (B) harbor
    (C) ship
    (D) barrier

22. an observer who is **neutral**
    (A) siding with rebels
    (B) taking neither side
    (C) siding with royalty
    (D) siding with the French

23. a **pewter** tray
    (A) gray metal
    (B) old-fashioned
    (C) expensive
    (D) elegant

24. a **quaint** village
    (A) modern
    (B) small
    (C) old-fashioned
    (D) run-down

25. an **urgent** message
    (A) late
    (B) loud
    (C) important
    (D) secret

Directions. For each item below, circle the letter of the choice that means the opposite, or about the opposite, of the boldface word.

26. to **confiscate** the evidence
    (A) give back
    (B) take away
    (C) forget
    (D) remember

27. to **generate** hope
    (A) cause
    (B) prevent
    (C) consider
    (D) remember

28. an **indelible** mark
    (A) black
    (B) interesting
    (C) erasable
    (D) memorable

29. an **obscure** individual
    (A) famous
    (B) forgotten
    (C) intelligent
    (D) dull

30. to **quench** your thirst
    (A) delight
    (B) satisfy
    (C) end
    (D) worsen

MAKING NEW WORDS YOUR OWN

Lesson 23 | CONTEXT: Voices of the United States
Music of the United States

Music reflects many different heritages. Popular music particularly shows the influence of all the peoples who have built this nation. From be-bop to bluegrass, from swing to salsa, musical styles that were once the property of a particular cultural group have become the standard fare for people of all ages and backgrounds.

In the following exercises, you will have the opportunity to expand your vocabulary by reading about popular music and musicians in the United States. Below are ten Vocabulary Words that will be used in these exercises.

activate	colossal	eccentric	invariable	pious
charitable	confide	intolerance	petty	tarnish

EXERCISE 1   *Wordbusting* ✍

Directions.   Follow these instructions for this word and the nine words on the next page.
- Figure out the word's meaning by looking at its **context,** its **structure,** and its **sound.** Fill in at least one of the three **CSS** boxes. Alternate which boxes you complete.
- Then, look up the word in a dictionary, read all of its meanings, and write the meaning of the word as it is used in the sentence.
- Follow this same process for each of the Vocabulary Words on the next page. You will need to draw your own map for each word. Use a separate sheet of paper.

1.

(activate) → If you would like to **activate** a lively discussion, just ask members of two different generations to discuss what they think good music is.

Context:	Structure:	Sound:

Dictionary:

2.

(charitable) ➜ When people want to be **charitable,** they will admit that another generation's music has value. Still, deep down most of us are convinced that the music we like is the best music.

3.

(colossal) ➜ However, we would be making a big mistake, a **colossal** blunder, to think that one form of music is better than another.

4.

(confide) ➜ No matter what people say in public, in private many will **confide** the realization that different kinds of music can enrich us all.

5.

(eccentric) ➜ People who enjoy unusual music often don't take part in the debate. They feel it is useless to defend their **eccentric** tastes.

6.

(intolerance) ➜ They know, from past experience, that many people show an **intolerance** for unusual music. Sometimes, people are just unwilling to hear music that differs from the kind they prefer.

7.

(invariable) ➜ The older generation's opposition to the younger generation's music seems to be an **invariable** truth of any society. The objections are as changeless as the hills—and almost as old.

8.

(petty) ➜ Arguing about whether country music is better than classical and jazz is a rather **petty** activity. There is room for all kinds of music, and it seems narrow-minded to try to prove that one form of music is better than another.

9.

(pious) ➜ Most of us are annoyed by people who are **pious** about, or devoted to, their personal taste in music and exclude all other types of music.

10.

(tarnish) ➜ You could **tarnish** your reputation as an intelligent person by getting into a silly discussion over whether swing is better than rock.

EXERCISE 2   Context Clues ✍

Directions. Scan the definitions in Column A. Then, think about how the boldface words are used in the sentences in Column B. To complete the exercise, match each definition in Column A with the correct Vocabulary Word from Column B. Write the letter of your choice on the line provided. Finally, write the Vocabulary Word on the line before the definition.

COLUMN A	COLUMN B

_____ **11.** word: _____
n. unwilling to accept beliefs that are different from one's own; sensitivity to a food or medicine

(A) Many popular recording artists do **charitable** work by contributing time and money to important causes.

_____ **12.** word: _____
v. to make active; to set in motion; to start

(B) Some musicians are **invariable** in their support of specific humanitarian causes. They appear at every major benefit.

_____ **13.** word: _____
adj. trivial or unimportant; spiteful; narrow-minded

(C) Their presence seems to **activate** something deep within us. It makes us remember that people have always believed in helping those who are in need.

_____ **14.** word: _____
adj. generous in giving gifts or helping with the needy; lenient when judging others

(D) Songs such as "We Are the World" have been **colossal** successes, helping to raise huge sums of money for worthy causes.

_____ **15.** word: _____
adj. suggesting real or affected devotion to religious beliefs; devout

(E) Musical styles are not religions that require **pious** devotion. Instead, they are interesting reflections of our different heritages.

_____ **16.** word: _____
adj. huge; gigantic; vast; extraordinary

(F) Only a **petty,** or small-minded, person would argue that people should listen to only one kind of music.

_____ **17.** word: _____
v. to dull or detract from the brightness of; to stain or disgrace; *n.* a film of chemically altered metal that dulls the surface

(G) It would certainly **tarnish** my enthusiasm for music if I could only listen to one kind. My interest would become dulled very rapidly.

_____ **18.** word: _____
adj. not changing; without exception

(H) However, I haven't always **confided** in my friends when it comes to music. I don't tell them, for example, of my interest in recordings of traditional Norwegian cow calls, because they might not understand.

_____ **19.** word: _____
adj. very odd in dress or behavior; unconventional; *n.* a person with these qualities

(I) They might think I am an **eccentric** because I listen to a pretty odd assortment of music, from North Carolina sea chanteys to old recordings of Appalachian folk music.

_____ **20.** word: _____
v. to tell in confidence; to hand over for safekeeping; to entrust with

(J) Everyone has the ability to appreciate many kinds of music. Few people have a true **intolerance** for a variety of music.

EXERCISE 3 *Like Meanings and Opposite Meanings* ✍

Directions. For each item below, circle the letter of the choice that means the same, or about the same, as the boldface word.

21. to **confide** to a friend
(A) regret telling
(B) entrust a secret
(C) refuse to speak
(D) listen carefully

22. an **intolerance** for penicillin
(A) inability to find
(B) dislike
(C) inability to take
(D) opposition

23. a **petty** mind
(A) small
(B) large
(C) unusual
(D) ordinary

24. a **pious** believer
(A) devout
(B) confused
(C) insincere
(D) new

25. to remove the **tarnish**
(A) cover
(B) paint
(C) dullness
(D) dirt

Directions. For each item below, circle the letter of the choice that means the opposite, or about the opposite, of the boldface word.

26. to **activate** the machine
(A) start
(B) stop
(C) repair
(D) watch

27. a **charitable** act
(A) forgivable
(B) generous
(C) selfish
(D) unforgiven

28. a **colossal** building
(A) elegant
(B) run-down
(C) tiny
(D) huge

29. an **eccentric** musician
(A) talented
(B) worthy
(C) strange
(D) typical

30. an **invariable** attitude
(A) changeable
(B) unchangeable
(C) confusing
(D) clear

MAKING NEW WORDS YOUR OWN

Lesson 24 | CONTEXT: Voices of the United States

A History of Humor in the United States

Humor and laughter have always been important, and the voice of the United States is as much the voice of its humorists as it is the voice of its serious scholars.

In the following exercises, you will have the opportunity to expand your vocabulary by reading about humor in the United States. Below are ten Vocabulary Words that will be used in these exercises.

apt	deduction	irk	sarcasm	summit
clarify	essay	proposal	successor	temperament

EXERCISE 1 | Wordbusting

Directions. Follow these instructions for this word and the nine words on the next page.
- Figure out the word's meaning by looking at its **context**, its **structure**, and its **sound.** Fill in at least one of the three **CSS** boxes. Alternate which boxes you complete.
- Then, look up the word in a dictionary, read all of its meanings, and write the meaning of the word as it is used in the sentence.
- Follow this same process for each of the Vocabulary Words on the next page. You will need to draw your own map for each word. Use a separate sheet of paper.

1.

(apt) → A sense of humor is important, even vital. In fact, studies have shown that laughter is an **apt** aid in overcoming cancer. It is a helpful tool in fighting many serious diseases.

Context:

Structure:

Sound:

Dictionary:

2.

clarify ➤ Humor can help **clarify** what is truly important. For when we can laugh about something, we can see clearly that what we thought was a grave problem is actually not so serious after all.

3.

deduction ➤ I arrived at this **deduction,** or conclusion, while reading my American history book.

4.

essay ➤ American writers are famous for the humorous **essay**. Benjamin Franklin, Mark Twain, James Thurber, E. B. White, Erma Bombeck, and Nora Ephron are just a few of the writers known for their funny compositions.

5.

irk ➤ These writers have learned to take annoying everyday things that **irk** most of us and show the humor in them.

6.

proposal ➤ When our teacher asked us for **proposals** for our research papers, I suggested that I write about humor in America.

7.

sarcasm ➤ My early research shows that U.S. citizens have always enjoyed a wide range of humor—everything from gentle ribbing to biting **sarcasm**.

8.

successor ➤ The humorists of each generation have had **successors** who have followed them and built on their work.

9.

summit ➤ Some people resent political humor, but most agree that anything can be viewed with humor, even an important **summit,** or meeting between world leaders.

10.

temperament ➤ Basically, people in the U.S. have a **temperament** that allows them to laugh at themselves. Perhaps the ability to poke fun at our own follies is part of human nature.

EXERCISE 2 *Context Clues*

Directions. Scan the definitions in Column A. Then, think about how the boldface words are used in the sentences in Column B. To complete the exercise, match each definition in Column A with the correct Vocabulary Word from Column B. Write the letter of your choice on the line provided. Finally, write the Vocabulary Word on the line before the definition.

COLUMN A	COLUMN B

COLUMN A

_____ **11.** word: _____
v. to make clear by removing impurities; to make understandable by explaining

_____ **12.** word: _____
v. to irritate; to tire out; to trouble

_____ **13.** word: _____
n. a short, often personal, composition on a single topic; an attempt; *v.* to try; to attempt; to test the quality of

_____ **14.** word: _____
n. a plan that is put forward for consideration; a suggestion; an offer of marriage

_____ **15.** word: _____
n. a sharp remark uttered to mock or make fun of something or someone; the use of such remarks

_____ **16.** word: _____
n. one who succeeds or follows another in an office or position; an heir

_____ **17.** word: _____
adj. fitting; likely; clever

_____ **18.** word: _____
n. the highest point; a peak; a meeting of heads of state

_____ **19.** word: _____
n. disposition; the manner in which a person thinks and responds

_____ **20.** word: _____
n. a conclusion based on reasoning; a subtraction; the amount subtracted

COLUMN B

(A) **Essays** by American humorists cover a variety of subjects. These short prose pieces may be about anything from basketball to politics.

(B) Styles of humor also vary and include everything from humorous observations to pointed **sarcasm,** a form of humor that sharply mocks its subject.

(C) Some humorists are more **apt** with certain styles of humor than others. Some might be more clever at using irony, for example.

(D) On the other hand, not every humorist will suit your **temperament**. For example, humor that is very physical might not appeal to you.

(E) Humorists like today's stand-up comics actually help us to **clarify** our values by poking fun at society. They help explain what is important to us and what is not.

(F) Some humor relies on the process of **deduction**. The joke depends on the audience being able to reason logically.

(G) Each generation seems to think that comedy has reached its **summit**. In fact, as time goes on, popular humor gets more and more daring but never peaks.

(H) Many of the things that might **irk** us and provide humor in this day would not have been funny 100 years ago. Modern inventions like the cell phone are the basis for jokes now that would not have been understood in the past.

(I) However, each new humorist is, in a way, a **successor** to the last generation of comics, an heir to a great American tradition.

(J) Humor is so important that I have a **proposal** for your consideration: Let's have special schools or colleges where people can earn degrees in humor!

EXERCISE 3   *Like Meanings and Opposite Meanings* ✍

Directions. For each item below, circle the letter of the choice that means the same, or about the same, as the boldface word.

21. **apt** to cause mildew
    - (A) never
    - (B) attempt
    - (C) likely
    - (D) possible

22. to **essay** the mountain peak
    - (A) avoid
    - (B) announce
    - (C) try
    - (D) remember

23. an unusual **proposal**
    - (A) suggestion
    - (B) indication
    - (C) problem
    - (D) result

24. with **sarcasm** in her voice
    - (A) enthusiasm
    - (B) tiredness
    - (C) good humor
    - (D) mockery

25. a gentle **temperament**
    - (A) person
    - (B) manner
    - (C) remark
    - (D) type of anger

Directions. For each item below, circle the letter of the choice that means the opposite, or about the opposite, of the boldface word.

26. to **clarify** the situation
    - (A) create
    - (B) destroy
    - (C) explain
    - (D) confuse

27. a small **deduction**
    - (A) amount added
    - (B) amount taken away
    - (C) problem created
    - (D) problem stated

28. the **summit** of the mountain
    - (A) price
    - (B) top
    - (C) base
    - (D) snow

29. a worthy **successor**
    - (A) one who comes after
    - (B) one who comes before
    - (C) one who is lost
    - (D) one who is found

30. to **irk** someone
    - (A) bother
    - (B) annoy
    - (C) please
    - (D) disgust

MAKING NEW WORDS YOUR OWN

Lesson 25 | CONTEXT: Voices of the United States

Writers of the United States

All nations have their writers and storytellers. The United States is no different. We have many writers whose different voices tell us stories, inform us about our world, and help us understand our past.

In the following exercises, you will have the opportunity to expand your vocabulary by reading about the role of writers in the United States. Below are ten Vocabulary Words that will be used in these exercises.

| anonymous | climax | famished | fragment | occurrence |
| casual | contemporary | fictitious | literal | therapy |

EXERCISE 1 | Wordbusting

Directions. Follow these instructions for this word and the nine words on the next page.
- Figure out the word's meaning by looking at its **context,** its **structure,** and its **sound.** Fill in at least one of the three **CSS** boxes. Alternate which boxes you complete.
- Then, look up the word in a dictionary, read all of its meanings, and write the meaning of the word as it is used in the sentence.
- Follow this same process for each of the Vocabulary Words on the next page. You will need to draw your own map for each word. Use a separate sheet of paper.

1.

anonymous → Some authors remain **anonymous**. We do not know the names of those who wrote many favorite stories and ballads.

| Context: | Structure: | Sound: |
| | | |

| Dictionary: |
| |

2.

casual →

It is incorrect to believe that people in the United States have only a **casual** interest in literature. Judging from the millions of books sold each year, it is clear that we have a serious interest in reading.

3.

climax →

American literature has not yet reached its peak, or **climax**. In many ways, it continues to reach for new ways to express ideas.

4.

contemporary →

Contemporary life is a great source of material for writers. The modern U.S. experience is interesting to readers as well.

5.

famished →

There is no reason for any person to be **famished** for good writing. Readers can go to any library to get their fill of classic U.S. literature.

6.

fictitious →

Many writers create **fictitious** voices to tell their stories. To readers, however, they often seem real.

7.

fragment →

In the past, some voices went unheard. For example, only a small **fragment** of Emily Dickinson's work was published in her lifetime. Of course, now we have access to her complete works.

8.

literal →

Even nonfiction writers do not always stick to the **literal** truth. They enjoy exaggerating and stretching the facts.

9.

occurrence →

U.S. writers examine important happenings—an **occurrence** such as a political scandal or the presidential election, for example.

10.

therapy →

Writers also give advice on our daily lives. There are books on **therapy,** or the treatment of emotional stress; books on money; and books on how to play golf.

EXERCISE 2 *Context Clues* ✍

Directions. Scan the definitions in Column A. Then, think about how the boldface words are used in the sentences in Column B. To complete the exercise, match each definition in Column A with the correct Vocabulary Word from Column B. Write the letter of your choice on the line provided. Finally, write the Vocabulary Word on the line before the definition.

COLUMN A	COLUMN B
____ **11.** word: _____ *adj.* living at the same time or period; modern; *n.* a person living in the same time period as another	(A) I told my parents that I was going to write a book about my **contemporaries,** or fellow teenagers. I planned to use myself and my friends as examples of today's typical teens.
____ **12.** word: _____ *n.* the point of greatest intensity in any series of events; the most exciting part; the final, most forceful statement	(B) My mother said that, if I did, I had better decide to remain **anonymous**. She didn't want anyone to know my name.
____ **13.** word: _____ *adj.* informal, relaxed; chance, unplanned; occasional; slight, superficial	(C) Dad said I might use a **fictitious** name, something like E. A. Twiddlethorpe.
____ **14.** word: _____ *adj.* by or of an unidentified person	(D) Then my mom said, very seriously, that she thought writing a book would be good **therapy** for me, that it would help me work out all my ~~age anxiety. I burst out laughing.~~
____ **15.** word: _____ *adj.* restricted to the exact meaning; not figurative; word-for-word, as a translation; concerned chiefly with fact	(E) Actually, ~~~~ done was make a **casual** remark while sett~~~~ the table for dinner. I didn't mean for them ~~~~ ke me seriously.
____ **16.** word: _____ *n.* something that takes place; an incident; the action or process of happening	(F) I don't know why I became s~~~~ritable about the whole thing. It was probably ~~~~use I was **famished**. I didn't get to eat lunch th~~~~
____ **17.** word: _____ *n.* treatment to soothe the body or mind; a method of healing	(G) Honestly, my parents have such **literal** minds sometimes. They think I actually mean everything I say.
____ **18.** word: _____ *adj.* extremely hungry; starving	(H) Still, if you had heard even a tiny **fragment** of the conversation, you'd realize that my parents love to joke.
____ **19.** word: _____ *n.* a part of a whole; portion of an incomplete manuscript; *v.* to break into bits	(I) "And what would be the **climax** of this book?" Mom asked. "The time you locked yourself in the basement or the day you accidentally dyed your hair green? I know those were high points in my life."
____ **20.** word: _____ *adj.* imaginary; false; not genuine	(J) My mom doesn't forget anything that happens to me, and Dad is almost as bad. I think they remember every embarrassing **occurrence** in my life.

EXERCISE 3 — *Like Meanings and Opposite Meanings* 👉

Directions. For each item below, circle the letter of the choice that means the same, or about the same, as the boldface word.

21. the **climax** of the story
(A) end
(B) high point
(C) beginning
(D) story

22. the **fragment** of the poem
(A) piece
(B) vision
(C) purpose
(D) memory

23. a **literal** translation
(A) loose
(B) strange
(C) exact
(D) original

24. a strange **occurrence**
(A) presentation
(B) evening
(C) person
(D) happening

25. **therapy** for the injury
(A) payment
(B) judgment
(C) treatment
(D) dependent

Directions. For each item below, circle the letter of the choice that means the opposite, or about the opposite, of the boldface word.

26. an **anonymous** donor
(A) generous
(B) selfish
(C) famous
(D) unknown

27. a **casual** dinner
(A) informal
(B) formal
(C) delicious
(D) unpleasant

28. a **contemporary** figure
(A) modern
(B) important
(C) unimportant
(D) historical

29. a **fictitious** tale
(A) made-up
(B) true
(C) ordinary
(D) unusual

30. the **famished** animal
(A) starving
(B) well-fed
(C) well-known
(D) unimportant

MAKING NEW WORDS YOUR OWN

Lesson 26 | **CONTEXT: Voices of the United States**

The Voice of the Press

An important voice in the United States is the voice of the free press. People sometimes get irritated with reporters and with news coverage. If no one gets upset, however, then the reporters are probably not doing their job. The founders of the United States knew this and made a free press part of the foundation of our Constitution.

In the following exercises, you will have the opportunity to expand your vocabulary by reading about news and reporters. Below are ten Vocabulary Words that will be used in these exercises.

| condemn | dilute | emphasize | falter | intrigue |
| dictate | dispatch | endorse | improvise | modify |

EXERCISE 1 *Wordbusting* 👉

Directions. Follow these instructions for this word and the nine words on the next page.
- Figure out the word's meaning by looking at its **context,** its **structure,** and its **sound.** Fill in at least one of the three **CSS** boxes. Alternate which boxes you complete.
- Then, look up the word in a dictionary, read all of its meanings, and write the meaning of the word as it is used in the sentence.
- Follow this same process for each of the Vocabulary Words on the next page. You will need to draw your own map for each word. Use a separate sheet of paper.

1.

(condemn) → Although we may criticize the actions of a particular reporter or newspaper, few people in the United States will ever **condemn** the idea of a free press.

| Context: | Structure: | Sound: |
| | | |

| Dictionary: |
| |

© Houghton Mifflin Harcourt Publishing Company

2.

(dictate) ➔ People know how important it is that the government not **dictate** what news can be printed or broadcast. A government that has total control over the news is a dangerous government indeed.

3.

(dilute) ➔ A government that controls the press can **dilute,** or weaken, the people's confidence in the press. Few readers believe what is written in newspapers controlled by the government.

4.

(dispatch) ➔ Reporters have serious responsibilities. When they send a **dispatch** to their newspapers, the facts contained in that report must be accurate and up-to-date.

5.

(emphasize) ➔ On the editorial page, the editors are free to **emphasize,** or stress, a certain point of view. However, the opposite point of view should also be addressed.

6.

(endorse) ➔ Newspapers do **endorse** particular political candidates. They show their support by printing favorable letters and editorials.

7.

(falter) ➔ Lack of support by a newspaper can cause a politician's campaign to **falter**. Moreover, once a candidate stumbles, the political race may be lost.

8.

(improvise) ➔ Good reporters go to an interview with prepared questions. They do not like to have to **improvise** their questions on the spot.

9.

(intrigue) ➔ People think reporters' lives are filled with **intrigue,** that they have inside knowledge of plots and schemes. Yet, most reporters wind up covering everyday stories, such as the opening of a new shopping mall or a city council meeting.

10.

(modify) ➔ Good editors do not tamper with the facts of a story; however, they may **modify** a story by changing some words or by cutting it to a certain length.

EXERCISE 2 *Context Clues* ✍

Directions. Scan the definitions in Column A. Then, think about how the boldface words are used in the sentences in Column B. To complete the exercise, match each definition in Column A with the correct Vocabulary Word from Column B. Write the letter of your choice on the line provided. Finally, write the Vocabulary Word on the line before the definition.

COLUMN A	COLUMN B

COLUMN A

_____ **11.** word: _____

v. to give support or approval to; to sign one's name on the back of a check or similar document for validation

_____ **12.** word: _____

v. to criticize or pass judgment against; to find guilty; to find unfit or unsafe

_____ **13.** word: _____

v. to hesitate; to stumble; to stammer

_____ **14.** word: _____

v. to recite something to be recorded; to require or order authoritatively

_____ **15.** word: _____

v. to compose or perform without preparation; to make something from whatever materials are available

_____ **16.** word: _____

n. a message; quickness; efficiency; *v.* to send; to finish quickly; to kill

_____ **17.** word: _____

n. sly or secret scheming; a conspiracy; *v.* to plot or scheme; to excite interest

_____ **18.** word: _____

v. to alter in form or character; in grammar, to qualify the meaning of

_____ **19.** word: _____

v. to denote as important; to stress

_____ **20.** word: _____

v. to thin or weaken by adding liquid; to lessen intensity, purity, strength

COLUMN B

(A) Editors usually make the assignments. They may **dispatch** a reporter to a crime scene or send the reporter to the city council meeting.

(B) Wanting to be certain that reporters get all the facts, editors will **condemn** any reporting that is sloppy or inaccurate.

(C) Usually a reporter's talents **dictate** what assignment he or she will get. One story may require a reporter with a science background, while another may require a reporter with Spanish-speaking skills.

(D) Editors **emphasize** that it is a reporter's duty to report accurately. They also stress thoroughness and good writing.

(E) Reporters frequently hit stumbling blocks that cause them to **falter** when reporting stories. However, a good reporter always charges on and follows a story to the end.

(F) The job of a reporter **intrigues** many people. They think it is fascinating work.

(G) Even after having written their stories, reporters may **modify** them, or make changes to them, based on new information.

(H) Like all other writers, reporters **endorse** the practice of revision. They strongly believe that good writers must rewrite.

(I) Good reporters know that too many words can **dilute** the impact of a story, so they edit to strengthen their work.

(J) While it is sometimes tempting to **improvise** a story—to throw it together with few real facts or quotations to back it up—a good reporter always tries to be truthful, accurate, and thorough.

EXERCISE 3   *Like Meanings and Opposite Meanings* ✍

Directions. For each item below, circle the letter of the choice that means the same, or about the same, as the boldface word.

21. to **dictate** the letter
- (A) read for another to record
- (B) record for another to read
- (C) write for another to read
- (D) be unable to read

22. to **dilute** the solution
- (A) strengthen
- (B) boil
- (C) weaken
- (D) analyze

23. to **endorse** the check
- (A) write something on
- (B) handle carefully
- (C) sign the back of
- (D) give away

24. to **falter** on the path
- (A) run
- (B) stumble
- (C) follow
- (D) hurry

25. to **modify** the report
- (A) write
- (B) change
- (C) continue
- (D) ignore

Directions. For each item below, circle the letter of the choice that means the opposite, or about the opposite, as the boldface word.

26. to **condemn** the action
- (A) discuss
- (B) criticize
- (C) praise
- (D) remember

27. to **emphasize** the point
- (A) ignore
- (B) stress
- (C) make
- (D) hurry

28. an **improvised** performance
- (A) rehearsed
- (B) special
- (C) unusual
- (D) offhand

29. to **intrigue** the audience
- (A) entertain
- (B) bore
- (C) interest
- (D) anger

30. to work with **dispatch**
- (A) speed
- (B) slowness
- (C) hope
- (D) unhappiness

MAKING NEW WORDS YOUR OWN

Lesson 27 **CONTEXT: Voices of the United States**

The Voice of Justice

The founders of this country understood the importance of a strong and fair system of courts. One basic principle of justice is that the accused is innocent until proven guilty. Another is that those accused shall have the opportunity to defend themselves in court. Such principles have made the U.S. system of justice a voice that speaks of democracy.

In the following exercises, you will have the opportunity to expand your vocabulary by reading about the U.S. legal system. Below are ten Vocabulary Words that will be used in these exercises.

articulate	demolish	detach	illuminate	testify
category	denial	distraction	inclination	upbraid

EXERCISE 1 *Wordbusting*

Directions. Follow these instructions for this word and the nine words on the next page.
- Figure out the word's meaning by looking at its **context,** its **structure,** and its **sound.** Fill in at least one of the three **CSS** boxes. Alternate which boxes you complete.
- Then, look up the word in a dictionary, read all of its meanings, and write the meaning of the word as it is used in the sentence.
- Follow this same process for each of the Vocabulary Words on the next page. You will need to draw your own map for each word. Use a separate sheet of paper.

1.

(articulate) → The voices in our justice system must be **articulate**. They must speak clearly for both the accuser and the accused.

Context:

Structure:

Sound:

Dictionary:

2.

category ➡ Lawyers may choose from several different kinds of law in which to specialize. One **category** is criminal law.

3.

demolish ➡ Often, lawyers have to **demolish,** or destroy, the statements made by witnesses against their clients.

4.

denial ➡ The courts are designed to give everyone a fair hearing. **Denial** of this basic right is dangerous to society—even when it is a guilty person who is refused the right.

5.

detach ➡ Judges are supposed to be fair and objective. Therefore, they try to **detach** themselves from the emotions of a situation and listen to the facts.

6.

distraction ➡ Some lawyers use **distraction** as a technique in court. If the facts are not in a client's favor, the lawyer tries to draw the jury's attention away from the facts.

7.

illuminate ➡ One purpose of a trial is to **illuminate** the truth surrounding the case. Ideally, all the facts are brought to light.

8.

inclination ➡ It may be against a lawyer's **inclination** to defend a client who appears to be guilty. But most lawyers are able to overcome this leaning.

9.

testify ➡ The lawyer is responsible for calling witnesses to **testify,** or give evidence, on behalf of the client.

10.

upbraid ➡ Sometimes lawyers must **upbraid,** or reproach, their clients for not telling them the complete truth. In order to defend clients properly, lawyers have to know all the facts before they enter the courtroom.

EXERCISE 2 *Context Clues* ☞

Directions. Scan the definitions in Column A. Then, think about how the boldface words are used in the sentences in Column B. To complete the exercise, match each definition in Column A with the correct Vocabulary Word from Column B. Write the letter of your choice on the line provided. Finally, write the Vocabulary Word on the line before the definition.

COLUMN A

_____ **11.** word: _____

n. a division or group in any classification system; a class

_____ **12.** word: _____

v. to provide with light; to make understandable; to clarify; to decorate a manuscript with colorful designs

_____ **13.** word: _____

v. to bear witness to, especially in court; to give evidence

_____ **14.** word: _____

v. to unfasten; to disconnect

_____ **15.** word: _____

n. a tendency; a personal preference or liking; a slant or slope

_____ **16.** word: _____

v. to tear down; to wreck; to ruin

_____ **17.** word: _____

n. something that diverts or draws attention away; the act of diverting attention; a condition of mental distress

_____ **18.** word: _____

n. a statement that something is false; a refusal of a request or a right; a rejection of a belief

_____ **19.** word: _____

adj. using distinct syllables or words; able to speak clearly; *v.* to speak clearly and distinctly; to express in words

_____ **20.** word: _____

v. to scold or criticize sharply

COLUMN B

(A) Because I can express myself so clearly, I think I would be a good lawyer. I would not be afraid to **articulate** my ideas in court.

(B) Because I want to be a lawyer, I study hard and avoid any **distraction** that might take my mind off my studies.

(C) When I study at night, I use an old-fashioned desk lamp to **illuminate** my books and papers.

(D) I study hard for every test, although sometimes that means fighting my **inclination** to go outside and play basketball.

(E) I admit that my attention often wanders, and that irritates me. Sometimes, I am forced to **upbraid** myself for not paying attention.

(F) My brother can **testify** that he has caught me shooting long shots into the wastepaper basket.

(G) I had better become a lawyer—because when I play basketball with my brother, he **demolishes** me. He has destroyed my dream of a basketball career.

(H) Of course, a dream of a basketball career means a **denial** of my 5'2" height. Lawyers, though, don't have to worry about refusing to accept the truth that they are short.

(I) Sometimes I try to figure out which **category** of law I might enjoy. Instead of working as a criminal lawyer in the courts, I could work in real estate law or tax law for the government.

(J) However, when I stay in my fantasy world too long, my brother reminds me that I have **detached** myself from reality again.

EXERCISE 3   *Like Meanings and Opposite Meanings*

Directions. For each item below, circle the letter of the choice that means the same, or about the same, as the boldface word.

21. a **category** of books
(A) hatred
(B) love
(C) study
(D) grouping

22. an interesting **distraction**
(A) something that draws away attention
(B) something that improves attention
(C) something that is boring
(D) something that destroys

23. the **inclination** of the cliff
(A) height
(B) trend
(C) difficulty
(D) slope

24. to **upbraid** the person
(A) feed
(B) jail
(C) scold
(D) ignore

25. to **testify** honestly
(A) reward
(B) listen
(C) declare
(D) ignore

Directions. For each item below, circle the letter of the choice that means the opposite, or about the opposite, of the boldface word.

26. to **detach** the pieces
(A) take off
(B) connect
(C) examine
(D) tape together

27. to **illuminate** the room
(A) discover
(B) paint
(C) brighten
(D) darken

28. to **demolish** the work
(A) create
(B) destroy
(C) remember
(D) finish

29. to **articulate** her wishes
(A) speak
(B) remain silent about
(C) read about
(D) agree with

30. a **denial** of his words
(A) description
(B) understanding
(C) support
(D) contradiction

MAKING NEW WORDS YOUR OWN

Lesson 28 | CONTEXT: Voices of the United States

Super Voices: The World of Comics

For several generations now, people in the United States have delighted in comic books. Superheroes have been especially popular, perhaps because they support many U.S. values. Superman, for example, believes in truth, justice, and the "American way."

In the following exercises, you will have the opportunity to expand your vocabulary by reading about comic books from the point of view of a collector. Below are ten Vocabulary Words that will be used in these exercises.

braggart	eligible	imply	secluded	tangible
derive	extensive	miscellaneous	superficial	unique

EXERCISE 1 Wordbusting ✍

Directions. Follow these instructions for this word and the nine words on the next page.
- Figure out the word's meaning by looking at its **context,** its **structure,** and its **sound.** Fill in at least one of the three **CSS** boxes. Alternate which boxes you complete.
- Then, look up the word in a dictionary, read all of its meanings, and write the meaning of the word as it is used in the sentence.
- Follow this same process for each of the Vocabulary Words on the next page. You will need to draw your own map for each word. Use a separate sheet of paper.

1.

(braggart) ➝ I have become quite the **braggart**. I now own about 500 comic books and love to boast about my varied collection.

Context:

Structure:

Sound:

Dictionary:

Name _____ Date _____ Class _____

2.
(derive) ➤ I **derive** a great deal of pleasure from my comic books. They are a good source of entertainment.

3.
(eligible) ➤ Few, if any, comic books are **eligible** to be called great literature, but many meet the requirements of good popular literature.

4.
(extensive) ➤ I have an **extensive** collection of comics. I have old comics, brand-new comics, and even some comics from other parts of the world.

5.
(imply) ➤ I don't want to **imply,** or suggest, that comics are all I read, but I do spend a lot of time with my favorite superheroes.

6.
(miscellaneous) ➤ When I began to collect comics, I also started collecting **miscella-neous** items associated with superheroes, anything from buttons to posters to action figures.

7.
(secluded) ➤ I like to read my comics in a **secluded** spot, a place where no one will bother me.

8.
(superficial) ➤ Not all comics are **superficial** entertainment. Some address serious issues that can touch readers at a deep level.

9.
(tangible) ➤ Many offer **tangible** support for important values. For example, they make the concepts of equality and justice more concrete by bringing those ideas to life on the page.

10.
(unique) ➤ One **unique** comic book hero is Flaming Carrot. There is no one else like him!

EXERCISE 2   *Context Clues* ✍

Directions. Scan the definitions in Column A. Then, think about how the boldface words are used in the sentences in Column B. To complete the exercise, match each definition in Column A with the correct Vocabulary Word from Column B. Write the letter of your choice on the line provided. Finally, write the Vocabulary Word on the line before the definition.

COLUMN A	COLUMN B

COLUMN A

____ **11.** word: _____
adj. cut off; remote; isolated; private

____ **12.** word: _____
adj. at the surface; shallow, not deep

____ **13.** word: _____
adj. capable of being touched; concrete; that can be understood; definite

____ **14.** word: _____
n. someone who brags excessively; a know-it-all; *adj.* boastful

____ **15.** word: _____
adj. being the only one of its kind; rare

____ **16.** word: _____
v. to receive or trace, as from a source; to arrive at by logic; to come (from)

____ **17.** word: _____
adj. fit or worthy to be chosen; qualified; suitable or desirable

____ **18.** word: _____
adj. far-reaching; vast; of wide scope

____ **19.** word: _____
v. to suggest without actually stating; to hint; to involve as necessary circumstance or logical necessity

____ **20.** word: _____
adj. made up of varied parts; possessing a variety of characteristics or abilities; varied; assorted

COLUMN B

(A) A character doesn't have to have fantastic powers to be **eligible** to be a superhero. Batman has no powers other than those of an ordinary human, yet he is worthy of the title superhero.

(B) The name X-Men seems to **imply** all male characters, but this group of comic-book heroes includes many females.

(C) Many superhero groups have **extensive** casts of characters. For example, there are too many X-Men for me to remember them all.

(D) Some heroes **derive** their names from characters in mythology. For example, Thor gets his name from a Scandinavian god.

(E) Generally, superheroes are not **braggarts**. Many of them have special powers but use them without boasting about them.

(F) Phoenix has the power to move objects. In fact, she can move any **tangible,** or solid, object with her mind.

(G) Superman operates from a **secluded** fortress in a freezing arctic region where no one can reach him.

(H) Many superheroes have had only **superficial** appeal, but others have had a deep and enduring appeal to generations of readers.

(I) Comic-book writers try to make their characters interesting. They give each character a **unique** personality. No two are alike.

(J) There are so many **miscellaneous** titles, so many varied heroes, that almost all of us can find a comic that suits our tastes.

EXERCISE 3 *Like Meanings and Opposite Meanings* ✍

Directions. For each item below, circle the letter of the choice that means the same, or about the same, as the boldface word.

21. to **derive** pleasure
    (A) get
    (B) spend
    (C) lose
    (D) save

22. to **imply** otherwise
    (A) announce
    (B) suggest
    (C) pretend
    (D) look

23. a **miscellaneous** collection
    (A) large
    (B) valuable
    (C) varied
    (D) organized

24. **tangible** proof
    (A) believed
    (B) mysterious
    (C) unusual
    (D) concrete

25. a **braggart** attitude
    (A) boastful
    (B) rude
    (C) brave
    (D) hostile

Directions. For each item below, circle the letter of the choice that means the opposite, or about the opposite, of the boldface word.

26. an **eligible** candidate
    (A) likely
    (B) unsuitable
    (C) available
    (D) interested

27. an **extensive** list
    (A) unusual
    (B) uninteresting
    (C) lengthy
    (D) limited

28. a **secluded** street
    (A) empty
    (B) busy
    (C) wide
    (D) narrow

29. a **superficial** interest
    (A) business
    (B) personal
    (C) shallow
    (D) deep

30. a **unique** characteristic
    (A) unusual
    (B) common
    (C) important
    (D) unimportant

MAKING NEW WORDS YOUR OWN

Lesson 29 | CONTEXT: Voices of the United States
Listening to the Radio

Long before television came into our homes, there was radio. People probably relied on it for music and news and entertainment. Once, radio was the voice of the United States, and today, in some ways, it still is.

In the following exercises, you will have the opportunity to expand your vocabulary by reading about radio. Below are ten Vocabulary Words that will be used in these exercises.

arrogant	congest	hypothesis	rebate	technology
commute	considerate	malfunction	synthetic	warranty

EXERCISE 1   Wordbusting 👉

Directions.   Follow these instructions for this word and the nine words on the next page.
- Figure out the word's meaning by looking at its **context,** its **structure,** and its **sound.** Fill in at least one of the three **CSS** boxes. Alternate which boxes you complete.
- Then, look up the word in a dictionary, read all of its meanings, and write the meaning of the word as it is used in the sentence.
- Follow this same process for each of the Vocabulary Words on the next page. You will need to draw your own map for each word. Use a separate sheet of paper.

1.

(arrogant) → Sometimes I can be **arrogant** about the radio programs I like. I definitely think that my favorite music stations are better than the talk radio Dad listens to.

Context:	Structure:	Sound:

Dictionary:

2.

commute ➤ My sister listens to the radio as she **commutes** back and forth to work. It's a two-hour round trip, so she knows every radio station in range.

3.

congest ➤ When traffic **congests** the freeway, she doesn't complain too much about the horns and the slow pace. She just cranks up the volume and sings along with the golden oldies station.

4.

considerate ➤ I try to be **considerate** of my parents and not play my radio too loud since I know they don't like it.

5.

hypothesis ➤ I have a **hypothesis** about hearing, but I haven't tested my theory. I suspect that at twenty-five years of age people grow new nerve endings in their ears. After that, they think everything is too loud.

6.

malfunction ➤ My mom teases me when she hears some of the music I listen to. She claims that my radio is making strange noises and that it must have a **malfunction**.

7.

rebate ➤ Dad listens to the radio, too. That's how he heard about the **rebate**, or cash-back offer, on a state-of-the-art radio. Naturally, he bought one.

8.

warranty ➤ The radio came with a **warranty**, but Dad didn't save it; he believes that nothing can go wrong with this radio.

9.

technology ➤ **Technology** has improved the quality of radio. Scientific discoveries have allowed for clearer broadcasting and reception.

10.

synthetic ➤ He hates music that sounds fake, or **synthetic**, like the mellow stuff played in grocery stores.

EXERCISE 2 Context Clues ✍

Directions. Scan the definitions in Column A. Then, think about how the boldface words are used in the sentences in Column B. To complete the exercise, match each definition in Column A with the correct Vocabulary Word from Column B. Write the letter of your choice on the line provided. Finally, write the Vocabulary Word on the line before the definition.

COLUMN A

_____ **11.** word: _____
v. to fail to function or act as expected;
n. a failure to work as expected

_____ **12.** word: _____
n. the technical methods of applying scientific and industrial skills to practical uses; applied science

_____ **13.** word: _____
n. an unproven theory

_____ **14.** word: _____
n. a guarantee by the seller that a product will maintain a certain standard or be replaced or repaired

_____ **15.** word: _____
n. a partial refund; *v.* to give back part of an original payment

_____ **16.** word: _____
adj. artificial; made by chemical process to imitate a natural product

_____ **17.** word: _____
adj. to be full of undue self-importance or feelings of superiority

_____ **18.** word: _____
v. to change; to change a penalty to a less severe one; to travel back and forth

_____ **19.** word: _____
v. to overcrowd; to clog, as with mucus

_____ **20.** word: _____
adj. thoughtful; kind; taking the needs of others into account

COLUMN B

(A) To be **considerate,** I agreed to listen to some tapes my granddad has of old radio shows. I didn't want to hurt his feelings.

(B) My **hypothesis** was that anything recorded before I was born was dull and boring. My theory was wrong.

(C) Granddad told me that his father's family used to have a big radio encased in maple wood. He dislikes the **synthetic,** plastic radios we have today.

(D) "No wonder they come with a **rebate,**" he says. "They'd definitely have to pay me to buy one."

(E) I don't want to sound **arrogant,** or overbearing, but I keep trying to convince Granddad that he would find the sound of those old radios intolerable today.

(F) I remind him that **technology** has improved radio a great deal. Because of applied sciences, sound is much better today.

(G) Granddad keeps expecting mine to **malfunction,** but it works fine.

(H) I also remind him that it came with a **warranty**. If it were to fail to work, the company would just give me another one.

(I) When I had a sore throat and a **congested** chest, I stayed in bed. To entertain myself, I listened to Granddad's tapes.

(J) At first, Mom said that I had to stay in all weekend because I was sick. However, on Sunday afternoon, she decided to **commute** my sentence to time already served, so I went to Granddad's house to borrow more tapes.

EXERCISE 3 *Like Meanings and Opposite Meanings* ✍

Directions. For each item below, circle the letter of the choice that means the same, or about the same, as the boldface word.

21. to **commute** the penalty
(A) change
(B) borrow
(C) recognize
(D) review

22. a strange **hypothesis**
(A) individual
(B) animal
(C) medicine
(D) theory

23. a new **technology**
(A) type of business
(B) application of science
(C) guarantee
(D) machine

24. a six-month **warranty**
(A) school term
(B) guarantee
(C) vacation
(D) return trip

25. to **malfunction** often
(A) prevent
(B) break down
(C) attend
(D) throw away

Directions. For each item below, circle the letter of the choice that means the opposite, or about the opposite, of the boldface word.

26. to **congest** the tunnel
(A) enter
(B) build
(C) crowd
(D) clear

27. a **considerate** person
(A) wealthy
(B) poor
(C) rude
(D) thoughtful

28. a **synthetic** rose
(A) artificial
(B) real
(C) lovely
(D) ugly

29. an **arrogant** attitude
(A) haughty
(B) rude
(C) pleasant
(D) sneering

30. to **rebate** the money
(A) give back
(B) divide
(C) subtract
(D) keep

MAKING NEW WORDS YOUR OWN

Lesson 30 | CONTEXT: Voices of the United States

Voices at Work

The voice of science is a powerful one. Science has brought about many changes in our lives—in our homes, in our schools, and in our places of work. Even now, changes are occurring that will affect the jobs and careers you will choose.

In the following exercises, you will have the opportunity to expand your vocabulary by reading about some of the differences science has made in the workplace. Below are ten Vocabulary Words that will be used in these exercises.

aeronautics	antibiotics	erosion	parasitic	planetarium
agenda	automaton	hydraulic	photogenic	respiration

EXERCISE 1   *Wordbusting* ✍

Directions. Follow these instructions for this word and the nine words on the next page.
- Figure out the word's meaning by looking at its **context,** its **structure,** and its **sound.** Fill in at least one of the three **CSS** boxes. Alternate which boxes you complete.
- Then, look up the word in a dictionary, read all of its meanings, and write the meaning of the word as it is used in the sentence.
- Follow this same process for each of the Vocabulary Words on the next page. You will need to draw your own map for each word. Use a separate sheet of paper.

1.

aeronautics → **Aeronautics** is an interesting field. People have been designing and building airplanes successfully only since the beginning of the twentieth century.

Context:

Structure:

Sound:

Dictionary:

2.

agenda ➡️ The conference **agenda** covered the most fascinating advances in software design.

3.

antibiotics ➡️ Think of the lives that have been saved as a result of the discovery of **antibiotics**. Before these medicines were discovered, even simple infections could lead to death.

4.

automaton ➡️ Thanks to science, much dull and repetitive work that was done by human beings can now be done by robots, or **automatons**.

5.

erosion ➡️ Studies of the causes of **erosion** have helped us to figure out how to stop land from washing away.

6.

hydraulic ➡️ My father operates a machine that runs on **hydraulic,** or liquid, pressure.

7.

parasitic ➡️ Think, too, of the work we have done in eliminating **parasitic** diseases, ailments caused by organisms that feed off host animals.

8.

photogenic ➡️ There have been many advances in photography, too. Even those of us who are not **photogenic** can be made to look good.

9.

planetarium ➡️ High-powered telescopes have made a trip to the **planetarium** even more exciting. Now, the projections of the stars and planets show things you never before knew existed!

10.

respiration ➡️ Thanks to scientists, we know more about everything—from the **respiration,** or breathing processes, of the horned lizard to the first moon of Jupiter.

EXERCISE 2 *Context Clues* ☞

Directions. Scan the definitions in Column A. Then, think about how the boldface words are used in the sentences in Column B. To complete the exercise, match each definition in Column A with the correct Vocabulary Word from Column B. Write the letter of your choice on the line provided. Finally, write the Vocabulary Word on the line before the definition.

COLUMN A	**COLUMN B**
_____ **11.** word: _____ *n.* a list of things to be done; things to be dealt with in a business meeting	(A) If you believe there has been an **erosion** of dedication in the U.S. workplace, consider these voices. They will prove that care and devotion have not deteriorated.
_____ **12.** word: _____ *adj.* living at the expense of or taking advantage of others; living on an organism and contributing nothing	(B) After the doctor examines her patient, she says, "His **respiration** is irregular. Get him on oxygen until he can breathe normally."
_____ **13.** word: _____ *n.* the science and practice of aircraft navigation; the engineering of aircraft	(C) "We had better start him on **antibiotics,** too. There is a danger of infection," the doctor adds.
_____ **14.** word: _____ *n.* a building with a domed ceiling onto which images of celestial bodies are projected	(D) "Has he been anywhere that he might have picked up a parasite? His blood work suggests that some **parasitic** creature may be living in his body."
_____ **15.** word: _____ *adj.* moved or operated by compressing water or some other liquid	(E) The foreman calls to a worker, "Get three crates from the warehouse. Use the **hydraulic** lift, but first make sure that it isn't leaking fluid again."
_____ **16.** word: _____ *adj.* having qualities that are attractive or suitable for photographing	(F) He adds, "Chester, you're beginning to look like an **automaton**. Let's put you to work at a task that will make you feel more like a human and less like a machine."
_____ **17.** word: _____ *n.* infection-fighting substances derived from microorganisms	(G) The director says, "I know he is **photogenic**. The camera loves him, but I want someone who can act. This is a serious film."
_____ **18.** word: _____ *n.* a gradual wearing away (as of the earth's surface); deterioration	(H) The engineer announces, "I have never regretted my decision to go into **aeronautics**. I love designing aircraft."
_____ **19.** word: _____ *n.* a robot; a person acting like a robot	(I) The architect says, "My favorite project is the **planetarium**. I designed it to produce the best possible model of the heavens."
_____ **20.** word: _____ *n.* breathing; a complete breath, including inhaling and exhaling	(J) "Make correcting the errors number one on your **agenda,**" the editor says. "Since thousands of students will be using these books, they need to be perfect!"

EXERCISE 3 *Like Meanings and Opposite Meanings* ✍

Directions. For each item below, circle the letter of the choice that means the same, or about the same, as the boldface word.

21. an interest in **aeronautics**
- (A) flying
- (B) medicine
- (C) astronomy
- (D) science

22. the cost of **antibiotics**
- (A) cameras
- (B) robots
- (C) science
- (D) medicine

23. with **hydraulic** pressure
- (A) decreasing
- (B) liquid
- (C) great
- (D) unfair

24. a view at the **planetarium**
- (A) robot for building machinery
- (B) expensive spacecraft
- (C) room for viewing the stars
- (D) factory for making microscopes

25. the rate of **respiration**
- (A) eating
- (B) breathing
- (C) sleeping
- (D) working

Directions. For each item below, circle the letter of the choice that means the opposite, or about the opposite, of the boldface word.

26. the **erosion** of hope
- (A) end
- (B) beginning
- (C) wearing away
- (D) building up

27. a **parasitic** being
- (A) dependent
- (B) independent
- (C) intelligent
- (D) ridiculous

28. a **photogenic** man
- (A) creative
- (B) unattractive
- (C) sick
- (D) well-behaved

29. a small **automaton**
- (A) robot
- (B) free-spirited person
- (C) problem
- (D) machine-like person

30. a review of the **agenda**
- (A) things to be done
- (B) things completed
- (C) items of business
- (D) listed in a series

© Houghton Mifflin Harcourt Publishing Company

INTRODUCTION

UNDERSTANDING NEW WORDS AND THEIR USES

Building Your Vocabulary

One way to build your vocabulary is to learn the different meanings of a single word. Another way is to learn how to make new words by using prefixes and suffixes. A third way is to learn about the origins of words. Learning about the origins of words will help you remember the words' meanings. The following exercises will help you build on, and remember, vocabulary.

HOW TO DO EXERCISE 1 *Multimeaning* 🖎

Words often have more than one meaning. In a Multimeaning exercise, you will read a boldface Vocabulary Word in a sentence. You will then read four more sentences that use the same Vocabulary Word. Your job is to choose the sentence that uses the Vocabulary Word in the same way as it is used in the first sentence. Here is an example of a Multimeaning exercise:

> The fog of nineteenth-century London was, in fact, **foul** air caused by pollution.
>
> **(A)** Soot from the city's many chimneys would also **foul** the air.
> **(B)** In this setting, Detective Sherlock Holmes tracks down **foul** murderers and other evil-doers.
> **(C)** Nothing keeps Holmes from the chase. He goes out into the streets of London even in a thunderstorm or other **foul** weather.
> **(D)** Waste dumped into London's river Thames had made the waterway **foul**.

In the first sentence, the air was **foul** because of pollution. Pollution makes things dirty or impure. **Foul** is used as an adjective to mean dirty or impure. How does this compare to the uses of the word in choices A, B, C, and D?

- In choice A, **foul** is a verb meaning to pollute or make dirty.
- In choice B, **foul** means evil, not dirty.
- In choice C, **foul** is used to describe weather, and it means unfavorable or stormy.
- In the correct choice, D, **foul** again describes something made dirty or impure.

HOW TO DO EXERCISE 2 *Word Analysis* 🖎

Prefixes and Suffixes

The following items will give you practice in identifying the kinds of prefixes and suffixes that you will run into again and again as you read. In each of these items, you will read two words. Both words will contain the same prefix or suffix. You will be asked to identify the choice that describes the meaning of the prefix or suffix as it is used in both words. Here is an example of a prefix exercise:

readjust   **re**write
(A) after
(B) with
(C) before
(D) again

Hint #1 The second word will usually be a word that you already know well. For example, you probably already know that *rewrite* means "to write again."

Hint #2 The first word or its root (in this case, *adjust*) is a Vocabulary Word in this program. When you remember that *rewrite* means "to write again," you can guess that *readjust* means "to adjust again." That leads you to the correct choice, D.

Note: The tables in the front of this book list some common prefixes and suffixes. These tables will help you to complete the exercises on *Prefixes* and *Suffixes* in the lessons that follow.

Word Origins

Many words in the English language come from Greek, Latin, French, and other languages. Word Origins exercises will give you practice in learning the roots of Vocabulary Words. In these exercises, you will be asked to identify the choice that best completes the sentence.

Here is an example of a Word Origins exercise:

debt   decrease   definite   descriptive

The Latin word *crescere*, "to grow," combined with the prefix *de–*, "away," gives us the word _____.

Hint #1 Compare the Latin root to the list of words provided above the item. If you remove *de–* from all of the choices, the part of the word left that most resembles the Latin root would be *–crease*, from the word *decrease*.

Hint #2 The choices in Word Origins will be Vocabulary Words you studied in *Making New Words Your Own*. In the introduction to *Making New Words Your Own*, you learned that to decrease means "to grow smaller." *Decrease* is the correct response.

UNDERSTANDING NEW WORDS AND THEIR USES

Lesson 1 | CONTEXT: The First Americans
Learning from American Indian Cultures

EXERCISE 1 *Multimeaning*

Directions. Read each numbered sentence below. Then, circle the letter of the choice that uses the boldface word in the same way as it is used in the numbered sentence.

1. American Indians have always believed that it is wrong to **abuse** the land.
   (A) They did not tolerate the **abuse** of animals either.
   (B) They killed animals only when they thought it was necessary. To kill for fun was considered an **abuse**.
   (C) Today many people are involved in the attempt to prevent **abuse** of the environment.
   (D) Many people follow the wisdom of the American Indian elders who teach them not to **abuse** the earth and its residents.

2. At first, the ways of the Europeans seemed to **baffle** American Indians.
   (A) On the other hand, the ways of the American Indians seemed to **baffle,** or confuse, the Europeans.
   (B) As Europeans moved westward, rugged mountains and raging rivers continued to **baffle** their progress.
   (C) The American Indians who occupied the land also **baffled** European settlers' plans for westward movement.
   (D) Some American Indians resisted and temporarily **baffled** the Europeans' settlement of their tribal lands, but ultimately the settlers prevailed.

EXERCISE 2 *Word Analysis*

Prefixes

Directions. Read the numbered pair of words below. Then, circle the letter of the choice that best describes the meaning of the underlined prefix as it is used in each pair.

3. **un**intentional   **un**certain
   (A) not
   (B) against
   (C) over
   (D) before

4. **im**probable   **im**possible
   (A) not
   (B) against
   (C) over
   (D) before

Suffixes

Directions. Read the numbered pair of words below. Then, circle the letter of the choice that best describes the meaning of the underlined suffix as it is used in each pair.

5. roman<u>ic</u>   poet<u>ic</u>
    (A) in the direction of
    (B) characteristic of
    (C) state of being
    (D) study of

6. sincer<u>ity</u>   possibil<u>ity</u>
    (A) state of being
    (B) study of
    (C) like
    (D) one who does

Word Origins

Directions. Read each of the following sentences. Then, from the vocabulary list below, choose the word that best completes the sentence. Write the word in the blank.

abuse	calamity	folklore	picturesque
appalling	contagious	intentional	probable
baffle	deceive	knoll	romantic
barbarism	eminent	myriad	ruthless
bewilder	epidemic	novelty	sincerity

7. We get a hint of the meaning of the word _____ when we learn that the Middle English word *appallen* means "to grow pale."

8. You may recognize the Greek word *barbaros,* meaning "foreign," in the Modern English word _____.

9. The German word *knollen,* meaning "lump," is closely related to our word _____.

10. You may recognize the Old French word *novel,* meaning "new," in our word _____.

UNDERSTANDING NEW WORDS AND THEIR USES

Lesson 2 | CONTEXT: The First Americans
When Cultures Intermingled

EXERCISE 1 *Multimeaning* ✍

Directions. Read each numbered sentence below. Then, circle the letter of the choice that uses the boldface word in the same way as it is used in the numbered sentence.

1. Many Europeans came to North America seeking **sanctuary** from religious persecution. They hoped to have a place where they were safe to practice their religion.
   (A) Cliff-dwelling Indians built underground chambers called *kivas,* a type of **sanctuary** where they held religious ceremonies.
   (B) Some cliff dwellers lived in caves which provided shelter and **sanctuary** for the families.
   (C) When Europeans first came to America, there was no need for a bird **sanctuary**. Because the land was not heavily populated by humans, a special place did not need to be set aside to protect the birds.
   (D) Some early North American Indians built mounds. A mound could be used for a burial place or as a foundation for a temple, a **sanctuary** for religious ceremonies.

2. American Indians helped the first Europeans **sustain** themselves by showing them how to plant crops.
   (A) Nevertheless, Europeans were to **sustain** many losses during their first years in the new land.
   (B) The American Indians could **sustain** themselves by hunting, fishing, and farming.
   (C) The American Indians would soon **sustain** great losses due to diseases that the Europeans brought.
   (D) Both peoples had to **sustain** many hardships.

EXERCISE 2 *Word Analysis* ✍

Prefixes

Directions. Read the numbered pair of words below. Then, circle the letter of the choice that best describes the meaning of the underlined prefix as it is used in each pair.

3. <u>mis</u>deed   <u>mis</u>understanding
   (A) good
   (B) same, identical
   (C) wrong, bad
   (D) late

4. <u>ad</u>vent   <u>ad</u>mit
   (A) to
   (B) before
   (C) bad
   (D) between

Suffixes

Directions. Read the numbered pair of words below. Then, circle the letter of the choice that best describes the meaning of the underlined suffix as it is used in each pair.

5. eco<u>logy</u>   geo<u>logy</u>
   (A) one who does
   (B) that which
   (C) study or theory of
   (D) like, resembling

6. pac<u>ify</u>   beaut<u>ify</u>
   (A) full of
   (B) characteristic of
   (C) to make
   (D) becoming

Word Origins

Directions. Read each of the following sentences. Then, from the vocabulary list below, choose the word that best completes the sentence. Write the word in the blank.

advent	defy	intelligible	pacify
aggressive	ecology	misdeed	sanctuary
alliance	ferocious	motivate	strategy
anthology	inevitable	mystical	sustain
catastrophe	integrity	nourish	valid

7. We get a hint of the meaning of _____ when we learn that the Latin word *sustinēre* means "to hold up."

8. You may recognize the Greek word *katastrophe*, meaning "an overthrowing," in our word _____.

9. The Latin word *ferox*, meaning "wild" or "untamed," is related to our word _____.

10. We get a hint of the meaning of _____ when we learn that the Latin word *intellegere* means "to perceive."

UNDERSTANDING NEW WORDS AND THEIR USES

Lesson 3 | CONTEXT: The First Americans
A Culture Rooted in Nature

EXERCISE 1 *Multimeaning*

Directions. Read each numbered sentence below. Then, circle the letter of the choice that uses the boldface word in the same way as it is used in the numbered sentence.

1. Many American Indian stories have animals such as the **badger,** the coyote, and the rabbit for characters.
   (A) European literature is also filled with animal characters, including the bear, the **badger,** and the squirrel.
   (B) In both cultures, children **badger** their parents to tell them stories. The children refuse to sleep until they have heard a bedtime tale.
   (C) In some stories, animals **badger,** or nag, humans into doing the right thing.
   (D) In some stories, the animals behave like humans. For example, the wolf parent might **badger** the wolf cub to behave, just as a human parent might nag a child to be good.

2. The relationships between American Indians and their environments were **harmonious.** American Indians worked with, not against, the environment.
   (A) Many peoples created **harmonious** proportions in their artistic work. This pleasing balance can be seen in a Navajo blanket or in a sand painting.
   (B) Their music was also **harmonious.** Though the music sounded strange to European ears, it was based on an underlying order.
   (C) The relationships between peoples were not always **harmonious.** Groups occasionally went to war against each other.
   (D) Today, elders still teach younger people the **harmonious** songs of their ancestors.

EXERCISE 2 *Word Analysis*

Prefixes

Directions. Read the numbered pair of words below. Then, circle the letter of the choice that best describes the meaning of the underlined prefix as it is used in each pair.

3. <u>inter</u>vene   <u>inter</u>national
   (A) before
   (B) following
   (C) between
   (D) well, good

4. <u>in</u>comparable   <u>in</u>complete
   (A) before
   (B) not
   (C) bad
   (D) with

Suffixes

Directions. Read the numbered pair of words below. Then, circle the letter of the choice that best describes the meaning of the underlined suffix as it is used in each pair.

5. custom**ary**   honor**ary**
   (A) of, relating to
   (B) act of
   (C) part, half
   (D) one who does

6. calcula**tion**   ac**tion**
   (A) study or theory of
   (B) full of
   (C) act or result of
   (D) to make

Word Origins

Directions. Read each of the following sentences. Then, from the vocabulary list below, choose the word that best completes the sentence. Write the word in the blank.

accessory	calculation	fragile	intervene
adjacent	complement	gallery	multicolored
artisan	convert	glorify	pulverize
attain	customary	harmonious	valor
badger	deceased	incomparable	vitality

7. We get a hint of the meaning of the word _____ when we learn that the Latin word *convertere* means "to turn in character or nature, transform."

8. You may recognize the Latin word *gloria*, meaning "glory," in our word _____.

9. We get a hint of the meaning of the word _____ when we learn that the Latin word *frangere* means "to break."

10. The Middle English word *deces*, meaning "death," is related to the Modern English word _____.

UNDERSTANDING NEW WORDS AND THEIR USES

Lesson 4 **CONTEXT:** The First Americans

An American Indian Woman Today

EXERCISE 1 *Multimeaning* ✍

Directions. Read each numbered sentence below. Then, circle the letter of the choice that uses the boldface word in the same way as it is used in the numbered sentence.

1. The elders have agreed to **delegate,** or entrust, the responsibility to her.
   (A) She is their chosen **delegate,** or representative.
   (B) She thinks of her ancestor, who was once a **delegate** to the Iroquois federation.
   (C) She remembers when another ancestor was the **delegate** to a convention.
   (D) Before she leaves, she has to **delegate** some of the work to others. She decides to entrust her duties to her brother.

2. She is **descended** from both the Cherokee and the Iroquois people.
   (A) As she **descended** the stairs of the convention hall, all eyes followed her movements down.
   (B) The stairs **descended** in a spiral.
   (C) The crowd **descended** on her as she reached the bottom. Everyone wanted to shake her hand.
   (D) Women played an important role in the Iroquois federation, and she is **descended** from a long line of courageous female ancestors.

EXERCISE 2 *Word Analysis* ✍

Prefixes

Directions. Read the numbered pair of words below. Then, circle the letter of the choice that best describes the meaning of the underlined prefix as it is used in each pair.

3. <u>fore</u>sight   <u>fore</u>runner
   (A) after
   (B) before
   (C) against
   (D) new

4. <u>con</u>federation   <u>con</u>current
   (A) away from
   (B) first, primary
   (C) against
   (D) with, together

Suffixes

Directions. Read the numbered pair of words below. Then, circle the letter of the choice that best describes the meaning of the underlined suffix as it is used in each pair.

5. isolat<u>ion</u>   prevent<u>ion</u>
    (A) one who does
    (B) process of
    (C) tending to
    (D) result of

6. advantage<u>ous</u>   courag<u>eous</u>
    (A) act of
    (B) full of
    (C) capable of being
    (D) suitable for

Word Origins

Directions. Read each of the following sentences. Then, from the vocabulary list below, choose the word that best completes the sentence. Write the word in the blank.

adequate	discord	incite	menagerie
advantageous	enhance	inflexible	mutual
confederation	feline	inherit	phenomenon
delegate	foresight	isolation	posterity
descend	gnarled	menace	revelation

7. We get a hint of the meaning of _____ when we learn that the Latin word *post* means "after."

8. The Middle English word *knore*, meaning "knot," is related to our Modern English word _____.

9. You may recognize the Latin word *flexus*, meaning "to bend," in our word _____.

10. The Greek word *phainomenons*, meaning "appearing," is closely related to our word _____.

UNDERSTANDING NEW WORDS AND THEIR USES

Lesson 5 | **CONTEXT:** The First Americans

Working with the System

EXERCISE 1 *Multimeaning*

Directions. Read each numbered sentence below. Then, circle the letter of the choice that uses the boldface word in the same way as it is used in the numbered sentence.

1. The American Indian group plans to **petition** the United States government to return the land.
   (A) People in neighboring communities have signed a **petition** in support of their cause.
   (B) In the meantime, lawyers plan to **petition** the state courts to reverse an earlier decision.
   (C) If the **petition** fails, the lawyers have another plan.
   (D) The group plans to send a **petition** to both the legislature and the governor. They hope that their earnest request will be taken seriously.

2. The lawyer in charge of the case is aware of **potential,** or possible, problems.
   (A) The group supported him in law school because they believed in his **potential**. In fact, he has turned out to be a superb lawyer.
   (B) He believes the case has the **potential** for appeal even if he loses in the lower courts, but he doesn't want to bank on this possibility.
   (C) He also thinks the attorney general is a **potential** ally. It may be possible to get her support.
   (D) He is relying for help on his assistants, who are all young lawyers with little experience but great **potential**.

EXERCISE 2 *Word Analysis*

Prefixes

Directions. Read the numbered pair of words below. Then, circle the letter of the choice that best describes the meaning of the underlined prefix as it is used in each pair.

3. <u>in</u>soluble   <u>in</u>sincere
   (A) away from
   (B) before
   (C) against
   (D) not

4. <u>re</u>store   <u>re</u>produce
   (A) back, again
   (B) away from
   (C) through
   (D) into, in

Suffixes

Directions. Read the numbered pair of words below. Then, circle the letter of the choice that best describes the meaning of the underlined suffix as it is used in each pair.

5. durabil<u>ity</u>   visibil<u>ity</u>
   (A) able to be
   (B) full of
   (C) state of being
   (D) in the direction of

6. creat<u>ive</u>   destruct<u>ive</u>
   (A) skill
   (B) tending to
   (C) somewhat
   (D) becoming

Word Origins

Directions. Read each of the following sentences. Then, from the vocabulary list below, choose the word that best completes the sentence. Write the word in the blank.

adapt	creative	immense	ordeal
assumption	diction	impel	petition
basis	durable	ingenious	potential
consecutive	feasible	insoluble	primitive
controversy	hilarious	omission	restore

7. You may recognize the Latin word *primus*, meaning "first," in our word

   _____.

8. We get a hint of the meaning of the word _____ when we learn that the Latin word *aptare* means "to fit" and the Latin word *ad* means "at" or "to."

9. The Old French word *faisible*, meaning "possible" is related to our word

   _____.

10. The Latin word *omittere*, meaning "to disregard," is closely related to our word

    _____.

UNDERSTANDING NEW WORDS AND THEIR USES

Lesson 6 | CONTEXT: Coming to North America
Leaving the "Old Country"

EXERCISE 1 *Multimeaning*

Directions. Read each numbered sentence below. Then, circle the letter of the choice that uses the boldface word in the same way as it is used in the numbered sentence.

1. Aboard the ship, the **multitude**—from the passengers to the deckhands—cheered as the Statue of Liberty came into view.
   (A) A **multitude** of people entered the United States over the past two hundred years.
   (B) They were escaping a **multitude** of problems such as hunger, religious persecution, and overcrowding.
   (C) They brought with them a **multitude** of strengths and talents.
   (D) The immigrant **multitude** helped build the nation. Without these masses the country's history would have taken a very different course.

2. John's grandfather came to the United States after the failure of a **boycott** he had organized.
   (A) He wanted to **boycott** a chain of stores that paid farmers unfairly low prices for their potatoes.
   (B) The owners heard of his plan to **boycott**.
   (C) They were determined that the **boycott** would fail.
   (D) They arranged for every store they owned to **boycott** all the farmers' produce.

EXERCISE 2 *Word Analysis*

Prefixes

Directions. Read the numbered pair of words below. Then, circle the letter of the choice that best describes the meaning of the underlined prefix as it is used in each pair.

3. <u>mal</u>nutrition   <u>mal</u>function
   (A) before
   (B) against
   (C) wrong, bad
   (D) like, of

4. <u>ir</u>resolute   <u>ir</u>responsible
   (A) over
   (B) all
   (C) after
   (D) not

Suffixes

Directions. Read the numbered pair of words below. Then, circle the letter of the choice that best describes the meaning of the underlined suffix as it is used in each pair.

5. censor**ship**   owner**ship**
(A) study or theory of
(B) resembling
(C) belief
(D) state of being

6. optim**ism**   hero**ism**
(A) state of being
(B) act or result of
(C) wrong, bad
(D) suitable for

Word Origins

Directions. Read each of the following sentences. Then, from the vocabulary list below, choose the word that best completes the sentence. Write the word in the blank.

anxiety	decade	morale	predicament
aristocrat	deport	multitude	propaganda
boycott	emigrate	nationality	refuge
burly	famine	naturalization	resolute
censorship	malnutrition	optimism	urban

7. The Middle English word *burlich,* meaning "strong," became our word

_____.

8. We get a hint of the meaning of the word _____ when we learn that the Latin word *urbs* means "city."

9. The Latin word *natio,* meaning "born," is related to our word _____.

10. The English word _____ comes from an incident in nineteenth-century Ireland, in which tenants refused to pay the high rents charged by a land agent named Charles C. Boycott.

UNDERSTANDING NEW WORDS AND THEIR USES

Lesson 7 | **CONTEXT:** Coming to North America
Freedom and Equality

EXERCISE 1 *Multimeaning* 🖎

Directions. Read each numbered sentence below. Then, circle the letter of the choice that uses the boldface word in the same way as it is used in the numbered sentence.

1. Most immigrants felt that it was a **privilege** to come to the United States; they often felt they were more fortunate than those they left behind.
   (A) Some came from countries in which only people who were born into a position of **privilege** had a chance for success.
   (B) In the "Old Country," the government might **privilege** one group over another.
   (C) Of course, in the United States, the government does not **privilege** particular groups. Rather, the government tries to create a level playing field for all groups.
   (D) This equality makes many people feel **privileged** to live here.

2. Last night I saw the **premiere** of a play about Russian immigrants to the United States. Since it was the first showing ever, the play had a few problems.
   (A) A young actor was to **premiere** last night. However, she became ill and now will have to begin her acting career another night.
   (B) Yesterday was an important date in the history of Russian Jews. That is why the director wanted to **premiere** the play last night.
   (C) Originally, the play was to **premiere** in Brookline, Massachusetts, where many of these immigrants settled. Instead, the play opened at a theater in Boston.
   (D) Many Russian Americans were in the audience. After the **premiere** ended, we all participated in a question-and-answer session.

EXERCISE 2 *Word Analysis* 🖎

Prefixes

Directions. Read the numbered pair of words below. Then, circle the letter of the choice that best describes the meaning of the underlined prefix as it is used in each pair.

3. <u>re</u>circulate   <u>re</u>appear
   (A) over, above
   (B) before
   (C) back, again
   (D) under, beneath

4. <u>in</u>hospitable   <u>in</u>complete
   (A) not
   (B) against
   (C) after
   (D) with

Suffixes

Directions. Read the numbered pair of words below. Then, circle the letter of the choice that best describes the meaning of the underlined suffix as it is used in each pair.

5. fraudul**ent**   depend**ent**
   (A) wrong, bad
   (B) full of
   (C) away from
   (D) showing

6. accept**ance**   disturb**ance**
   (A) act of
   (B) becoming
   (C) like, resembling
   (D) study or theory of

Word Origins

Directions. Read each of the following sentences. Then, from the vocabulary list below, choose the word that best completes the sentence. Write the word in the blank.

acceptance	dilapidated	immigrate	privilege
accessible	exaggeration	impulsive	prosecute
bankrupt	fraudulent	intensity	riotous
boisterous	grieve	jubilation	thrive
circulate	hospitable	premiere	transit

7. You may recognize the Old French word *rihoter,* meaning "to make a disturbance," in the Modern English word _____.

8. The Middle English word *boistous,* meaning "rude," became the Modern English word _____.

9. We get a hint of the meaning of the word _____ when we learn that the Latin word *jubilare* means "to raise a shout of joy."

10. The Latin word *migrare,* meaning "to move," is closely related to our word _____.

UNDERSTANDING NEW WORDS AND THEIR USES

| Lesson 8 | **CONTEXT:** Coming to North America

Learning to Speak English

EXERCISE 1 *Multimeaning*

Directions. Read each numbered sentence below. Then, circle the letter of the choice that uses the boldface word in the same way as it is used in the numbered sentence.

1. Most immigrants find that it is **imperative,** or absolutely necessary, to learn the language.
   (A) English teachers explain the indicative, subjunctive, and **imperative** moods of verbs.
   (B) The **imperative** sentence is a command.
   (C) Immigrants soon discover that to learn English, it is **imperative** to use the language every day.
   (D) The English teacher used an **imperative** tone of voice, but her students liked her anyway.

2. Not learning the language can **hamper** an immigrant's progress.
   (A) On the other hand, a lack of money could **hamper** an immigrant's opportunity to learn the language.
   (B) One English teacher brought a **hamper** filled with picnic items.
   (C) The students ate the food from the **hamper** after they had learned what the items were called.
   (D) The next day, the teacher brought a **hamper** of clothes to teach the students the English words for different items of clothing.

EXERCISE 2 *Word Analysis*

Prefixes

Directions. Read the numbered pair of words below. Then, circle the letter of the choice that best describes the meaning of the underlined prefix as it is used in each pair.

3. <u>de</u>pose   <u>de</u>crease
   (A) undo
   (B) repeat
   (C) all
   (D) toward

4. <u>im</u>pose   <u>im</u>polite
   (A) into; not
   (B) against
   (C) away from
   (D) for

Suffixes

Directions. Read the numbered pair of words below. Then, circle the letter of the choice that best describes the meaning of the underlined suffix as it is used in each pair.

5. spac<u>ious</u>   luxur<u>ious</u>
   - (A) state of being
   - (B) able to be
   - (C) full of
   - (D) away from

6. neglig<u>ent</u>   intellig<u>ent</u>
   - (A) part, half
   - (B) one who does
   - (C) showing
   - (D) study or theory of

Word Origins

Directions. Read each of the following sentences. Then, from the vocabulary list below, choose the word that best completes the sentence. Write the word in the blank.

dedicate	hamper	inconsiderate	presume
depose	haven	intercept	recuperate
dispense	humidity	liable	restrain
dissect	imperative	memento	spacious
exertion	impose	negligent	tumult

7. The Old English word *haefen*, meaning "port," became our word _____.

8. We get a hint of the meaning of our word _____ when we learn that the Latin word *humidus* means "moist."

9. The Latin word *recuperare*, meaning "to recover," is closely related to our word _____.

10. The Latin word *dispendere*, meaning "to weigh out," carries over into Modern English as the word _____.

■ UNDERSTANDING NEW WORDS AND THEIR USES ■

Lesson 9 ▏ CONTEXT: Coming to North America

A Day in the Life

EXERCISE 1 ▏ *Multimeaning*

Directions. Read each numbered sentence below. Then, circle the letter of the choice that uses the boldface word in the same way as it is used in the numbered sentence.

1. The family lived in the **capital** city of the old country. Because the government is centered there, many people work in government jobs.
   (A) They moved to the United States with very little **capital**, or money, to invest.
   (B) They hoped to visit the U.S. **capital** area of Washington, D.C.
   (C) The children thought the visit was a **capital** idea. They couldn't wait to go.
   (D) The grandparents, on the other hand, thought it might be a **capital** mistake.

2. Grandmother's recipe calls for **basting** the tomatoes with oil.
   (A) Mother is in the living room **basting** together a blouse for Aunt Jennifer.
   (B) If it fits, she will replace the **basting** with permanent stitches.
   (C) Grandfather is watching TV and **basting** the coach of the losing team with barbed remarks about his coaching decisions.
   (D) The next step in the recipe is **basting** the pastry dough with butter.

EXERCISE 2 ▏ *Word Analysis*

Prefixes

Directions. Read each numbered pair of words below. Then, circle the letter of the choice that best describes the meaning of the underlined prefix as it is used in each pair.

3. <u>pre</u>arrange   <u>pre</u>paid
   (A) for
   (B) against
   (C) after
   (D) before

4. <u>dis</u>mantle   <u>dis</u>like
   (A) opposite
   (B) before
   (C) many
   (D) across

Suffixes

Directions. Read each numbered pair of words below. Then, circle the letter of the choice that best describes the meaning of the underlined suffix as it is used in each pair.

5. grac*ious*   ambit*ious*
   (A) full of
   (B) study of
   (C) becoming
   (D) resembling

6. manage**able**   accept**able**
   (A) resembling
   (B) capable of being
   (C) cause to be
   (D) full of

Word Origins

Directions. Read each of the following sentences. Then, from the vocabulary list below, choose the word that best completes the sentence. Write the word in the blank.

aroma	elegant	manageable	probation
baste	embarrass	monopoly	remote
capital	frequency	occupant	rigid
diminish	gracious	populate	saturate
dismantle	haughty	prearrange	sedate

7. We get a hint of the meaning of the word _____ when we learn that the Middle English word *diminuen* means "to make smaller."

8. The Latin word *saturare*, meaning "to fill up," is closely related to our word _____.

9. You may recognize the Greek word *monos*, meaning "one," in our word _____.

10. The Latin word *populus*, meaning "people," is closely related to our word _____.

UNDERSTANDING NEW WORDS AND THEIR USES

Lesson 10 | CONTEXT: Coming to North America
"Old Country" Cooking

EXERCISE 1 *Multimeaning* ✍

Directions. Read each numbered sentence below. Then, circle the letter of the choice that uses the boldface word in the same way as it is used in the numbered sentence.

1. New immigrants like to have easy **access** to the ingredients they used in their traditional cooking.
   (A) Today we can **access** information about almost anything from the Internet.
   (B) Even those who do not yet read English can **access** information by that method.
   (C) Immigrants who cannot read English might **access** Web pages in their first language.
   (D) To be sure of **access** to familiar languages, foods, and customs, many immigrants tried to settle in neighborhoods with people from their original countries.

2. Different people consider different foods to be basic, necessary **provisions**.
   (A) Neighborhood grocery stores made **provision** for their customers' special needs.
   (B) **Provisions** could be bought within the neighborhood.
   (C) If the immigrant had to live far away, he or she had to make **provision** for a trip to the grocery store.
   (D) Often, friends would make **provision** to help each other with the shopping and cooking.

EXERCISE 2 *Word Analysis* ✍

Prefixes

Directions. Read each numbered pair of words below. Then, circle the letter of the choice that best describes the meaning of the underlined prefix as it is used in each pair.

3. <u>dis</u>agreeable   <u>dis</u>pleasure
   (A) after
   (B) opposite
   (C) over
   (D) before

4. <u>circum</u>navigate   <u>circum</u>ference
   (A) beneath
   (B) over
   (C) around
   (D) through

Suffixes

Directions. Read each numbered pair of words below. Then, circle the letter of the choice that best describes the meaning of the underlined suffix as it is used in each pair.

5. thrif<u>ty</u>   jealous<u>y</u>
   (A) characterized by
   (B) somewhat
   (C) becoming
   (D) resembling

6. not<u>ify</u>   just<u>ify</u>
   (A) full of
   (B) act of
   (C) to make
   (D) like

Word Origins

Directions. Read each of the following sentences. Then, from the vocabulary list below, choose the word that best completes the sentence. Write the word in the blank.

access	disagreeable	maroon	regime
accommodations	evacuate	notify	remorse
adept	humiliate	persistent	thrifty
circumnavigate	jeopardize	pleasantry	titanic
dingy	liberate	provision	verify

7. We get a hint of the meaning of the word _____ when we learn that the Latin word *liber* means "free."

8. The French word *plaisanterie*, meaning "pleasant remarks," is closely related to our word _____.

9. The Latin word *humiliare*, meaning "to humble," is closely related to our word _____.

10. We get a hint of the meaning of the word _____ when we learn that the Latin word *vacare* means "to make empty."

© Houghton Mifflin Harcourt Publishing Company

UNDERSTANDING NEW WORDS AND THEIR USES

Lesson 11 | **CONTEXT:** Voices of the United States

Reading About United States History

EXERCISE 1 *Multimeaning* ✍

Directions. Read each numbered sentence below. Then, circle the letter of the choice that uses the boldface word in the same way as it is used in the numbered sentence.

1. The voices that tell the story of history are not always **neutral**.
   (A) Even if a historian is not personally **neutral** about an issue, he or she will usually try not to take sides.
   (B) I just read a book that examines the U.S. attempt to be a **neutral** in the early days of World War II.
   (C) It was interesting, but I have read other books that were so dull that my brain went into **neutral**.
   (D) One of the problems with many books is that they are not eye-catching; they're either black and white, or they use only **neutral** colors. I prefer to look at books with vivid colors.

2. I have read about the **blockade** of Confederate ports by the Union Navy in the Civil War.
   (A) Historians have also written about the attempts of students in the 1960s to **blockade** streets in protest marches.
   (B) I saw an old photograph of a river dammed by a **blockade** of debris.
   (C) Countries have decided to **blockade** various ports throughout history.
   (D) I wonder what the first **blockade** in United States military history was?

EXERCISE 2 *Word Analysis* ✍

Prefixes

Directions. Read each numbered pair of words below. Then, circle the letter of the choice that best describes the meaning of the underlined prefix as it is used in each pair.

3. <u>re</u>generate   <u>re</u>marry
   (A) before
   (B) across
   (C) through
   (D) again

4. <u>fore</u>word   <u>fore</u>thought
   (A) after
   (B) against
   (C) before
   (D) all

Suffixes

Directions. Read each numbered pair of words below. Then, circle the letter of the choice that best describes the meaning of the underlined suffix as it is used in each pair.

5. diplomat<u>ic</u>   dramat<u>ic</u>
   (A) one who
   (B) tending to
   (C) characterized by
   (D) state of being

6. satir<u>ize</u>   standard<u>ize</u>
   (A) to carry
   (B) to subject to
   (C) study or theory of
   (D) full of

Word Origins

Directions. Read each of the following sentences. Then, from the vocabulary list below, choose the word that best completes the sentence. Write the word in the blank.

aspiration	generate	pewter	sable
blockade	indelible	premier	salutation
confiscate	neutral	pun	satire
diplomat	obituary	quaint	tariff
foreword	obscure	quench	urgent

7. You may recognize the Latin word *obitus*, meaning "death," in our word
   _____.

8. We get a hint of the meaning of the word _____ when we learn that the Italian word *puntiglio* means "verbal hairsplitting."

9. The Latin word *indelibilis*, meaning "not capable of being destroyed," is closely related to our word _____.

10. The Italian word *tariffa*, meaning "rate," is closely related to our word
   _____.

UNDERSTANDING NEW WORDS AND THEIR USES

Lesson 12 | CONTEXT: Voices of the United States
Essaying the Essay

EXERCISE 1 *Multimeaning*

Directions. Read each numbered sentence below. Then, circle the letter of the choice that uses the boldface word in the same way as it is used in the numbered sentence.

1. Many professional writers are **apt** to write about topics they know well.
   (A) For instance, **apt** topics may include a hobby or interest, a personal event, or a favorite place.
   (B) Before beginning an article, writers are **apt** to brainstorm many possible topics.
   (C) Writers also consider to whom they are writing when choosing a topic. Knowing the audience helps the writer to make an **apt** choice.
   (D) An **apt** student can use the same strategies as a professional writer to choose a topic.

2. Some essayists write about a local **eccentric**. Neighborhood characters seem to be an endless source of inspiration for writers.
   (A) Essayists need not follow a fixed form. They can take an **eccentric** path.
   (B) Essayists sometimes offer **eccentric** opinions.
   (C) I read an essay on the art of the boomerang that was written by a true **eccentric**.
   (D) Of course, I think it's a bit **eccentric** to read nothing but essays.

EXERCISE 2 *Word Analysis*

Prefixes

Directions. Read the numbered pair of words below. Then, circle the letter of the choice that best describes the meaning of the underlined prefix as it is used in each pair.

3. <u>in</u>variable   <u>in</u>complete
   (A) many
   (B) after
   (C) not
   (D) almost

4. <u>re</u>activate   <u>re</u>appoint
   (A) again
   (B) over
   (C) against
   (D) toward

Suffixes

Directions. Read the numbered pair of words below. Then, circle the letter of the choice that best describes the meaning of the underlined suffix as it is used in each pair.

5. charit**able**   believ**able**
   (A) capable of
   (B) tending to
   (C) becoming
   (D) making

6. deduct**ion**   restrict**ion**
   (A) capable of
   (B) condition of
   (C) pertaining to
   (D) resembling

Word Origins

Directions. Read each of the following sentences. Then, from the vocabulary list below, choose the word that best completes the sentence. Write the word in the blank.

activate	confide	invariable	sarcasm
apt	deduction	irk	successor
charitable	eccentric	petty	summit
clarify	essay	pious	tarnish
colossal	intolerance	proposal	temperament

7. We get a hint of the meaning of the word _____ when we learn that the Latin word *pius* means "dutiful."

8. The Middle English word *petit*, meaning "small," became our Modern English word _____.

9. The Latin word *summus*, meaning "highest," is related to our word _____.

10. The Latin word *succedere*, meaning "to follow after," is closely related to our word _____.

UNDERSTANDING NEW WORDS AND THEIR USES

Lesson 13 | CONTEXT: Voices of the United States
Writing and Publishing

EXERCISE 1 Multimeaning ✍

Directions. Read each numbered sentence below. Then, circle the letter of the choice that uses the boldface word in the same way as it is used in the numbered sentence.

1. Writers know how to **intrigue** the reading public.
   - (A) Some write novels of political **intrigue** that tell of plots against corrupt governments.
   - (B) Some write about lovers engaged in romantic but secret **intrigue**.
   - (C) Some writers **intrigue** us with tales of adventure around the globe.
   - (D) In writing their novels, some writers fulfill their wish for a life of excitement and **intrigue**.

2. Some writers finish their novels with **dispatch** and move on to the next.
   - (A) Some writers **dispatch,** or do away with, the villain in the last chapter.
   - (B) Writers **dispatch** their manuscripts to publishers with either relief or nervousness.
   - (C) Writers always wish editors would read with more **dispatch**. They hate waiting to hear what the editors think.
   - (D) Sometimes a writer will strongly disagree with the **dispatch** he or she receives from an editor, especially if the letter contains a rejection.

EXERCISE 2 Word Analysis ✍

Prefixes

Directions. Read each numbered pair of words below. Then, circle the letter of the choice that best describes the meaning of the underlined prefix as it is used in each pair.

3. <u>con</u>temporary   <u>con</u>tain
   - (A) before
   - (B) through
   - (C) against
   - (D) with

4. <u>non</u>literal   <u>non</u>living
   - (A) many
   - (B) before
   - (C) not
   - (D) after

Suffixes

Directions. Read each numbered pair of words below. Then, circle the letter of the choice that best describes the meaning of the underlined suffix as it is used in each pair.

5. occurr**ence**   confer**ence**
   (A) act or state of
   (B) resembling
   (C) pertaining to
   (D) one who

6. emphas**ize**   computer**ize**
   (A) to study
   (B) to make
   (C) having to do with
   (D) full of

Word Origins

Directions. Read each of the following sentences. Then, from the vocabulary list below, choose the word that best completes the sentence. Write the word in the blank.

anonymous	dictate	falter	intrigue
casual	dilute	famished	literal
climax	dispatch	fictitious	modify
condemn	emphasize	fragment	occurrence
contemporary	endorse	improvise	therapy

7. The Middle English word *modifien,* meaning "to limit," became the Modern English word _____.

8. We get a hint of the meaning of the word _____ when we learn that the Greek word *klimax* means "ladder."

9. The Middle English word *faltren,* meaning "to stagger," became the Modern English word _____.

10. The Latin word *dictare,* meaning "to speak," is closely related to our word _____.

UNDERSTANDING NEW WORDS AND THEIR USES

Lesson 14 | CONTEXT: Voices of the United States

Writing About Experience

EXERCISE 1 *Multimeaning*

Directions. Read each numbered sentence below. Then, circle the letter of the choice that uses the boldface word in the same way as it is used in the numbered sentence.

1. Reading about others' experiences in the United States can **illuminate,** or make clear, our own lives.
   (A) Some writers **illuminate** or celebrate their past experiences as they retell them.
   (B) Others use their writings as a way to **illuminate** or clarify problems they have had.
   (C) Long ago in the Middle Ages, artists would **illuminate** manuscripts with beautiful colors.
   (D) If they painted at night, these artists had to **illuminate** the manuscripts with candles or oil lamps.

2. Many writers **derive,** or receive, satisfaction from writing about their early experiences in the United States.
   (A) What conclusions might you **derive,** or arrive at by logic, from a study of these writers?
   (B) They seem to **derive** some very similar conclusions about life in a new country.
   (C) Readers **derive** great pleasure from their books.
   (D) Some of my opinions **derive,** or come, from my study of writers from eastern Europe.

EXERCISE 2 *Word Analysis*

Prefixes

Directions. Read each numbered pair of words below. Then, circle the letter of the choice that best describes the meaning of the underlined prefix as it is used in each pair.

3. <u>super</u>ficial   <u>super</u>visor
   (A) over
   (B) under
   (C) without
   (D) after

4. <u>de</u>tach   <u>de</u>frost
   (A) toward
   (B) together
   (C) undo
   (D) around

Suffixes

Directions. Read each numbered pair of words below. Then, circle the letter of the choice that best describes the meaning of the underlined suffix as it is used in each pair.

5. extens**ive**   expens**ive**
   (A) to make
   (B) relating to
   (C) becoming
   (D) without

6. tang**ible**   collect**ible**
   (A) full of
   (B) familiar with
   (C) similar to
   (D) capable of being

Word Origins

Directions. Read each of the following sentences. Then, from the vocabulary list below, choose the word that best completes the sentence. Write the word in the blank.

articulate	derive	illuminate	superficial
braggart	detach	imply	tangible
category	distraction	inclination	testify
demolish	eligible	miscellaneous	unique
denial	extensive	secluded	upbraid

7. We get a hint of the meaning of the word _____ when we learn that the Latin *de* means "down" and *moliri* means "build."

8. The Latin word *unus,* meaning "one," is related to our word _____.

9. The Middle English word *implien,* meaning "to involve," became the Modern English word _____.

10. The Middle English word *secluden,* meaning "to set apart," became the Modern English word _____.

UNDERSTANDING NEW WORDS AND THEIR USES

Lesson 15 | CONTEXT: Voices of the United States

Reading and Learning

EXERCISE 1 | Multimeaning

Directions. Read each numbered sentence below. Then, circle the letter of the choice that uses the boldface word in the same way as it is used in the numbered sentence.

1. Here's an article by a writer discussing how many people now **commute** to work.
   (A) Another article discusses whether or not to **commute,** or make less severe, a bank robber's prison sentence.
   (B) This writer discusses how he was able to **commute** an idea for a little feature story into major front-page news.
   (C) Another writer is discussing what it is like to **commute** between the East Coast and the West Coast.
   (D) After hearing the lawyer's argument, the judge decided to **commute** the prisoner's sentence.

2. Another article describes the effect of traffic on our already **congested** highways.
   (A) The writer tells how flash flooding **congested** the river road.
   (B) Here's an article on what to do when you are **congested** from a cold or the flu.
   (C) The writer points out that most of us feel miserable when our heads are **congested** from allergies, which usually are not serious.
   (D) My head is as **congested** as a highway at rush hour; it's crowded with too many facts about traffic and head colds.

EXERCISE 2 | Word Analysis

Prefixes

Directions. Read each numbered pair of words below. Then, circle the letter of the choice that best describes the meaning of the underlined prefix as it is used in each pair.

3. <u>anti</u>biotics   <u>anti</u>freeze
   (A) across
   (B) two
   (C) good
   (D) against

4. <u>mal</u>function   <u>mal</u>formation
   (A) single
   (B) bad; wrong
   (C) new
   (D) near

Suffixes

Directions. Read each numbered pair of words below. Then, circle the letter of the choice that best describes the meaning of the underlined suffix as it is used in each pair.

5. synthet**ic**   volcan**ic**
    (A) characteristic of
    (B) against
    (C) capable of
    (D) without

6. techno**logy**   bio**logy**
    (A) study of
    (B) having the nature
    (C) in the direction of
    (D) state of being

Word Origins

Directions. Read each of the following sentences. Then, from the vocabulary list below, choose the word that best completes the sentence. Write the word in the blank.

aeronautics	commute	hypothesis	rebate
agenda	congest	malfunction	respiration
antibiotics	considerate	parasitic	synthetic
arrogant	erosion	photogenic	technology
automaton	hydraulic	planetarium	warranty

7. We get a hint of the meaning of the word _____ when we learn that the Greek word *hupothesis* means "to suppose."

8. The Latin word *erodere,* meaning "to gnaw off," is related to our word
_____ .

9. We get a hint of the meaning of the word _____ when we learn that the Greek word *hydraulis* means "a water organ."

10. You may recognize the Greek words *para,* meaning "beside," and *sitos,* meaning "food," in our English word _____ .

Why We Practice Analogies

Practice with analogies builds logic skills. To answer analogy questions correctly, you think about two words and discover the relationship between them. Then you match that relationship with one shared by another pair of words. In addition, when you study analogies, you think about the precise meanings of words and fix these definitions in your memory.

Understanding Word Analogies

A word analogy is a comparison between two pairs of words. Here is how word analogies are written:

Example 1 FIND : LOCATE :: lose : misplace

The colon (:) stands for the phrase "is related to." Here is how to read the relationships in Example 1:

> FIND [is related to] LOCATE
> lose [is related to] misplace

The double colon [::] between the two pairs of words stands for the phrase "in the same way that." Here is how to read the complete analogy:

> FIND [is related to] LOCATE
> [in the same way that]
> lose [is related to] misplace

Here is another way:

> FIND is to LOCATE as lose is to misplace.

A properly constructed analogy, then, tells us that the relationship between the first pair of words is the same as the relationship between the second pair of words. In Example 1, *find* and *locate* are synonyms, just as *lose* and *misplace* are synonyms.

Let's look at another example:

Example 2 GIFT : JOY :: grief : tears

What is the relationship here? A *gift* causes *joy*, just as *grief* causes *tears*. These two pairs of words have the same relationship, a cause-and-effect relationship. The chart on page 156 will help you to identify analogy relationships. No chart could list all possible relationships between words, but the twelve relationships on the chart are the ones most often used. Also, they are the only relationships used in the analogy lessons.

TYPES OF ANALOGIES		
RELATIONSHIP	**EXAMPLE**	**EXPLANATION**
Synonym	DRY : ARID :: find : locate	*Dry* is similar in meaning to *arid*, just as *find* is similar in meaning to *locate*.
Antonym	KIND : CRUEL :: find : lose	A *kind* action is the opposite of a *cruel* action, just as to *find* something is the opposite of to *lose* it.
Cause and Effect	GIFT : JOY :: rain : flood	A *gift* can cause *joy*, just as *rain* can cause a *flood*.
Part and Whole	CHAPTER : BOOK :: fender : automobile	A *chapter* is a part of a *book*, just as a *fender* is a part of an *automobile*.
Classification	POLKA : DANCE :: frog : amphibian	A *polka* may be classified as a *dance*, just as a *frog* may be classified as an *amphibian*.
Characteristic Quality	PUPPIES : FURRY :: fish : slippery	*Puppies* are *furry*, just as *fish* are *slippery*.
Degree	CHUCKLE : LAUGH :: whimper : cry	A *chuckle* is a little *laugh*, just as a *whimper* is a little *cry*.
Function	KNIFE : CUT :: pen : write	The function of a *knife* is to *cut*, just as the function of a *pen* is to *write*.
Performer and Action	AUTHOR : WRITE :: chef : cook	You expect an *author* to *write*, just as you expect a *chef* to *cook*.
Performer and Object	CASHIER : CASH :: plumber : pipe	A *cashier* works with *cash*, just as a *plumber* works with *pipe*.
Action and Object	BOIL : EGG :: throw : ball	You *boil* an *egg*, just as you *throw* a *ball*.
Location	FISH : SEA :: moose : forest	A *fish* can be found in the *sea*, just as a *moose* can be found in a *forest*.

A Process for Solving Analogies

Your job in solving multiple-choice analogy questions is to identify the relationship between the first two words and then to find the pair of words that has the most similar relationship. Keep in mind that a word pair has the same relationship no matter in which order the two words appear. For example, both CHAPTER : BOOK and BOOK : CHAPTER have a part-and-whole relationship. Here is a hint for identifying relationships. Try using word pairs in the explanation sentences on the chart. When a word pair makes sense in the explanation sentence for a particular relationship, you have found the relationship that the two words have to each other.

Here is a process that will help you with analogy questions:

Answering Analogy Questions: A 4-Step Method

1. Identify the relationship between the capitalized pair of words.
2. Identify the relationship between the pair of words in each possible answer.
3. Eliminate answer choices that have relationships that do not match the relationship between the capitalized words.
4. Choose the remaining possible answer. This answer will have the same relationship as the capitalized pair.

Let's apply this pattern to a sample question.

Example 3

WRITE : PEN :: _F_   [*Function*]

(A)	toe : foot _PW_	[*Part and Whole*—does not match]
(B)	toss : salad _AO_	[*Action and Object*—does not match]
(C)	gymnast : mat _PO_	[*Performer and Object*—does not match]
(D)	sky : blue _CQ_	[*Characteristic Quality*—does not match]
(E)	shine : sun _F_	[*Function*—does match]

None of relationships (A) through (D) match that of the capitalized pair. They can be eliminated. Choice E must be the correct answer. Notice that the words make sense in the explanation sentence: The function of a *pen* is to *write* just as the function of the *sun* is to *shine*.

A Final Word

Analogies are easier and more fun if you tackle them with a sense of adventure. Allow yourself to discover the relationship between the first pair of words and to explore the relationships between the words in the answer choices. Keep in mind that some words can represent more than one part of speech and that many words have several meanings. Remember, these little verbal puzzles call for flexibility as well as logic.

CONNECTING NEW WORDS AND PATTERNS

Lesson 1 | ANALOGIES

Directions. On each line, write the letter or letters that describe the type of relationship the words have to each other. Choose from the following types:

S synonym A antonym PW part and whole PA performer and action
F function L location CE cause and effect PO performer and object
D degree C classification CQ characteristic quality AO action and object

Circle the letter of the pair of words that has the same relationship as the capitalized words. Each relationship is used no more than once in each numbered item.

1. ABUSE : CRUEL :: _____
   (A) valuable : priceless _____
   (B) eraser : erase _____
   (C) bake : potato _____
   (D) shutter : camera _____
   (E) celebration : joyful _____

2. APPALLING : UPSETTING :: _____
   (A) sculptor : statue _____
   (B) fascinating : interesting _____
   (C) pineapple : fruit _____
   (D) criticism : disappointment _____
   (E) iceberg : sea _____

3. BAFFLE : CONFUSE :: _____
   (A) sweat : exercise _____
   (B) instrument : tuba _____
   (C) green : grass _____
   (D) attempt : try _____
   (E) pitcher : team _____

4. CALAMITY : DISTRESS :: _____
   (A) banker : money _____
   (B) orange : pumpkin _____
   (C) winning : happiness _____
   (D) grocer : sell _____
   (E) lawn : mow _____

5. DECEIVE : LIAR :: _____
   (A) speeding : dangerous _____
   (B) bound : free _____
   (C) coin : quarter _____
   (D) rescue : hero _____
   (E) pitch : throw _____

6. EPIDEMIC : FEAR :: _____
   (A) puzzle : confusion _____
   (B) baker : bread _____
   (C) rub : scrub _____
   (D) tool : hammer _____
   (E) slumber : sleep _____

7. KNOLL : MOUNTAIN :: _____
   (A) brook : fish _____
   (B) point : pen _____
   (C) ditch : canyon _____
   (D) disk : flat _____
   (E) bushes : trim _____

8. NOVELTY : INVENTOR :: _____
   (A) symphony : composer _____
   (B) space : satellite _____
   (C) programmer : type _____
   (D) oven : rack _____
   (E) improvement : practice _____

9. PROBABLE : UNLIKELY :: _____
   (A) bat : cave _____
   (B) thermometer : nurse _____
   (C) join : stapler _____
   (D) fruit : grape _____
   (E) sad : happy _____

10. RUTHLESS : MERCILESS :: _____
    (A) rule : king _____
    (B) famous : well-known _____
    (C) soft : pillow _____
    (D) rich : poor _____
    (E) praise : pride _____

CONNECTING NEW WORDS AND PATTERNS

Lesson 2 ANALOGIES

Directions. On each line, write the letter or letters that describe the type of relationship the words have to each other. Choose from the following types:

S synonym	A antonym	PW part and whole	PA performer and action
F function	L location	CE cause and effect	PO performer and object
D degree	C classification	CQ characteristic quality	AO action and object

Circle the letter of the pair of words that has the same relationship as the capitalized words. Each relationship is used no more than once in each numbered item.

1. ADVENT : ARRIVAL :: _____
   (A) old : ancient _____
   (B) compass : direct _____
   (C) football : sport _____
   (D) faithfulness : loyalty _____
   (E) lemon : yellow _____

2. AGGRESSIVE : BULLY :: _____
   (A) clip : cut _____
   (B) crime : fear _____
   (C) enrage : annoy _____
   (D) confident : expert _____
   (E) shelf : bookcase _____

3. CATASTROPHE : CONFUSION :: _____
   (A) potter : clay _____
   (B) death : sorrow _____
   (C) clear : cluttered _____
   (D) sleeve : dress _____
   (E) insect : ant _____

4. ECOLOGY : SCIENCE :: _____
   (A) canoe : lake _____
   (B) beverage : quench _____
   (C) gymnast : athletic _____
   (D) actor : script _____
   (E) algebra : mathematics _____

5. FEROCIOUS : GENTLE :: _____
   (A) pleased : dissatisfied _____
   (B) clerk : receipt _____
   (C) toss : ring _____
   (D) sprint : jog _____
   (E) dolphin : sea _____

6. MOTIVATE : DISCOURAGE :: _____
   (A) mix : blender _____
   (B) silk : smooth _____
   (C) puck : hockey player _____
   (D) warn : caution _____
   (E) tarnished : polished _____

7. NOURISH : FOOD :: _____
   (A) guitar : strum _____
   (B) surprised : shocked _____
   (C) instrument : guitar _____
   (D) protect : raincoat _____
   (E) receiver : telephone _____

8. PACIFY : PROVOKE :: _____
   (A) dog : poodle _____
   (B) producer : script _____
   (C) juggler : circus tent _____
   (D) warm : hot _____
   (E) refuse : accept _____

9. SANCTUARY : CHURCH :: _____
   (A) past : previous _____
   (B) hammer : pound _____
   (C) axle : truck _____
   (D) actor : perform _____
   (E) lilac : fragrant _____

10. STRATEGY : METHOD :: _____
    (A) boredom : yawning _____
    (B) intention : purpose _____
    (C) rehearse : actor _____
    (D) gem : emerald _____
    (E) snout : dog _____

CONNECTING NEW WORDS AND PATTERNS

Lesson 3 ANALOGIES

Directions. On each line, write the letter or letters that describe the type of relationship the words have to each other. Choose from the following types:

S synonym	A antonym	PW part and whole	PA performer and action
F function	L location	CE cause and effect	PO performer and object
D degree	C classification	CQ characteristic quality	AO action and object

Circle the letter of the pair of words that has the same relationship as the capitalized words. Each relationship is used no more than once in each numbered item.

1. ACCESSORY : BELT :: _____
   (A) shine : shoes _____
   (B) large : roomy _____
   (C) comedian : entertain _____
   (D) jewelry : bracelet _____
   (E) disagreement : tension _____

2. ARTISAN : POTTERY :: _____
   (A) square : shape _____
   (B) gain : lose _____
   (C) dampness : dew _____
   (D) trim : lawn _____
   (E) architect : blueprint _____

3. BADGER : ANIMAL :: _____
   (A) penguin : Antarctica _____
   (B) striped : zebra _____
   (C) honk : goose _____
   (D) granite : rock _____
   (E) conductor : baton _____

4. CALCULATION : MATH WHIZ :: _____
   (A) comment : remark _____
   (B) formula : chemist _____
   (C) mane : lion _____
   (D) breezy : windy _____
   (E) pride : praise _____

5. CUSTOMARY : UNUSUAL :: _____
   (A) hands : clock _____
   (B) thoughtful : inconsiderate _____
   (C) cut : scissors _____
   (D) fiddler : violin _____
   (E) ostrich : bird _____

6. FRAGILE : EGG :: _____
   (A) birth : celebration _____
   (B) release : capture _____
   (C) invent : create _____
   (D) accountant : calculator _____
   (E) dry : desert _____

7. GALLERY : PAINTING :: _____
   (A) blade : lawn mower _____
   (B) fan : breeze _____
   (C) tiny : small _____
   (D) studio : easel _____
   (E) flannel : warm _____

8. GLORIFY : DEGRADE :: _____
   (A) gold : shiny _____
   (B) desert : cactus _____
   (C) succeed : fail _____
   (D) derby : hat _____
   (E) heat : stove _____

9. MULTICOLORED : RAINBOW :: _____
   (A) shallow : deep _____
   (B) coal : underground _____
   (C) eyes : see _____
   (D) soft : pillow _____
   (E) horse : neigh _____

10. VITALITY : ENERGY :: _____
    (A) colorful : plaid _____
    (B) escape : prisoner _____
    (C) picture : take _____
    (D) beak : bird _____
    (E) sadness : sorrow _____

CONNECTING NEW WORDS AND PATTERNS

Lesson 4 ANALOGIES

Directions. On each line, write the letter or letters that describe the type of relationship the words have to each other. Choose from the following types:

S synonym	A antonym	PW part and whole	PA performer and action
F function	L location	CE cause and effect	PO performer and object
D degree	C classification	CQ characteristic quality	AO action and object

Circle the letter of the pair of words that has the same relationship as the capitalized words. Each relationship is used no more than once in each numbered item.

1. ADEQUATE : EXCELLENT :: _____
   (A) gap : opening _____
   (B) artist : draw _____
   (C) year : month _____
   (D) paint : enamel _____
   (E) tired : frazzled _____

2. DELEGATE : REPRESENT :: _____
   (A) dog : fox terrier _____
   (B) moment : brief _____
   (C) actor : perform _____
   (D) fence : separate _____
   (E) exist : live _____

3. DESCEND : RISE :: _____
   (A) clown : makeup _____
   (B) delicate : flower _____
   (C) tell : brag _____
   (D) shove : pull _____
   (E) minute : hour _____

4. DISCORD : HARMONY :: _____
   (A) wheelchair : mobile _____
   (B) mixer : stir _____
   (C) war : peace _____
   (D) boat : canoe _____
   (E) apple : stem _____

5. ENHANCE : DECORATION :: _____
   (A) ginger : spice _____
   (B) deliver : mail _____
   (C) enrich : fertilizer _____
   (D) frantic : upset _____
   (E) foul : penalty _____

6. FELINE : WHISKERS :: _____
   (A) announcer : microphone _____
   (B) sincere : honest _____
   (C) kitten : paw _____
   (D) telephone : answer _____
   (E) metal : silver _____

7. INHERIT : HEIRESS :: _____
   (A) beaten : defeated _____
   (B) steal : thief _____
   (C) shell : beach _____
   (D) game : rules _____
   (E) vinegar : sour _____

8. ISOLATION : LONELINESS :: _____
   (A) captain : lead _____
   (B) experience : confidence _____
   (C) trunk : tree _____
   (D) traffic light : street corner _____
   (E) sailor : compass _____

9. MENACE : FRIGHTENING :: _____
   (A) assist : help _____
   (B) crime : offensive _____
   (C) scold : praise _____
   (D) blow : fan _____
   (E) racket : tennis player _____

10. MENAGERIE : CAGED :: _____
    (A) apart : separate _____
    (B) crime : illegal _____
    (C) wick : candle _____
    (D) singer : tenor _____
    (E) match : strike _____

CONNECTING NEW WORDS AND PATTERNS

Lesson 5 | ANALOGIES

Directions. On each line, write the letter or letters that describe the type of relationship the words have to each other. Choose from the following types:

S synonym	A antonym	PW part and whole	PA performer and action
F function	L location	CE cause and effect	PO performer and object
D degree	C classification	CQ characteristic quality	AO action and object

Circle the letter of the pair of words that has the same relationship as the capitalized words. Each relationship is used no more than once in each numbered item.

1. ADAPT : MODIFY :: ____
   (A) thoughtful : considerate ____
   (B) library : quiet ____
   (C) pencil : sharpen ____
   (D) writer : notebook ____
   (E) drowsiness : nap ____

2. BASIS : FOUNDATION :: ____
   (A) slippers : comfortable ____
   (B) automobile : transport ____
   (C) door : cabinet ____
   (D) delay : prevent ____
   (E) sign : indication ____

3. CONSECUTIVE : INTERRUPTED :: ____
   (A) skim : read ____
   (B) slack : loose ____
   (C) teeth : crocodile ____
   (D) lamp : living room ____
   (E) fresh : stale ____

4. CONTROVERSY : DISPUTE :: ____
   (A) sleeper : snore ____
   (B) soft : cushion ____
   (C) compose : song ____
   (D) promise : pledge ____
   (E) turtle : reptile ____

5. CREATIVE : ARTIST :: ____
   (A) dentist : teeth ____
   (B) germ : illness ____
   (C) idle : inactive ____
   (D) scientific : chemist ____
   (E) palm : tropics ____

6. DURABLE : LEATHER :: ____
   (A) brim : hat ____
   (B) hear : ears ____
   (C) keep : secret ____
   (D) ocean : octopus ____
   (E) gritty : sand ____

7. HILARIOUS : FUNNY :: ____
   (A) police officer : arrest ____
   (B) lighthearted : gloomy ____
   (C) toes : feet ____
   (D) nasty : unpleasant ____
   (E) pain : sunburn ____

8. IMMENSE : LARGE :: ____
   (A) architect : blueprint ____
   (B) snake : hole ____
   (C) frantic : nervous ____
   (D) awkward : clumsy ____
   (E) eagle : bird ____

9. INGENIOUS : INVENTOR :: ____
   (A) lampshade : lamp ____
   (B) artist : draw ____
   (C) antlers : protect ____
   (D) curious : monkey ____
   (E) microscope : biologist ____

10. PRIMITIVE : CRUDE :: ____
    (A) bell : telephone ____
    (B) orchid : jungle ____
    (C) guitarist : strum ____
    (D) complex : complicated ____
    (E) skunk : animal ____

CONNECTING NEW WORDS AND PATTERNS

Lesson 6 ANALOGIES

Directions. On each line, write the letter or letters that describe the type of relationship the words have to each other. Choose from the following types:

S synonym   A antonym   PW part and whole   PA performer and action
F function   L location   CE cause and effect   PO performer and object
D degree   C classification CQ characteristic quality AO action and object

Circle the letter of the pair of words that has the same relationship as the capitalized words. Each relationship is used no more than once in each numbered item.

1. ARISTOCRAT : PRINCESS :: ____
   (A) unlock : door ____
   (B) outdoors : inside ____
   (C) pilot : fly ____
   (D) vessel : sailboat ____
   (E) stick : lollipop ____

2. BURLY : FOOTBALL PLAYER :: ____
   (A) graceful : ballet dancer ____
   (B) plead : beg ____
   (C) science : forestry ____
   (D) trot : horse ____
   (E) entertain : movie ____

3. DECADE : YEAR :: ____
   (A) house : roof ____
   (B) partially : entirely ____
   (C) loneliness : sadness ____
   (D) sandals : footwear ____
   (E) instructor : explain ____

4. FAMINE : WAR :: ____
   (A) forbid : allow ____
   (B) colorful : parrot ____
   (C) sculpture : museum ____
   (D) destruction : hurricane ____
   (E) tap : push ____

5. MALNUTRITION : DEATH :: ____
   (A) bore : hole ____
   (B) kitchen : kettle ____
   (C) monarch : rule ____
   (D) fever : sweating ____
   (E) hold : release ____

6. MULTITUDE : CROWD :: ____
   (A) turn : key ____
   (B) chef : pan ____
   (C) ceremony : service ____
   (D) metal : iron ____
   (E) genius : intelligent ____

7. PROPAGANDA : PERSUADE :: ____
   (A) plow : tool ____
   (B) outburst : attention ____
   (C) knee : leg ____
   (D) computer : office ____
   (E) newspaper : inform ____

8. REFUGE : SAFE :: ____
   (A) anchor : heavy ____
   (B) sack : bag ____
   (C) weave : loom ____
   (D) fountain : park ____
   (E) drizzle : downpour ____

9. RESOLUTE : DETERMINED :: ____
   (A) fat : thin ____
   (B) fruit : plum ____
   (C) playwright : script ____
   (D) steady : regular ____
   (E) irrigate : soil ____

10. URBAN : RURAL :: ____
    (A) hive : bee ____
    (B) child : tricycle ____
    (C) firm : unsteady ____
    (D) game : baseball ____
    (E) claws : defend ____

CONNECTING NEW WORDS AND PATTERNS

Lesson 7 | ANALOGIES

Directions. On each line, write the letter or letters that describe the type of relationship the words have to each other. Choose from the following types:

S synonym	A antonym	PW part and whole	PA performer and action
F function	L location	CE cause and effect	PO performer and object
D degree	C classification	CQ characteristic quality	AO action and object

Circle the letter of the pair of words that has the same relationship as the capitalized words. Each relationship is used no more than once in each numbered item.

1. ACCESSIBLE : UNOBTAINABLE :: _____
   (A) cat : pounce _____
   (B) mast : sailboat _____
   (C) shout : whisper _____
   (D) ball : juggler _____
   (E) lieutenant : officer _____

2. BANKRUPT : RICH :: _____
   (A) torn : mended _____
   (B) luxurious : comfortable _____
   (C) limestone : rock _____
   (D) supermarket : groceries _____
   (E) puddle : muddy _____

3. BOISTEROUS : CALM:: _____
   (A) violent : peaceful _____
   (B) thief : steal _____
   (C) mix : cement _____
   (D) hour : second _____
   (E) sculptor : clay _____

4. DILAPIDATED : OLD RUINS :: _____
   (A) parking lot : car _____
   (B) glee : sadness _____
   (C) harmonica : instrument _____
   (D) towel : absorb _____
   (E) dangerous : parachuting _____

5. FRAUDULENT : EMBEZZLER :: _____
   (A) post office : letter _____
   (B) stingy : miser _____
   (C) buzz : bee _____
   (D) comrade : enemy _____
   (E) tag : game _____

6. GRIEVE : MOURN :: _____
   (A) haul : carry _____
   (B) cyclone : damage _____
   (C) party : celebrate _____
   (D) brush : hair _____
   (E) vitamins : healthful _____

7. HOSPITABLE : CIVIL :: _____
   (A) search : peek _____
   (B) dishonest : burglar _____
   (C) sport : bowling _____
   (D) worry : stress _____
   (E) air : breathe _____

8. JUBILATION : VICTORY :: _____
   (A) needle : tailor _____
   (B) scream : yell _____
   (C) leap : deer _____
   (D) sadness : loss _____
   (E) train : transport _____

9. RIOTOUS : LIVELY :: _____
   (A) veterinarian : vaccine _____
   (B) unhappiness : pouting _____
   (C) shudder : quiver _____
   (D) duck : migrate _____
   (E) greeting : farewell _____

10. TRANSIT : PASSAGE :: _____
    (A) winner : boast _____
    (B) faithful : disloyal _____
    (C) ripe : mature _____
    (D) looking : glaring _____
    (E) cliff : steep _____

CONNECTING NEW WORDS AND PATTERNS

Lesson 8 ANALOGIES

Directions. On each line, write the letter or letters that describe the type of relationship the words have to each other. Choose from the following types:

S synonym	A antonym	PW part and whole	PA performer and action
F function	L location	CE cause and effect	PO performer and object
D degree	C classification	CQ characteristic quality	AO action and object

Circle the letter of the pair of words that has the same relationship as the capitalized words. Each relationship is used no more than once in each numbered item.

1. DISSECT : BIOLOGIST :: _____
   (A) teach : professor _____
   (B) exercise : strengthen _____
   (C) honest : truthful _____
   (D) dribble : basketball _____
   (E) success : jealousy _____

2. HAVEN : SAFE :: _____
   (A) leg : chair _____
   (B) love : hate _____
   (C) delighted : satisfied _____
   (D) farmer : tractor _____
   (E) treasure : valuable _____

3. HAMPER : HELP :: _____
   (A) England : country _____
   (B) moose : Canada _____
   (C) ignore : disregard _____
   (D) criticize : praise _____
   (E) dog : howl _____

4. HUMIDITY : DAMP :: _____
   (A) cold : cool _____
   (B) wagonload : haul _____
   (C) sleet : cold _____
   (D) desk : office _____
   (E) flour : cake _____

5. INCONSIDERATE : SELFISH :: _____
   (A) fasting : hunger _____
   (B) evil : wicked _____
   (C) vegetable : carrot _____
   (D) keyboard : computer _____
   (E) feathered : duck _____

6. MEMENTO : REMIND :: _____
   (A) helicopter : police officer _____
   (B) heel : foot _____
   (C) pouring : dripping _____
   (D) exploration : discover _____
   (E) heavy : rhinoceros _____

7. RECUPERATE : PATIENT :: _____
   (A) lobster : shellfish _____
   (B) examine : physician _____
   (C) evil : bad _____
   (D) petal : flower _____
   (E) boredom : restlessness _____

8. RESTRAIN : SEAT BELT :: _____
   (A) clutch : hold _____
   (B) lend : borrow _____
   (C) limb : tree _____
   (D) hold : reservoir _____
   (E) loafer : lazy _____

9. SPACIOUS : MANSION :: _____
   (A) bake : bread _____
   (B) salty : sea _____
   (C) train : locomotive _____
   (D) strong : powerful _____
   (E) chef : chop _____

10. TUMULT : UPROAR :: _____
    (A) trunk : attic _____
    (B) tanned : sunburned _____
    (C) feather : light _____
    (D) locker : store _____
    (E) confusion : disorder _____

CONNECTING NEW WORDS AND PATTERNS

Lesson 9 | ANALOGIES

Directions. On each line, write the letter or letters that describe the type of relationship the words have to each other. Choose from the following types:

S synonym   A antonym   PW part and whole   PA performer and action
F function   L location   CE cause and effect   PO performer and object
D degree   C classification   CQ characteristic quality   AO action and object

Circle the letter of the pair of words that has the same relationship as the capitalized words. Each relationship is used no more than once in each numbered item.

1. AROMA : BAKING :: _____
   (A) wash : dishes _____
   (B) hat : protect _____
   (C) accident : speeding _____
   (D) chef : recipe _____
   (E) car : vehicle _____

2. BASTE : TURKEY :: _____
   (A) soldier : defend _____
   (B) trim : tree _____
   (C) cruelty : suffering _____
   (D) forest : owl _____
   (E) black : crow _____

3. CAPITAL : INVESTOR :: _____
   (A) fishing : sport _____
   (B) thirst : salty food _____
   (C) land : realtor _____
   (D) underground : oil _____
   (E) teeth : saw _____

4. ELEGANT : CRUDE :: _____
   (A) exchange : trade _____
   (B) publication : magazine _____
   (C) pond : turtle _____
   (D) engine : carburetor _____
   (E) serious : amusing _____

5. HAUGHTY : FRIENDLY :: _____
   (A) pouring : drizzling _____
   (B) transport : airplane _____
   (C) paint : mix _____
   (D) wealthy : poor _____
   (E) striped : skunk _____

6. OCCUPANT : RESIDENT :: _____
   (A) poem : line _____
   (B) nail : join _____
   (C) flower : daisy _____
   (D) scrape : gash _____
   (E) shrub : bush _____

7. REMOTE : DISTANT :: _____
   (A) hard : difficult _____
   (B) reptile : snake _____
   (C) clean : scour _____
   (D) driver : license _____
   (E) egg : nest _____

8. RIGID : FLEXIBLE :: _____
   (A) baby : bottle _____
   (B) damaged : repaired _____
   (C) water : seedling _____
   (D) advisor : suggest _____
   (E) song : concert _____

9. SEDATE : ROWDY :: _____
   (A) protect : endanger _____
   (B) automobile : horn _____
   (C) delays : impatience _____
   (D) lunch : meal _____
   (E) sprint : run _____

10. SATURATE : MOISTEN :: _____
   (A) wool : warm _____
   (B) elephant : jungle _____
   (C) pour : sprinkle _____
   (D) bass : fish _____
   (E) marry : wed _____

Name _____ Date _____ Class _____

*L*esson 10 **ANALOGIES**

Directions. On each line, write the letter or letters that describe the type of relationship the words have to each other. Choose from the following types:

S synonym   A antonym   PW part and whole   PA performer and action
F function   L location   CE cause and effect   PO performer and object
D degree   C classification   CQ characteristic quality   AO action and object

Circle the letter of the pair of words that has the same relationship as the capitalized words. Each relationship is used no more than once in each numbered item.

1. DINGY : SHABBY :: _____
  (A) chess : game _____
  (B) blame : forgive _____
  (C) joke : amuse _____
  (D) private : personal _____
  (E) wall : fort _____

2. DISAGREEABLE : HORRIBLE :: _____
  (A) repair expert : fix _____
  (B) entrance : exit _____
  (C) difficult : impossible _____
  (D) sticky : tape _____
  (E) window : house _____

3. EVACUATE : BUILDING :: _____
  (A) hasty : speedy _____
  (B) separate : join _____
  (C) entertain : crowd _____
  (D) otter : lake _____
  (E) millionaire : wealthy _____

4. HUMILIATE : FLATTER :: _____
  (A) quail : prairie _____
  (B) criticize : compliment _____
  (C) introduction : essay _____
  (D) swimmer : goggles _____
  (E) hurt : harm _____

5. LIBERATE : CAPTURE :: _____
  (A) feed : starve _____
  (B) burn : heat _____
  (C) marshy : swampy _____
  (D) answer : telephone _____
  (E) tusk : elephant _____

6. MAROON : COLOR :: _____
  (A) fly : kite _____
  (B) alarm clock : wake _____
  (C) pigeon : plaza _____
  (D) diamond : gem _____
  (E) knuckle : finger _____

7. NOTIFY : INFORM :: _____
  (A) scarf : outfit _____
  (B) unhappy : miserable _____
  (C) pupil : eraser _____
  (D) misconduct : punishment _____
  (E) fasten : attach _____

8. REMORSE : WRONGDOING :: _____
  (A) scarecrow : frighten _____
  (B) toss : ball _____
  (C) forgiveness : apology _____
  (D) cuff : shirt _____
  (E) refugee : flee _____

9. THRIFTY : MISERLY :: _____
  (A) wipe : napkin _____
  (B) pink : flamingo _____
  (C) joke : laughter _____
  (D) mischievous : wicked _____
  (E) sport : diving _____

10. VERIFY : WITNESS :: _____
  (A) athlete : play _____
  (B) salt : white _____
  (C) breakfast : meal _____
  (D) note : melody _____
  (E) hay : stable _____

© Houghton Mifflin Harcourt Publishing Company

CONNECTING NEW WORDS AND PATTERNS

Lesson 11 ANALOGIES

Directions. On each line, write the letter or letters that describe the type of relationship the words have to each other. Choose from the following types:

S synonym	A antonym	PW part and whole	PA performer and action
F function	L location	CE cause and effect	PO performer and object
D degree	C classification	CQ characteristic quality	AO action and object

Circle the letter of the pair of words that has the same relationship as the capitalized words. Each relationship is used no more than once in each numbered item.

1. ASPIRATION : AMBITION :: _____
   (A) letter : communicate _____
   (B) wish : desire _____
   (C) whistle : shrill _____
   (D) attack : fort _____
   (E) cricket : insect _____

2. CONFISCATE : WEAPON :: _____
   (A) rob : bank _____
   (B) car : fender _____
   (C) counselor : advise _____
   (D) cave : dark _____
   (E) tree frog : jungle _____

3. DIPLOMAT : REPRESENT :: _____
   (A) gap : opening _____
   (B) captain : lead _____
   (C) tuba player : band _____
   (D) octagon : shape _____
   (E) enter : invade _____

4. FOREWORD : INTRODUCE :: _____
   (A) conclusion : summarize _____
   (B) light : dark _____
   (C) inch : foot _____
   (D) sea : shrimp _____
   (E) punctuate : sentence _____

5. GENERATE : PRODUCE :: _____
   (A) firefly : wings _____
   (B) illustrator : draw _____
   (C) sick : healthy _____
   (D) dalmatian : spotted _____
   (E) contribute : give _____

6. OBSCURE : CLEAR :: _____
   (A) bagpipes : Scotland _____
   (B) cyclone : storm _____
   (C) private : public _____
   (D) polite : courteous _____
   (E) dentist : cavity _____

7. PEWTER : GRAY :: _____
   (A) allergy : sneeze _____
   (B) lemon : sour _____
   (C) folks : people _____
   (D) following : leading _____
   (E) money : bank teller _____

8. QUENCH : BEVERAGE :: _____
   (A) absorb : sponge _____
   (B) spinach : vegetable _____
   (C) dainty : lace _____
   (D) painter : ladder _____
   (E) dessert : meal _____

9. SABLE : MAMMAL :: _____
   (A) shy : bashful _____
   (B) infection : fever _____
   (C) write : book _____
   (D) maple : tree _____
   (E) bird : sing _____

10. SALUTATION : LETTER :: _____
    (A) trunk : tree _____
    (B) deed : act _____
    (C) optometrist : glasses _____
    (D) striped : zebra _____
    (E) take : seize _____

© Houghton Mifflin Harcourt Publishing Company

CONNECTING NEW WORDS AND PATTERNS

Lesson 12 ANALOGIES

Directions. On each line, write the letter or letters that describe the type of relationship the words have to each other. Choose from the following types:

S synonym	A antonym	PW part and whole	PA performer and action
F function	L location	CE cause and effect	PO performer and object
D degree	C classification	CQ characteristic quality	AO action and object

Circle the letter of the pair of words that has the same relationship as the capitalized words. Each relationship is used no more than once in each numbered item.

1. CHARITABLE : STINGY :: _____
   (A) stubborn : flexible _____
   (B) lean : thin _____
   (C) mirror : breakable _____
   (D) scale : weigh _____
   (E) city : village _____

2. COLOSSAL : LARGE :: _____
   (A) roaming : wandering _____
   (B) senator : politician _____
   (C) pound : nail _____
   (D) surgeon : gloves _____
   (E) demand : suggest _____

3. CONFIDE : SECRET :: _____
   (A) measure : ruler _____
   (B) cups : cupboard _____
   (C) watermelon : pink _____
   (D) tell : tale _____
   (E) shade : lamp _____

4. ESSAY : CONCLUSION :: _____
   (A) spider : spin _____
   (B) quartz : rock _____
   (C) textbook : chapter _____
   (D) wrinkled : smooth _____
   (E) wobbly : unsteady _____

5. IRK : IRRITATE :: _____
   (A) satin : fabric _____
   (B) build : construct _____
   (C) effort : accomplishment _____
   (D) cluttered : tidy _____
   (E) win : lottery _____

6. PETTY : IMPORTANT :: _____
   (A) bee : wax _____
   (B) pattern : design _____
   (C) grapes : vineyard _____
   (D) innocent : guilty _____
   (E) snail : slow _____

7. PIOUS : BELIEVER :: _____
   (A) student : lunch box _____
   (B) pond : goldfish _____
   (C) looking glass : mirror _____
   (D) carry : books _____
   (E) talented : artist _____

8. SUMMIT : MOUNTAIN :: _____
   (A) watchdog : bark _____
   (B) swings : park _____
   (C) mouth : river _____
   (D) whole : broken _____
   (E) weaver : cloth _____

9. TARNISH : DISGRACE :: _____
   (A) need : require _____
   (B) perspiration : exercise _____
   (C) instrument : cello _____
   (D) florist : vase _____
   (E) leg : body _____

10. TEMPERAMENT : MANNER :: _____
    (A) athlete : train _____
    (B) region : area _____
    (C) eel : slippery _____
    (D) prehistoric : old _____
    (E) flower : bouquet _____

CONNECTING NEW WORDS AND PATTERNS

Lesson 13 | ANALOGIES

Directions. On each line, write the letter or letters that describe the type of relationship the words have to each other. Choose from the following types:

S synonym   A antonym   PW part and whole   PA performer and action
F function   L location   CE cause and effect   PO performer and object
D degree   C classification   CQ characteristic quality   AO action and object

Circle the letter of the pair of words that has the same relationship as the capitalized words. Each relationship is used no more than once in each numbered item.

1. CASUAL : INFORMAL :: ____
    (A) tunnel : dark ____
    (B) photographer : lens ____
    (C) regular : ordinary ____
    (D) water filter : purify ____
    (E) damaged : ruined ____

2. CONDEMN : BUILDING :: ____
    (A) sign : contract ____
    (B) spin : twirl ____
    (C) minnow : fish ____
    (D) hen : cluck ____
    (E) fade : brighten ____

3. DISPATCH : AMBULANCE :: ____
    (A) anger : argument ____
    (B) hurry : rush ____
    (C) comet : space ____
    (D) piece : pie ____
    (E) send : telegram ____

4. EMPHASIZE : STRESS :: ____
    (A) almond : nut ____
    (B) dolphin : swim ____
    (C) tall : ostrich ____
    (D) mice : barn ____
    (E) realize : understand ____

5. ENDORSE : CHECK :: ____
    (A) teacher : faculty ____
    (B) child : pretend ____
    (C) gelatin : wobbly ____
    (D) raise : taxes ____
    (E) mean : merciless ____

6. FAMISHED : HUNGRY :: ____
    (A) skinny : slim ____
    (B) yellow : daffodil ____
    (C) juror : courtroom ____
    (D) helicopter : aircraft ____
    (E) always : never ____

7. FICTITIOUS : REAL :: ____
    (A) quarterback : team ____
    (B) florist : deliver ____
    (C) shake : hand ____
    (D) taste : eat ____
    (E) worried : unconcerned ____

8. FRAGMENT : INCOMPLETE :: ____
    (A) reckless : careful ____
    (B) load : camera ____
    (C) crumb : cookie ____
    (D) chrome : shiny ____
    (E) tension : headache ____

9. IMPROVISE : ACTOR :: ____
    (A) alligator : swamp ____
    (B) recite : poet ____
    (C) instructions : directions ____
    (D) lullaby : song ____
    (E) nozzle : hose ____

10. MODIFY : ALTER :: ____
    (A) car : roller coaster ____
    (B) teacher : computer ____
    (C) earn : medal ____
    (D) copy : imitate ____
    (E) chilly : freezing ____

CONNECTING NEW WORDS AND PATTERNS

Lesson 14 | ANALOGIES

Directions. On each line, write the letter or letters that describe the type of relationship the words have to each other. Choose from the following types:

S synonym	A antonym	PW part and whole	PA performer and action
F function	L location	CE cause and effect	PO performer and object
D degree	C classification	CQ characteristic quality	AO action and object

Circle the letter of the pair of words that has the same relationship as the capitalized words. Each relationship is used no more than once in each numbered item.

1. BRAGGART : BOAST :: _____
   (A) insect : ant _____
   (B) perform : musician _____
   (C) clothing : closet _____
   (D) rose : fragrant _____
   (E) suggest : insist _____

2. DEMOLISH : DAMAGE :: _____
   (A) attorney : courtroom _____
   (B) trespassing : illegal _____
   (C) accomplishment : satisfaction _____
   (D) wing : bird _____
   (E) recover : improve _____

3. DENIAL : ACCEPTANCE :: _____
   (A) helmet : protect _____
   (B) strut : rooster _____
   (C) encouragement : disapproval _____
   (D) stinger : wasp _____
   (E) convict : prison _____

4. DETACH : DISCONNECT :: _____
   (A) dripping : streaming _____
   (B) conductor : ticket _____
   (C) pajamas : comfortable _____
   (D) mend : repair _____
   (E) law : profession _____

5. ELIGIBLE : QUALIFIED :: _____
   (A) ready : prepared _____
   (B) disgusted : delighted _____
   (C) toys : nursery _____
   (D) enraged : annoyed _____
   (E) strawberry : fruit _____

6. ILLUMINATE : LANTERN :: _____
   (A) stub : toe _____
   (B) chill : refrigerator _____
   (C) strict : lenient _____
   (D) eye : iris _____
   (E) ice : slippery _____

7. SECLUDED : PUBLIC :: _____
   (A) inspector : examine _____
   (B) star : night sky _____
   (C) dig : spade _____
   (D) mask : diver _____
   (E) deserted : crowded _____

8. SUPERFICIAL : SCRAPE :: _____
   (A) deep : gash _____
   (B) ship : ocean _____
   (C) handle : tea kettle _____
   (D) frog : croak _____
   (E) snapshot : remind _____

9. TANGIBLE : TOUCHABLE :: _____
   (A) tourist : luggage _____
   (B) odd : strange _____
   (C) crisis : stress _____
   (D) operate : surgeon _____
   (E) open : package _____

10. TESTIFY : WITNESS :: _____
   (A) sticky : glue _____
   (B) spend : shopper _____
   (C) orchard : cultivate _____
   (D) tap : pound _____
   (E) flute : instrument _____

CONNECTING NEW WORDS AND PATTERNS

Lesson 15 ANALOGIES

Directions. On each line, write the letter or letters that describe the type of relationship the words have to each other. Choose from the following types:

S synonym   A antonym   PW part and whole   PA performer and action
F function   L location   CE cause and effect   PO performer and object
D degree   C classification   CQ characteristic quality   AO action and object

Circle the letter of the pair of words that has the same relationship as the capitalized words. Each relationship is used no more than once in each numbered item.

1. ANTIBIOTICS : FIGHT :: ____
    (A) waiting : impatience ____
    (B) stretcher : rescuer ____
    (C) ordinary : unusual ____
    (D) red : strawberry ____
    (E) vaccinations : protect ____

2. AUTOMATON : ROBOT :: ____
    (A) bureau : dresser ____
    (B) kickstand : support ____
    (C) signer : signature ____
    (D) robin : bird ____
    (E) page : book ____

3. CONGEST : CLOG :: ____
    (A) genuine : fake ____
    (B) employ : hire ____
    (C) grove : forest ____
    (D) old : antiques ____
    (E) member : organization ____

4. HYPOTHESIS : UNPROVEN :: ____
    (A) horse : hay ____
    (B) sloppy : neat ____
    (C) nostril : nose ____
    (D) lie : untrue ____
    (E) direct : administrator ____

5. PARASITIC : INDEPENDENT :: ____
    (A) sea : starfish ____
    (B) kill : insecticide ____
    (C) damaged : perfect ____
    (D) alley : narrow ____
    (E) strayed : wandered ____

6. PHOTOGENIC : FASHION MODEL :: ____
    (A) journalist : newspaper ____
    (B) limb : body ____
    (C) climb : ladder ____
    (D) strong : steel ____
    (E) sight : sense ____

7. PLANETARIUM : BUILDING :: ____
    (A) mound : hill ____
    (B) orange : fruit ____
    (C) baker : bread ____
    (D) yellow : lemon ____
    (E) headboard : bed ____

8. RESPIRATION : BREATHING :: ____
    (A) count : teller ____
    (B) movie : theater ____
    (C) sharp : nail ____
    (D) clean : wound ____
    (E) exchange : trade ____

9. SYNTHETIC : NATURAL :: ____
    (A) commentator : speak ____
    (B) ill : healthy ____
    (C) metal : gold ____
    (D) fire : carelessness ____
    (E) wing : airplane ____

10. WARRANTY : ASSURE :: ____
    (A) investigation : solve ____
    (B) pouch : bag ____
    (C) squirrel : scamper ____
    (D) wrap : gift ____
    (E) soothing : breeze ____

READING NEW WORDS IN CONTEXT

Why We Read Strategically

Reading is active. As you read, you step into the writer's world. When you come across a new idea, you usually look for a clue to help you determine the writer's meaning. You move ahead to see if the idea is explained, or you retrace your steps to look for any signs you missed.

You can use these same strategies to build your vocabulary. If you do not know the meaning of a word, you should look in the passage surrounding the word for hints. These hints are called context clues. The more you practice hunting for context clues, the better you become at reading new words, and the larger your vocabulary will grow. Remember, strengthening your vocabulary skills will help you to score higher on standardized vocabulary tests.

The following reading selection shows the kinds of context clues you will find in the Reading New Words in Context lessons.

Strategic Reading: An Example

Long, long ago, long before there were humans on Earth—much less humans who could record history—dinosaurs walked the earth. During these **prehistoric** times, strange and wonderful creatures ruled the entire earth. All in all, *this* **reign** lasted 135 million years.

Note that a *summary* indicates the meaning of **prehistoric**.

A *pronoun* (*this*) refers us to the meaning of **reign**.

The dinosaur was one **descendant** of the thecodonts, mighty reptiles whose *later generations* also included many other reptiles, as well as all of today's birds. One of these relatives was a huge flying reptile. Another was a creature with a body like that of a turtle but with a 25-foot-long neck. Like the dinosaurs, these unusual *and* **extraordinary** creatures became extinct. Any of these creatures has the power to *stun,* **astonish,** *and amaze* us, but it is the dinosaurs that most people find especially fascinating.

The meaning of **descendant** is made clear through *restatement*, that is, through saying the same thing in a different way.

A *coordinating conjunction* (*and*) provides a clue to the meaning of **extraordinary**. The words *but, or,* and *nor* are other coordinating conjunctions.

Note that a clue to the meaning of **astonish** is provided by using the word in a *series* of words that have similar meanings.

Some dinosaurs were **mammoth** creatures. *The euhelopus, for example, was 60 feet tall and weighed 50,000 pounds.* In contrast, the 20-foot, 7,000-pound stegosaurus seems almost small. Although enormous size *was* a **characteristic** of many dinosaurs, others were much, much smaller, no bigger than a chicken or a duck. Some of these smaller ones looked much like either the iguana or the komodo dragon, two reptiles that inhabit Earth today.

An *example* provides the key to understanding **mammoth**.

A form of the verb *to be* (*was*) links an example of a quality to the word **characteristic**.

Some of the dinosaurs were fierce, meat-eating creatures. Often, other *milder and gentler dinosaurs were unable to defend themselves from the more savage ones and thus became their* **victims**. Even the vegetarian dinosaurs who roamed about peacefully snacking on plants could be quite frightening to other species that shared the planet. A 55-ton brachiosaurus lumbering across the countryside would have presented a real **threat**, *a clear danger,* to any unsuspecting creature who got in its way. The huge Triceratops had frightening horns on its nose and over both of its eyes. The sight of this 10-ton animal bounding along at 30 miles per hour certainly scared the newly emerging mammals that had to scurry out of its way. Nevertheless, it was also a threat to any other dinosaur that tried to attack it.

Although groups of dinosaurs might be in **competition** with each other, *cooperation within a group was also common.* Members of a species might travel in a herd, eat and nest together, share responsibility for the young, and present a united defense against enemies.

Scientists are still debating about why the dinosaurs disappeared. We do not know for sure. All we know is that **twilight** *arrived for these creatures at the same time all across the earth. Then, in a twinkling, it was night,* and the dinosaurs were gone.

In a *cause-and-effect* relationship, one thing causes another thing to happen. The meaning of **victims** is established through a cause-and-effect relationship. *Thus* is a cause-and-effect clue word.

An *appositive phrase* contains a noun or pronoun that explains the noun or pronoun beside it. An appositive phrase indicates the meaning of **threat**.

Note that the meaning of **competition** is established through *contrast,* the placement of opposites near each other to point out their difference. The word *although* indicates contrast.

The meaning of **twilight** is established through *figurative language.* Figurative language is language that imaginatively describes one thing by comparing it to something else.

A Final Note

How can you learn strategic reading? Practice is a great way to improve your skill. The following lessons will help you learn the different context clues a writer uses. As you complete each lesson, you will become a more effective reader.

READING NEW WORDS IN CONTEXT

Lesson 1 | CONTEXT: Coming to the United States

Introduction. We know with certainty that Columbus came to North America in 1492. We also know that the Vikings first came to North America on or around A.D. 1000. However, the date that the very first people set foot on the North American continent is hotly debated. Guesses differ by as much as sixty thousand years. What we do know is that the first Americans arrived a very long time ago.

The following article gives you an opportunity to read about the first Americans and their encounters with Europeans. It also gives you an opportunity to expand your vocabulary. Below are twenty Vocabulary Words that are used in the article and in the exercise that follows it.

abuse	bewilder	eminent	knoll	probable
appalling	calamity	epidemic	myriad	romantic
baffle	contagious	folklore	novelty	ruthless
barbarism	deceive	intentional	picturesque	sincerity

North America Meets Europe

Some scientists believe that human beings first began to call North America home twelve thousand years ago. Others believe that twenty-five thousand years is a more likely guess. Still others say that it is most **probable** (1) that people began to arrive here thirty thousand years ago. In any case, the continent has been home to **myriad** (2) groups of people for thousands of years. No one knows for sure exactly how many different groups lived here before the Europeans came five hundred years ago, but the groups numbered well into the hundreds.

Some of the First Americans
Long before Europeans began to arrive, people in the Arctic reaches of the continent traveled by dog sled and kayak. Far to the south, the Anasazi built multilevel cliff dwellings and irrigated their crops. In the southeast, the Choctaw made textiles and buried their dead in elaborate mounds. Many of these **knolls** (3)

are still visible today. In the northeast, the Hurons built stockades and farmed the land. In the continent's heartland, the peoples of the plains grew crops, traded, and hunted bison.

The idea that Christopher Columbus or the Vikings somehow discovered a new world **baffles** (4) many people. Such a one-sided view of history confuses them. Today, we realize that people had discovered the Americas thousands and thousands of years before either the Vikings' or Columbus's arrival.

Some of the First Americans
The original inhabitants were sometimes confused and **bewildered** (5) by the Europeans' strange ways, but they could not know that the arrival of the Europeans would be a **calamity** (6) for them. European weapons and diseases soon began to destroy the native people. Thousands were killed by violence and disease, and entire cultures were

wiped out. The **abuse** (7) began almost as soon as Columbus set foot in the Americas.

Destructive Policies

Throughout the Americas, the original inhabitants were the victims of **ruthless** (8) policies. They were forced into slavery; they were killed if they did not convert to Christianity; and they lost their lives in wars. These terrible events are **appalling** (9) to historians.

Not all of the suffering caused by the Europeans was **intentional** (10). Some of it was accidental. For example, many American Indians died as a result of **contagious** (11) diseases. They had never been exposed to mumps or measles or other illnesses that the Europeans brought with them. As a result, some diseases reached **epidemic** (12) proportions, wiping out entire communities.

Unfortunately, Europeans often approached American Indians without **sincerity** (13), or good faith. Too often, acts of friendship were designed to **deceive** (14). The European Americans often gained the American Indians' trust in order to betray it. In fact, the story of the relationship between European Americans and American Indians is one of the saddest in U.S. history. The **folklore** (15) that North America's native peoples have passed down from generation to generation reflects this fact. Many American Indians tell tales of the conquerors who came from across the sea and changed forever the native peoples' way of life.

Understanding Cultural Differences

While some Europeans respected the cultures they encountered, many did not. They thought that anyone who did not live the way they did must be a savage. As a result, they considered customs of the American Indians to be **barbarisms** (16).

Of course, not all Europeans were so blind. Many respected the native cultures. Some were simply curious about a culture they thought was **picturesque** (17). They were interested in a way of life that seemed charming and pleasant. Others were interested in **novelty** (18), in exploring what was, to them, strange, different, and new. These Europeans had a **romantic** (19) notion of American Indians. They weren't really interested in the realities or difficulties of their daily lives. However, some Europeans understood American Indian cultures' **eminent** (20) worth. They recognized these cultures as remarkable and noteworthy.

EXERCISE *Reading Strategically* ✍

Directions. Answer each of the following items by circling the letter of the correct answer. You may need to refer to the selection as you answer the items. The numbers of the items are the same as the numbers of the boldface Vocabulary Words in the selection.

1. Some people think that it is **probable** that human beings have lived in North America for more than seventy-five thousand years. Here, **probable** means
   (A) likely
   (B) possible
   (C) unlikely
   (D) interesting

2. The writer gives us a clue to the meaning of **myriad**. What is the clue?
   (A) Human beings have lived on the continent for thousands of years.
   (B) Many different groups lived in North America before the Europeans arrived.
   (C) The Europeans came to North America five hundred years ago.
   (D) Scientists disagree about when human beings first lived in North America.

3. You can tell from the article that **knolls** means

(A) visible
(B) mounds
(C) stockades
(D) textiles

4. The writer states, "The idea that Columbus or the Vikings somehow discovered a new world **baffles** many people." Here, **baffles** means

(A) disturbs
(B) confuses
(C) crosses
(D) ignores

5. You can tell from the article that **bewildered** means

(A) frequently
(B) strange
(C) entertained
(D) confused

6. How does the writer let us know that a **calamity** is an event that causes great misery and distress?

(A) The writer tells us that the Europeans arrived.
(B) The writer tells us that the Europeans brought both weapons and disease.
(C) The writer tells us that thousands died and that entire cultures disappeared.
(D) The writer tells us that the Europeans had strange ways.

7. The writer states, "The **abuse** began almost as soon as Columbus set foot in the Americas." Here, **abuse** means

(A) disease
(B) greeting
(C) mistreatment
(D) culture

8. All of the following are good definitions of **ruthless** *except*

(A) cruel
(B) hardhearted
(C) without mercy
(D) unbelievable

9. The writer says that historians today find the actions **appalling**. Here, **appalling** means

(A) deadly
(B) historic
(C) horrifying
(D) warlike

10. How does the writer let us know that **intentional** means deliberate?

(A) The writer lets us know that diseases are only severe if they are deliberate.
(B) The writer contrasts **intentional** with the word *accidental*.
(C) The writer tells us that the Europeans brought the diseases.
(D) The writer says that Europeans destroyed American Indians.

11. According to the article, _____ is an example of something **contagious**.

(A) European Americans
(B) starvation
(C) measles
(D) a result

12. How does the writer let us know that **epidemic** means widespread?

(A) The writer tells us that diseases wiped out whole communities.
(B) The writer tells us that the diseases were severe.
(C) The writer tells us that the Europeans brought the diseases.
(D) The writer tells us that no one was exposed to the diseases.

© Houghton Mifflin Harcourt Publishing Company

13. The writer says that many Europeans did not approach American Indians with **sincerity,** or good faith. Here, **sincerity** means
   (A) actions
   (B) friendliness
   (C) value
   (D) honesty

14. How does the writer let us know that **deceive** means to mislead?
   (A) The writer tells us that friends deceive one another.
   (B) The writer implies we should trust our own judgment.
   (C) The writer says that some European Americans gained American Indians' trust in order to betray it.
   (D) The writer makes it clear that the relationship between American Indians and European Americans has occasionally been good.

15. The writer mentions that **folklore** has been passed down through generations. Here, **folklore** means
   (A) fact
   (B) traditional stories
   (C) sadness
   (D) historical relationships

16. The writer tells us that many Europeans considered American Indian customs to be **barbarisms.** Here, **barbarisms** means
   (A) historical realities
   (B) uncivilized activities
   (C) un-American actions
   (D) cultural customs

17. The writer states, "Some were simply curious about a culture they thought was **picturesque.**" Here **picturesque** means
   (A) charming
   (B) artistic
   (C) interesting
   (D) honest

18. The writer states, "Others were interested in **novelty,** in exploring what was, to them, strange, different, and new." Here, **novelty** means
   (A) cultures
   (B) something new and unusual
   (C) exploration
   (D) something charming and pleasant

19. The writer of this article gives a clue to the meaning of **romantic.** What is the clue?
   (A) The writer lets us know that the Europeans had notions about American Indians that were different from reality.
   (B) The writer makes it clear that daily life is difficult.
   (C) The writer tells us that some of the Europeans weren't interested in the realities of daily life.
   (D) The writer reminds us that some Europeans continued to explore American Indian cultures.

20. In this article, **eminent** means
   (A) useful
   (B) visible
   (C) wealthy
   (D) noteworthy

READING NEW WORDS IN CONTEXT

Lesson 2 | CONTEXT: The First Americans

Introduction. The American Indian people called the Dakotas were not a single, close-knit group. They were divided into several subgroups. Some Dakotas called themselves Mdewakanto, or Spirit Lake People. Others were Sisseton, or People of the Boggy Ground. In all, there were fourteen Dakota groups living in North America.

The following article gives you an opportunity to learn more about the Dakota culture and to expand your vocabulary. Below are twenty Vocabulary Words that are used in the article and in the exercise that follows it.

advent	catastrophe	inevitable	motivate	sanctuary
aggressive	defy	integrity	mystical	strategy
alliance	ecology	intelligible	nourish	sustain
anthology	ferocious	misdeed	pacify	valid

The Dakotas

Some of the knowledge we have of the Dakota people comes from collections of myths and legends found in **anthologies** (1). Most of it, however, is from well-documented research. For example, it is known that before the Europeans came, before the **advent** (2) of the French in Canada and the British in New England, the Dakotas made their homes in areas of what is now the United States and Canada. The several different groups that together are called the Dakotas formed an **alliance** (3), an agreement between nations with a common cause, to govern and protect themselves from enemies. One of the enemies was the Ojibwa people, with whom the Dakotas warred from time to time. A typical Dakota might scorn the Ojibwa for believing they could threaten the Dakotas' security. However, an even more powerful threat to the Dakotas was on its way.

The Beginning of Trouble

The Dakotas first began to encounter Europeans in the 1600s. In the summers, many Dakotas lived in what is now Minnesota, where they found an abundant supply of wild rice, fruits, and vegetables to **nourish** (4) themselves and their children. In the fall, they broke into smaller bands and hunted for game to **sustain** (5) them through the winter.

The Europeans were friendly to the Dakotas, but they were even friendlier to the Dakotas' enemies, the Ojibwas—to whom they sold guns. The Dakotas were concerned that the armed Ojibwas might become **aggressive** (6) and attack them, so the Dakotas moved. By 1750, they established new territory that stretched from the upper Mississippi Valley into the Black Hills. They continued their defensive **strategy** (7) of keeping lodges of soldiers to protect them from any invaders.

Life on the Plains

Like most American Indian peoples, the Dakotas considered the earth as having **mystical** (8) qualities. They thought of it in a spiritual way and, therefore, they respected earth's **ecology** (9), the complex relationship among living things. They never destroyed anything for which they did not have a **valid** (10) use. An animal for which they had a real need was the bison. The Dakotas depended upon the bison for survival. They used the flesh for food; the hides became clothing and shelter; the horns were made into spoons and cups; the muscle tendon was used to make bowstrings and thread. No part of the bison was wasted.

For almost a hundred years the Dakotas lived in relative peace. They traded with the few white merchants who lived near them. They did not know that the presence of trading posts meant that **catastrophe** (11) was **inevitable** (12). They did not know that once a few white people came, wave after wave of land-hungry settlers would follow, demanding the Dakotas' land. They did not know that white hunters would slaughter all the bison. Perhaps they would not have believed it possible. The concept of wasteful slaughter might not have been **intelligible** (13) to a people who used their resources wisely, wasting nothing. The Dakota must have wondered what would **motivate** (14) someone to act so irresponsibly. Soon the Dakotas would have to wage a fierce, sometimes **ferocious** (15) battle in defense of their homeland.

The Coming of the Settlers

By 1850, the number of white settlers pouring west began to alarm the Dakotas. The United States government hoped to **pacify** (16) the Dakotas and avoid war with them by signing three treaties.

The Dakotas gave up more than ten million acres of land in Minnesota and Iowa. In return, they were promised yearly payments. They were also promised that the land along the upper Minnesota River would remain Dakota land. The Dakotas thought of the land as a **sanctuary** (17), a place of shelter that the whites would not enter. Peace, however, was not assured.

In 1854, the first in a long series of battles between the United States and the Dakotas took place near Fort Laramie in Wyoming. A white settler claimed that the Dakotas had stolen one of his cows. He wanted the Dakotas to pay for this **misdeed** (18). When the U.S. troops arrived at the camp to demand payment, the Dakotas chose to **defy** (19) them. They attacked the troops. It was the beginning of almost forty years of struggle.

For several years, the proud Dakotas struggled to maintain the **integrity** (20) of their culture, to keep it whole against overwhelming odds. By 1880, however, most of the Dakotas had been disarmed. Their horses had been taken from them, they were confined to reservation land, and they were dependent on the U.S. government for food and clothing. Today, the Sioux tribes, to which the Dakotas belong, continue to discuss with the federal government the possibilities of a settlement for the lands that were taken from them.

EXERCISE *Reading Strategically*

Directions. Answer each of the following items by circling the letter of the correct answer. You may need to refer to the selection as you answer the items. The numbers of the items are the same as the numbers of the boldface Vocabulary Words in the selection.

1. You can tell from the article that **anthologies** means
   (A) research
   (B) a collection
   (C) legends
   (D) bound books

2. The writer uses **advent** when discussing the French and British. Here, **advent** means
   (A) settling
   (B) push
   (C) arrival
   (D) delivery

3. The writer says that the Dakotas formed an **alliance**. Here, **alliance** means
   (A) an agreement between nations with a common cause
   (B) a group of peoples living in the same general area
   (C) an enemy that threatens a number of different groups
   (D) a declaration of war between two groups that share a region

4. How does the writer let us know that **nourish** means to feed with healthful substances?
   (A) The writer tells us the Dakotas spent summers in what is now Minnesota.
   (B) The writer says Dakota children gathered the food.
   (C) The writer says that fruits and vegetables were in short supply.
   (D) The writer says that the Dakotas found wild rice, fruits, and vegetables.

5. In this article, **sustain** means
   (A) hunt
   (B) search and destroy
   (C) support
   (D) divide

6. All of the following are good definitions of **aggressive** *except*
   (A) hostile
   (B) quick to attack
   (C) ready to fight
   (D) willing to trade

7. The writer of this article gives us a clue to the meaning of **strategy**. What is the clue?
   (A) The Dakotas established new territory.
   (B) The Dakotas moved to the upper Mississippi Valley.
   (C) The Dakotas were concerned by the Ojibwa threat.
   (D) The Dakotas maintained lodges of soldiers to protect them from attackers.

8. The writer says that the Dakotas considered the earth as having **mystical** qualities. Here, **mystical** means
   (A) occult
   (B) mysterious
   (C) secret
   (D) spiritual

9. You can tell from the article that **ecology** means
   (A) the complex relationship among living things
   (B) American Indian cultures
   (C) a kind of religion
   (D) the use of nature for survival

10. In this article, **valid** means
    (A) reasonable
    (B) valuable
    (C) independent
    (D) ordinary

11. _____ is an example of a **catastrophe** that is mentioned in the article.
    (A) The efficient use of bison
    (B) The slaughter of the bison
    (C) A hundred years of peace
    (D) Dakota land

12. How does the writer let us know that **inevitable** means certain to happen?
    (A) The writer tells us that land-hungry settlers demanded Dakota land.
    (B) The writer says that once a few white people came, wave after wave would surely follow.
    (C) The Dakotas would not have believed what would happen.
    (D) The writer refers to trading posts and merchants as **catastrophes**.

13. The writer suggests that the concept of wasteful slaughter might not have been **intelligible** to the Dakotas. Here, **intelligible** means
    (A) understandable
    (B) interesting
    (C) available
    (D) useful

14. The writer says that the Dakota would wonder "what would **motivate** someone to act so irresponsibly." Here, **motivate** means

(A) cause
(B) advise
(C) suggest
(D) join

15. You can tell from the article that **ferocious** means

(A) defensive
(B) very fierce
(C) always better
(D) skillful

16. The writer of this article gives us a clue to the meaning of **pacify**. What is the clue?

(A) The number of settlers alarmed the Dakotas.
(B) No matter how well armed one might be, it is impossible to defeat the United States Army.
(C) The U.S. government signed treaties with the Dakotas to avoid war.
(D) The Dakotas were a powerful military force.

17. The writer tells us that the Dakotas thought of the land as a **sanctuary**. Here, **sanctuary** means

(A) church
(B) gift
(C) long-lasting peace
(D) place of shelter

18. The writer states, "He wanted the Dakotas to pay for this **misdeed**." Here, **misdeed** means

(A) payment
(B) claim
(C) cow
(D) wrongdoing

19. The writer states, "When the U.S. troops arrived at the camp to demand payment, the Dakotas chose to **defy** them." Here, **defy** means

(A) resist
(B) answer
(C) ignore
(D) claim

20. In the last paragraph, **integrity** means

(A) loyalty
(B) wholeness
(C) resistance
(D) bitterness

READING NEW WORDS IN CONTEXT

Lesson 3 | CONTEXT: The First Americans

Introduction. Four Corners is the name given to the point where Arizona, Colorado, New Mexico, and Utah meet. For many centuries the area has been home to several groups of American Indians. Among these groups are the various Pueblo peoples, the Navajos, and the Apaches.

The following essay gives you an opportunity to read about the people who live at Four Corners. It also enables you to expand your vocabulary. Below are twenty Vocabulary Words that are used in the essay and in the exercise that follows it.

accessory	badger	customary	glorify	multicolored
adjacent	calculation	deceased	harmonious	pulverize
artisan	complement	fragile	incomparable	valor
attain	convert	gallery	intervene	vitality

Cultures of Four Corners

Much land in the Four Corners area, particularly in New Mexico and Arizona, is reservation land. Some reservations are **adjacent** (1) to each other. For example, the Zuni reservation borders on the Navajo reservation, and the Hopi reservation is actually surrounded by the Navajo land. The area also includes reservations for Apaches and Utes. The Hopis and Zunis of the Pueblo peoples, however, have lived there the longest.

If you visit the Four Corners area, you are sure to get a sense of how old life there is. It's easy to imagine people there a thousand years ago grinding corn, **pulverizing** (2) the grain to make flour. You might imagine a basket weaver at work or a priest preparing for a ceremony. The peoples who have lived there have shown an amazing ability to endure and survive. The **vitality** (3) of these cultures is admired throughout the world.

The Pueblos of the Four Corners Area: Hopis and Zunis

Pueblo was the name the Spanish gave to the nineteen different groups of American Indians who lived in villages in New Mexico and northeastern Arizona. Although these are separate peoples, they have much in common. For example, each group is made up of clans. Each clan may be named after an animal such as the deer or the **badger** (4). Each clan has its own role within the tribe. For example, a clan may perform a particular ceremony. Although many Pueblos became Christians, some chose not to **convert** (5) to Christianity, and each clan plays an important role in traditional religious ceremonies.

Life in a Pueblo culture is **harmonious** (6). The Pueblos do not approve of disagreement within the group. Although they are capable of fighting, and they honor war gods, they do not

glorify (7) war. They honor the values of peace and harmony. Perhaps they are able to live together so easily because they participate in a ceremony sometimes called the rites of rebellion. During this ceremony, it is **customary** (8), or usual, for priests to dress as clowns, sometimes called Mudheads, and to pretend to engage in behavior that is normally forbidden. This ceremony helps relieve tension that might lead to disagreements.

The Pueblos have many other ceremonies. One ceremony honors the **deceased** (9) by paying tribute to the souls of the dead. At these ceremonies, dancers may wear **multicolored** (10) costumes, each color having a special meaning.

Neighboring Navajos

The **calculations** (11) of anthropologists and archaeologists indicate that the Pueblos have lived in the Four Corners region for thousands of years. However, scientists figure that the Navajos arrived in the Southwest much more recently, about five or six hundred years ago.

Although the Pueblos probably did not try to **intervene** (12) directly in the affairs of their new neighbors, over the centuries the Navajos have felt the influence of the Pueblo cultures. The Pueblos have, to some extent, been influenced by the Navajos, as well. Each group seems to have selected what would **complement** (13), or add to, their own culture. Yet they are distinctly different peoples.

The Navajos believe the world is **fragile** (14) and that people must treat it with love and care.

They believe that evil is a real presence on the earth and that people must guard against it to remain pure. The Navajos work to achieve *hohzo*. *Hohzo* is a difficult concept for a non-Navajo to understand. It includes beauty, happiness, harmony, and goodness. *Hohzo* is the goal all Navajos reach for, but it is difficult to **attain** (15).

Today, the Navajo nation is the largest American Indian group within the United States, including more than 200,000 people. They have played a major role in twentieth-century history. Many demonstrated their **valor** (16) by bravely serving as soldiers in World War II. The "Code Talkers" were of special importance. They used the Navajo language as a code to prevent the enemy from understanding American radio messages.

American Art

Anyone who is familiar with American Indian art is familiar with the art of the cultures of the Four Corners region. The area has long been home to **artisans** (17) of **incomparable** (18) skill who create rugs, pottery, statuary, and sand paintings of matchless beauty. A **gallery** (19) of this art would include not only these items but also bracelets, necklaces, and other jewelry too beautiful to be worn simply as **accessories** (20). The rich artistic tradition of the Four Corners area is an important part of the fascinating cultures that live in this historic region.

EXERCISE *Reading Strategically* 👉

Directions. Answer each of the following items by circling the letter of the correct answer. You may need to refer to the selection as you answer the items. The numbers of the items are the same as the numbers of the boldface Vocabulary Words in the selection.

1. The writer gives a clue to the meaning of **adjacent**. What is the clue?
   (A) New Mexico and Arizona are home to many reservations.
   (B) The Zuni reservation borders the Navajo reservation.
   (C) There are several reservations.
   (D) The people who have lived there the longest are the Pueblos.

2. The writer says that it's easy to imagine someone grinding corn, **pulverizing** it to make flour. Here, **pulverizing** means
   (A) imagining
   (B) cooking
   (C) borrowing
   (D) grinding

3. The writer of this essay gives a clue to the meaning of **vitality**. What is the clue?
   (A) The peoples of the Four Corners area have an amazing ability to endure and survive.
   (B) The cultures are admired throughout the world.
   (C) You can imagine a basket weaver at work or a priest preparing for a ceremony.
   (D) A visitor to the Four Corners area can sense how old life is there.

4. In the passage, **badger** means
   (A) a deer
   (B) to pester
   (C) an animal
   (D) to imagine

5. According to the writer, "Although many Pueblos became Christians, some chose not to **convert** to Christianity." Here, **convert** means
   (A) change
   (B) build
   (C) complain
   (D) dislike

6. How does the writer let us know that **harmonious** means showing agreement in attitudes and feelings?
   (A) The writer comments that the Pueblos are capable of fighting.
   (B) The writer implies that the Pueblo culture is religious.
   (C) The writer notes that the Pueblos disapprove of disagreement within the community.
   (D) The writer shows how the Pueblos honor war gods.

7. You can tell from the essay that to **glorify** means
   (A) to apologize for
   (B) to go to
   (C) to give honor to
   (D) to fight in

8. The writer indicates that at special times it is **customary** for priests to dress as clowns. Here, **customary** means
   (A) usual
   (B) ceremonial
   (C) honorable
   (D) understandable

9. The writer states, "One ceremony honors the **deceased**. . . ." Here, **deceased** means
   (A) forbidden
   (B) things
   (C) dead
   (D) dancers

10. The writer states, "At these ceremonies, dancers may wear **multicolored** costumes, each color having a special meaning." Here, **multicolored** means
    (A) black and white only
    (B) having different colors
    (C) honorable
    (D) having special colors

11. The writer gives a clue to the meaning of **calculations**. What is the clue?
    (A) Scientists figure that the Navajos arrived five or six hundred years ago.
    (B) The Pueblos live in the Four Corners region.
    (C) The writer hints that no one has lived in the region longer than the Pueblos have.
    (D) The **calculations** are made by anthropologists and archaeologists.

12. You can tell from the essay that **intervene** means
    (A) control
    (B) interfere
    (C) overlook
    (D) live

13. The writer says that each group se-
lected what would **complement** their
own culture. Here, **complement**
means to
(A) take away from
(B) add to
(C) differ from
(D) contest

14. All of the following are good defini-
tions of **fragile** *except*
(A) frail
(B) easily damaged
(C) delicate
(D) broken

15. All of the following are good defini-
tions of **attain** *except*
(A) to achieve
(B) to reach
(C) to avoid
(D) to gain

16. The writer states, "Many demon-
strated their **valor** by serving as sol-
diers in World War II." Here, **valor**
means
(A) worth
(B) service
(C) wisdom
(D) courage

17. In this essay, **artisans** means people
(A) of the Four Corners region
(B) who are the best
(C) with special abilities
(D) who create hand-made art

18. Another word that means about the
same thing as **incomparable** is
(A) unfriendly
(B) useful
(C) incomplete
(D) matchless

19. You can tell from the essay that a
gallery is
(A) rugs, pottery, statuary, and sand
paintings
(B) American Indian art
(C) a place where art is displayed
(D) a large amount

20. Which of the following are examples
of **accessories**?
(A) artistic traditions
(B) bracelets
(C) beautiful things
(D) sand paintings

READING NEW WORDS IN CONTEXT

Lesson 4 | CONTEXT: The First Americans

Introduction. Long before the United States formed Congress, the several groups that made up the Iroquois nations had formed the League of Five Nations. The league was founded in the early 1600s, and each member group had elected representatives. The council was not intended to be a strong, centralized authority, but it was a model of representative government.

The following article gives you an opportunity to learn more about the Iroquois nations. The article also enables you to expand your vocabulary. Below are twenty Vocabulary Words that are used in the article and in the exercise that follows it.

adequate	descend	foresight	inherit	mutual
advantageous	discord	gnarled	isolation	phenomenon
confederation	enhance	incite	menace	posterity
delegate	feline	inflexible	menagerie	revelation

The Five Nations

East of the Great Lakes, in country that is now partly in Canada and partly in the United States, the woods once swarmed with animals. There were moose and beavers and bears—creatures that many of us no longer see except in wildlife parks or caged in **menageries** (1). The lakes and rivers were filled with fish, and the air was alive with the songs of birds. Here, five nations of the Iroquois—the Mohawk, the Seneca, the Oneida, the Cayuga, and the Ondaga—made their homes.

Here, in the sixteenth century, the prophet Deganwidah dreamed of a huge evergreen tree. He understood the dream to be a **revelation** (2), a dramatic sign showing him a path the Iroquois should follow. The roots of the tree were the many groups that formed the Iroquois nation, and the tree itself was the sisterhood of the Iroquois women. The Iroquois nations had lived in **discord** (3), often quarreling with one another. Deganwidah interpreted the dream to mean that the nations should end their differences and band together for support.

Achieving the Dream

It was Hiawatha who made Deganwidah's dream of a **confederation** (4) a reality. From village to village he traveled, encouraging the Iroquois to form a league. He convinced five groups of Iroquois that it would be **advantageous** (5) to adopt the plan. They saw that the league would be to their benefit. In 1570, the League of the Five Nations was formed.

Rules for the league were established, and the Iroquois passed a law saying that **delegates** (6) from each nation had to meet every fifth summer to discuss the needs of the people. The men chosen to represent the people were called sachem, and they were selected by the women. The rule about meeting every five years was **inflexible** (7). In addition to the fixed five-year schedule, however, delegates could meet at other times as they saw fit.

For the most part, the league was **adequate** (8) for the needs of the five nations. The Iroquois

© Houghton Mifflin Harcourt Publishing Company

were able to settle most of their differences. However, the council did not put an end to war.

The Iroquois and Their Neighbors

From time to time, a group of Iroquois **descended** (9) on another tribe, like a hawk coming down on its prey, and engaged in a quick battle. They did this for glory and to capture prisoners. The prisoners were used as laborers or were adopted into families as replacements for family members who had died.

These attacks were usually brief but violent. Europeans said that the Iroquois, like wild cats, sneaked up on their victims quietly and then attacked and fought ferociously. Stories of this **feline** (10) stealth and ferocity spread throughout European and American Indian communities. The mere thought of the **menace** (11) of an Iroquois raiding party was enough to **incite** (12) fear and terror in the hearts of many.

The Iroquois were among the first people European settlers encountered in North America. The two groups wondered about the other's customs. This **mutual** (13) curiosity led the two groups to have extensive contact with each other.

The Iroquois Heritage

Iroquois culture was impressive in many ways. For example, the Iroquois interpreted dreams with great skill and wisdom, and they used dreams to **enhance** (14), or improve upon, their understanding of themselves and others. In addition, the Iroquois people had the **foresight** (15) to look ahead and plan for future generations. This planning for **posterity** (16) was based on a basic principle of American Indian wisdom: Always consider how any decision you make will affect the seventh generation following you.

Women played a major role in the Iroquois nation. In addition to choosing delegates to the meetings of the League of Five Nations, women owned all the property, and daughters **inherited** (17) it from their mothers. Almost everything in the culture was passed from one generation of women to the next.

The basic social unit of the Iroquois was the *owachiras,* which consisted of a woman and her children. The Iroquois family never experienced the sense of **isolation** (18) that contemporary families may feel. Several families lived together in one long house. They may have been crowded by our standards, but they were never lonely, and parents always had help in caring for their children.

The Iroquois believed that the spirit world revealed itself in the physical world. In other words, the spiritual was not separate from the physical, but was a **phenomenon** (19) that could be sensed in the material world. For example, the face of a spirit might reveal itself in the trunk of a **gnarled** (20) and twisted tree. Thus, the world of the Iroquois—rich in natural and cultural beauty—was also a magical place.

EXERCISE *Reading Strategically* 👉

Directions. Answer each of the following items by circling the letter of the correct answer. You may need to refer to the selection as you answer the items. The numbers of the items are the same as the numbers of the boldface Vocabulary Words in the selection.

1. The writer says that some animals are now seen only in **menageries**. Here **menageries** means
   (A) collections of caged animals
   (B) areas east of the Great Lakes
   (C) the Iroquois nation
   (D) lakes and rivers

2. In the second paragraph, **revelation** means
   (A) a dramatic disclosure or sign
   (B) a clear view of the past
   (C) a plan to cooperate with the enemy
   (D) a dream of a beautiful garden

3. The writer gives us a clue to the meaning of **discord**. What is the clue?
   (A) Deganwidah interpreted the dreams.
   (B) The groups often quarreled with one another.
   (C) No one can live in peace.
   (D) The nations should band together for support.

4. You can tell from the article that **confederation** means
   (A) reality
   (B) a league
   (C) a dream
   (D) travel

5. All of the following are good definitions of **advantageous** *except*
   (A) favorable
   (B) useful
   (C) profitable
   (D) convincing

6. The writer indicates that the **delegates** were to meet every five years. Here, **delegates** means
   (A) meetings
   (B) people
   (C) representatives
   (D) membership dues

7. You can tell from the article that **inflexible** means
   (A) not enforced
   (B) unworkable
   (C) unchangeable
   (D) not broken

8. The writer of the article gives a clue to the meaning of **adequate**. What is the clue?
   (A) There were only five nations.
   (B) The league was effective most of the time.
   (C) The sachem were required to abide by a strict, five-year meeting schedule.
   (D) The Iroquois attacked other groups.

9. The writer says that the way the Iroquois **descended** on another tribe was most like
   (A) a quick battle
   (B) an occasional burst of aggression
   (C) a hawk coming down on its prey
   (D) adopting a new family member

10. The writer uses **feline** when talking about how the Iroquois attacked their enemies. Here, **feline** means
    (A) polite
    (B) clumsy
    (C) catlike
    (D) fearful

11. The writer shows that **menace** means a threat by saying that
    (A) the mere thought of an Iroquois raiding party caused fear and terror
    (B) the Europeans and other American Indians thought of the Iroquois as ferocious fighters
    (C) the attacks from the Iroquois were usually brief but violent
    (D) the Iroquois were among the first people European settlers encountered in North America

12. The writer tells us that the mere thought of an Iroquois raiding party was enough to **incite** fear and terror in many people. Here, **incite** means
    (A) arouse
    (B) drown out
    (C) think about
    (D) include

13. The writer says that the two groups had **mutual** curiosity. Here, **mutual** means
    (A) normal
    (B) shared
    (C) cultural
    (D) strange

14. The writer states, "They used dreams to **enhance,** or improve upon, their understanding of themselves and others." Here, **enhance** means
(A) to improve
(B) to create
(C) to remove
(D) to interpret

15. The writer states, "In addition, the Iroquois people had the **foresight** to look ahead and plan for future generations." Here, **foresight** means
(A) intense desire
(B) concern for the future
(C) plan of government
(D) affection for their relatives

16. In this article, **posterity** means
(A) wisdom
(B) American Indians
(C) future generations
(D) decisions

17. The writer of the article gives a clue to the meaning of **inherited**. What is the clue?
(A) Women owned property.
(B) Women chose sachems.
(C) The *owachiras* was the basic social unit of the Iroquois people.
(D) Things were passed from one generation of women to the next.

18. Which of the following is the most likely reason that families never experienced a sense of **isolation**?
(A) Women owned virtually all the property.
(B) The basic family unit consisted of a mother and her child.
(C) The Iroquois believed that the spirit world was evident in the physical world.
(D) Several families lived together in a long house.

19. You can tell from the article that a **phenomenon** is
(A) another way of saying separateness
(B) the face of a spirit
(C) something that can be sensed or experienced
(D) the beliefs of the Iroquois

20. The writer states, "For example, the face of a spirit might reveal itself in the trunk of a **gnarled** and twisted tree." Here, **gnarled** means
(A) growing
(B) misshapen
(C) revealed
(D) carved

READING NEW WORDS IN CONTEXT

Lesson 5 | CONTEXT: The First Americans

Introduction. The first Americans that Europeans encountered were those who dwelled in the upper reaches of the North American continent. In A.D. 1005, Vikings met the Inuits, perhaps somewhere around Labrador in Canada. The Inuits of Canada and the Inupiats and Yu'piks of Alaska are the major groups of native peoples that live in upper North America, on or near the icy northern coasts of the continent.

The following article gives you an opportunity to learn about Inupiat and Yu'pik peoples of Alaska, the northernmost part of the United States. The article also enables you to expand your vocabulary. Below are twenty Vocabulary Words that are used in the article and in the exercise that follows it.

adapt	controversy	feasible	ingenious	petition
assumption	creative	hilarious	insoluble	potential
basis	diction	immense	omission	primitive
consecutive	durable	impel	ordeal	restore

Far to the North: Native Peoples of Alaska

Together, the Inuits, the Inupiats, the Yu'piks, and the Siberian Yuits make up the group that for decades has been called *Eskimos*. No one is sure where the term *Eskimo* came from. One source says that the term was given to the native people of Labrador by fishermen from the Basque region of France and that it means snowshoe net maker. Another story has it that *Eskimo* is an American Indian word originally used by one group of native people to describe their neighbors. When Europeans first heard the term, their **assumption** (1) was that it was, in fact, the correct name. They simply took it for granted that *Eskimo* was the name by which these people, who were probably Inuits, called themselves.

For several centuries, small settlements of people have been scattered along the Arctic coast, which stretches for more than six thousand miles from Alaska to Greenland—an **immense** (2) territory. Among these early settlers were the Inupiat and the Yu'piks. There is no **controversy** (3) about where the Inupiats and Yu'piks originally came from; the evidence is clear that they migrated to North America from Asia. However, there is some debate about how they came. Perhaps they walked across on a land bridge. Perhaps they came by sea. Regardless, these cultures went through several **consecutive** (4), or successive, stages before evolving into the modern Inupiat and Yu'pik cultures.

Creativity in a Harsh Environment

People from warmer climates look at the frozen world of the Arctic and wonder how it is **feasible** (5), or possible, for people to survive in an environment that is so barren. To people from warmer places, the problems of finding food and shelter appear to be **insoluble** (6), and these difficulties seem to be a terrible **ordeal** (7).

However, the **ingenious** (8) people who live in

the Arctic learned how to make the most of their environment. They are highly resourceful in using what is available to **adapt** (9) themselves to the harsh environment. To travel across the frozen terrain, they invented the dog sled. To survive the long months without light in a land with no wood to burn, they invented oil lamps. To prevent snow blindness, they created goggles.

The Inupiats and the Yu'piks are **creative** (10) in other ways, too. Of course, their clothing has to be warm and waterproof. It has to be **durable** (11) because it is needed year in and year out. They also make their clothing—and their other belongings—beautiful. For these peoples, art is essential to life.

Traditionally, the Inupiats and the Yu'piks live in groups in small villages. Today, most of these people live in modern homes, but some live in traditional dwellings. The traditional summer dwelling for most Eskimos is a tent made of caribou skin and sealskin. In Alaska, the Inupiats and the Yu'piks traditionally spend the winter in houses made of sod. (Only in Canada do some Inuits make their permanent homes in ice houses, or igloos). These sod houses, made of pieces of earth, may seem rough and crude, even **primitive** (12), to those used to a different kind of shelter. Actually, however, they are warm and cozy and a testament to the resourcefulness of people who had to carve a home out of a hostile environment.

The Importance of Cooperation

Farming is impossible in this cold environment, so the Inupiats and Yu'piks are **impelled** (13) to hunt. They have no other choice. Surviving by hunting in the frozen north is difficult at best. Game is scarce, and there is a constant possibility of starvation. As a result, sharing is the **basis** (14) of Eskimo society.

Without a foundation of cooperation and generosity, these people could not survive.

Because the native people of northern Alaska depend on each other for survival, they have to avoid disagreements. For times of conflict, they have developed a clever way to handle **potential** (15) violence and to regain harmony. The two people who disagree engage in a duel of songs. However, this is one performance when **diction** (16), or pronouncing the words clearly, is not important. Here, they sing insults to one another while the rest of the group watches. The insults usually take the form of jokes. As a result, a situation that might have ended in violence often ends in **hilarious** (17) laughter instead, and harmony is **restored** (18).

Spiritual Beliefs

Balance and harmony are important to the Inupiats and the Yu'piks, and this is reflected in their religious beliefs. They have many rules that enable them to maintain this positive balance. Some are rules for duties and activities that must be performed. The **omission** (19) of an act that should be performed could displease the spirits. When the spirits are displeased, a spiritual leader and the sinner take part in a ceremony to **petition** (20) the spirits to forgive the sinner. The villagers also join in the ceremony, entering their pleas for the sinner's forgiveness.

The world of the Inupiats and the Yu'piks is a very different world from the one most of us know. They are not concerned with being on time. They are not concerned with money or shopping or cars. Rather, they focus on their life in their cold world, on cooperating with one another, and on living in harmony with nature.

EXERCISE *Reading Strategically* 👉

Directions. Answer each of the following items by circling the letter of the correct answer. You may need to refer to the selection as you answer the items. The numbers of the items are the same as the numbers of the boldface Vocabulary Words in the selection.

1. The writer explains that Europeans made the **assumption** that all Arctic peoples were called *Eskimo*. Here, **assumption** means the act of
   (A) correcting an error in translation
   (B) deriving a new word from an old word
   (C) creating a problem with pronunciation
   (D) taking something for granted

2. The writer gives a clue to the meaning of **immense**. What is the clue?
   (A) Inupiats and Yu'piks live in Alaska.
   (B) A meeting between Inuits and Vikings occurred.
   (C) Native peoples have lived on the coast for centuries.
   (D) Inupiat, Yu'pik, and Inuit territory covers thousands of miles.

3. Which of the following is the most likely reason that there is no **controversy** about where people who settled the Arctic coast came from?
   (A) They cover a vast territory along the Arctic coast.
   (B) The evidence is clear that they migrated from Asia.
   (C) No one knows how they came to North America.
   (D) They might have come to North America by sea.

4. The writer states that Arctic cultures went through several **consecutive** stages before evolving into modern cultures. Here, **consecutive** means
   (A) ancient
   (B) successive
   (C) cultural
   (D) modern

5. You can tell from the article that **feasible** means
   (A) livable
   (B) warm enough
   (C) possible
   (D) suitable

6. In the third paragraph, **insoluble** means
   (A) unable to be dissolved
   (B) difficult
   (C) unsolvable
   (D) preventable

7. The writer indicates that finding food and shelter in the Arctic appears to be a terrible **ordeal** to people from warmer climates. Here, **ordeal** means
   (A) an impossible plan
   (B) a barren plot
   (C) a possible starvation
   (D) a difficult situation

8. The writer gives a clue to the meaning of **ingenious** by saying that
   (A) the people of the region are highly resourceful
   (B) it is possible to travel by dog sled
   (C) we should make the most of our environment
   (D) there are long months without light in the Arctic

9. Which of the following is an example of a way the people of the Arctic **adapt** to their environment?
   (A) They found a harsh environment.
   (B) Traveling across frozen terrain was very difficult.
   (C) They created goggles to prevent snow blindness.
   (D) There were long months of darkness and no firelight.

10. The writer states, "The Inupiats and the Yu'piks are **creative** in other ways, too." Here, **creative** means
   (A) waterproof
   (B) warming
   (C) inventive
   (D) hopeful

11. The writer indicates that **durable** means long lasting by saying that clothes have to
   (A) be warm
   (B) be waterproof
   (C) be artistic
   (D) last for years

12. The writer gives a clue to the meaning of **primitive** by saying that sod houses
   (A) are warm and cozy
   (B) seem rough and crude
   (C) are not common today
   (D) are winter homes

13. The writer indicates that the Inupiats and the Yu'piks are **impelled** to hunt. Here, **impelled** means
   (A) born
   (B) forced
   (C) urged
   (D) understood

14. All of the following are good definitions of **basis** *except*
   (A) foundation
   (B) base
   (C) chief support
   (D) culture

15. You can tell from the article that **potential** means
   (A) serious
   (B) possible
   (C) powerful
   (D) unending

16. Which of the following is the most likely reason **diction** is not important when the two people are engaged in a duel of songs?
   (A) The manner of speaking is not the main purpose of the singing.
   (B) The singers are singing insults to amuse one another.
   (C) The insults usually take the form of jokes.
   (D) The main purpose in the singing is not to entertain.

17. Which of the following is the most likely reason that a disagreement between members of the community often ends in **hilarious** laughter?
   (A) Members of the community depend on each other for survival.
   (B) The whole community watches the two people work out their conflict.
   (C) Two people often end a conflict by exchanging joking insults.
   (D) A conflict might end in laughter, or it might end in violence.

18. All of the following are good definitions of **restored** *except*
   (A) removed
   (B) brought back
   (C) regained
   (D) reestablished

19. In this article, **omission** means
   (A) adding to
   (B) observing
   (C) doing
   (D) leaving out

20. The writer says that the spiritual leader and the sinner **petition** the spirits. Here, **petition** means
   (A) to collect enough signatures for
   (B) to argue with
   (C) to make a serious request of
   (D) to prepare for

READING NEW WORDS IN CONTEXT

Lesson 6 | CONTEXT: Coming to the United States

Introduction. In the last two hundred years, groups of people from many different countries have come to the shores of the United States. The country has been made stronger and richer by each of them. Between 1820 and 1870, a wave of Irish people, fleeing a food shortage in Ireland, came to the United States. Today, Irish Americans are active in every aspect of public life in the country.

The following article gives you an opportunity to expand your vocabulary. Below are twenty Vocabulary Words that are used in the article and in the exercise that follows it.

anxiety	censorship	famine	nationality	propaganda
aristocrat	decade	malnutrition	naturalization	refuge
boycott	deport	morale	optimism	resolute
burly	emigrate	multitude	predicament	urban

Leaving the Emerald Isle

The History of the Irish

One **nationality** (1) that has greatly helped to shape the United States is the Irish. Historically, the Irish have shown a gift for surviving troubled times and a talent for speaking and writing expressively of their struggles. Many of the world's best playwrights, novelists, and poets have been Irish, including Samuel Beckett, James Joyce, and William Butler Yeats. Irish literature tends to reflect a peculiar mixture of **optimism** (2) and negative thinking. The Irish have the faith and hope of people born to a land that seems almost enchanted, but experience tells them that the worst can and sometimes does happen.

Serious difficulties for the Irish people began in the 1600s. The English drove the Irish **aristocrats** (3) out of their castles and off their estates and replaced them with an English ruling class. The English treated Ireland as a colony, and they restricted the rights of the Irish people. For example, **censorship** (4) was common. Irish newspapers were not allowed to criticize the English government.

The people of Ireland suffered in other ways, as well. In the early 1800s, they experienced a dozen crop failures in three **decades** (5), or thirty years. Toward the end of the 1840s, Ireland suffered a terrible **famine** (6). Within three years, 500,000 people starved to death. Thousands watched their loved ones suffer from **malnutrition** (7) due to the lack of food.

The situation seemed hopeless, and hundreds of thousands fled the country. In this case, they were not **deported** (8) but chose to leave the country in hopes of finding a better life. Some headed for Canada and other destinations, but the vast **multitude** (9) went to the United States.

Life in a New Country

The decision to **emigrate** (10) caused great **anxiety** (11). As bad as life in Ireland had become, it was still difficult to leave home for a new country. On the long ocean voyage, the **emigrants** worried about how they would get along in a new world. The Irish were a rural people. They lived on farms and in small villages. When they came to the United States, however, they settled in **urban** (12) areas in the Northeast, especially New York City, Boston, and Philadelphia. In the cities, they took **refuge** (13) in neighborhoods where other Irish newcomers had already settled, where they felt more secure and comfortable living around people from home.

Like members of other incoming groups, many of the Irish were victims of **propaganda** (14). They had been led to believe that the United States offered unlimited opportunities and that any hard-working person could get rich quickly. Of course, that was not the case.

Life in the United States was difficult. It was hard for even the most **resolute** (15) individuals to maintain their **morale** (16). It took great determination to remain courageous and confident in the face of hardships. New arrivals to the United States were usually offered only the lowest paying, least desirable jobs. Most Irish worked at first as laborers and did backbreaking physical labor. There were so many Irish laborers that the image of the Irish American became linked in many people's minds with the image of the **burly** (17), powerful worker. It is true that Irish American laborers helped build U.S. cities.

The Irish Americans remained connected to their culture. In Irish American neighborhoods, reading rooms sprang up with books, newspapers, and magazines that reminded Irish Americans of their heritage. In addition, they did not forgive the injustices they had suffered at the hands of the English. When the Prince of Wales visited the United States in 1860, the Irish **boycotted** (18) the parade that was held in his honor. They refused to participate in any activities that honored the English prince.

Most Irish Americans chose **naturalization** (19), but, like all recent immigrants, they faced the **predicament** (20) of deciding how to be loyal to their past while becoming citizens of a new country. Like most other new citizens, they eventually found a way to balance old and new, and in doing so, they greatly enriched the United States.

EXERCISE *Reading Strategically* 👉

Directions. Answer each of the following items by circling the letter of the correct answer. You may need to refer to the selection as you answer the items. The numbers of the items are the same as the numbers of the Vocabulary Words in the selection.

1. An example of a **nationality** that is mentioned in the first paragraph of the article is
   (A) expressive writing
   (B) gifts
   (C) survival
   (D) the Irish

2. The writer explains that Irish literature mixes **optimism** and negative thinking. Here, **optimism** means
   (A) the belief that things will work out for the best
   (B) a belief in magic
   (C) a special form of literature
   (D) the belief that the worst is likely to happen

3. You can tell from the article that **aristocrats** means
(A) the English
(B) the upper class
(C) the Irish
(D) the castles and estates

4. The writer of this article gives a clue to the meaning of **censorship**. What is the clue?
(A) The writer mentions that the English treated Ireland as a colony.
(B) The writer notes that Irish newspapers were forbidden to criticize the English government.
(C) The writer regrets that the people of Ireland suffered in other ways.
(D) The writer explains that the English became the ruling class.

5. The writer indicates that the crops failed twelve times in three **decades**. Here, **decade** means
(A) twelve times
(B) the 1800s
(C) crop failures
(D) ten years

6. How does the writer let us know that **famine** means a widespread shortage of food?
(A) The writer tells us that the **famine** occurred toward the end of the 1840s.
(B) The writer refers to a period of just three years.
(C) The writer tells us that 500,000 people starved to death.
(D) The writer uses the adjective *terrible*.

7. The most likely reason that **malnutrition** occurred is that
(A) there was not enough food
(B) the children had to be buried
(C) the end of the **decade** arrived
(D) people told stories

8. The writer states, "In this case they were not **deported** but chose to leave the country in hopes of finding a better life." Here, **deported** means
(A) anxious to leave the country
(B) forced to leave the country
(C) sent away
(D) homeless

9. The writer states that the vast **multitude** fled to the United States. Here, **multitude** means
(A) great number of people
(B) people who believe the best will happen
(C) pessimistic people
(D) destination

10. The writer indicates that choosing to **emigrate** can create problems. Here, **emigrate** means
(A) to move to the United States
(B) to continue to worry beyond a reasonable point
(C) to move from one country to another
(D) to travel by ship

11. All of the following are good definitions of **anxiety** *except*
(A) worry
(B) uneasiness
(C) stress
(D) homesickness

12. The writer states that the Irish people settled in **urban** areas. Here, **urban** means having to do with

(A) villages
(B) cities
(C) the Irish people
(D) farms

13. The writer of this article gives us a clue to the meaning of **refuge**. What is the clue?

(A) that the newly arrived Irish felt safer with people from home
(B) that the cities were unsafe
(C) that cities offered nearly unlimited opportunities to hard-working people
(D) that the newly arrived Irish were generally rural people

14. You can tell that **propaganda** means

(A) hard work
(B) misleading information
(C) mistaken identities
(D) a terrible food shortage

15. All of the following are good definitions of **resolute** *except*

(A) immediate
(B) determined
(C) resolved
(D) purposeful

16. The writer of this article gives a clue to the meaning of **morale**. What is the clue?

(A) that there were no real hardships
(B) that some people might get rich quickly
(C) the phrase "remain courageous and confident"
(D) the word *maintain*

17. The writer uses **burly** when talking about workers. Here, **burly** means

(A) poetic and beautiful
(B) twisted and gnarled
(C) big and strong
(D) small and weak

18. The writer of this article gives a clue to the meaning of **boycotted**. What is the clue?

(A) The Prince of Wales visited the United States.
(B) The Irish remembered their heritage.
(C) The Irish suffered injustices at the hands of the English government.
(D) The Irish refused to participate in honoring the English royalty.

19. In this article, **naturalization** means

(A) a new country
(B) freedom
(C) the act of behaving naturally
(D) the process of becoming a citizen

20. The writer explains that Irish Americans faced a **predicament**. Here, **predicament** means

(A) prediction
(B) problem
(C) option
(D) old saying

READING NEW WORDS IN CONTEXT

Lesson 7   CONTEXT: Coming to the United States

Introduction. Italians came to the United States before 1870, but only in small numbers, and most of them were from northern Italy. Beginning in 1871, people from southern Italy began to arrive in large numbers. Tens of thousands arrived in the country between 1871 and 1925.

The following article gives you an opportunity to read about the experiences of Italian immigrants and to expand your vocabulary. Below are twenty Vocabulary Words that are used in the article and in the exercise that follows it.

acceptance	circulate	grieve	intensity	prosecute
accessible	dilapidated	hospitable	jubilation	riotous
bankrupt	exaggeration	immigrate	premiere	thrive
boisterous	fraudulent	impulsive	privilege	transit

From Roma, Napoli, and Palermo to Ellis Island

Like most people who came to live in the United States in the late nineteenth and early twentieth centuries, southern Italians **immigrated** (1) by way of Ellis Island in New York Harbor. The familiar image of immigrants arriving after their long **transit** (2) across the Atlantic Ocean is that of men and women gazing in wonder at the New York skyline. The city must have seemed an almost magical place. Many Italians did experience a sense of **jubilation** (3) as the ships drew near the city.

All too often, however, their joy turned into frustration. The streets were not paved with gold as many had been led to believe. Because they found themselves in a strange country where they did not speak the language and where jobs were difficult to find, Italian immigrants sometimes **grieved** (4) over their decision to leave Italy.

Some Reactions

Some U.S. citizens were not **accessible** (5) or even **hospitable** (6) to the Italian immigrants. These people did not welcome the immigrants because of opinions about Italians that were not based in reality. They believed that Italians were too **impulsive** (7), or spontaneous. Further, they did not approve of people who did not speak English. Such prejudice against Italians varied in **intensity** (8). Some people wanted to limit the kinds of jobs Italians could hold. Others wanted to prevent Italians from entering the country altogether. Fortunately, not everyone had such misguided notions. It is hard to imagine the United States today without its Italian heritage.

The new citizens faced other problems as well. Many were the victims of people who hired poor immigrants to work in the United States in order to take advantage of them. Some of these people were involved in **fraudulent** (9) schemes that tricked the newcomers out of their wages. These individuals were morally **bankrupt** (10)—that is, they had no morals and did not care about the harm they did to innocent people. They caught the immigrants in a system of continual debt. It was unfortunate that these actions were rarely, if ever, **prosecuted** (11) in the courts.

Italian Neighborhoods

Italian Americans were usually forced to live in **dilapidated** (12) old apartments in run-down neighborhoods. However, these small neighborhoods preserved something of the flavor of village life in southern Italy and enabled the culture of southern Italy to **thrive** (13) in the United States.

At first, survival was the main goal of the families in these neighborhoods. The rule was loyalty to family above all else. Outsiders were viewed with suspicion. Italian American children might be criticized or even punished if they forgot their loyalties. Such were the ways of families struggling to survive.

Because the Italian Americans lived in crowded apartments, much of life was lived on front stoops and out in the streets, especially in the summertime. On warm days, people opened what windows they had to allow the air to **circulate** (14) through the building. The noisy, lively laughter of **boisterous** (15) children drifted in with the fresh air. There was also **riotous** (16) laughter from the adults as they exchanged jokes and gossip. Life was very hard for these new citizens, but they found joy in their close communities.

Education

Italian American communities began to change when the children began to attend school. At first, some parents saw the schools as a threat to the preservation of their Italian heritage. However, **acceptance** (17) of the public schools soon led to outright enthusiasm for them. The immigrants began to see school as a **privilege** (18), as an honor that would give their children an advantage. Education proved useful in escaping the cycle of poverty in which so many Italian Americans had become trapped.

Today, Italian Americans play significant roles in all aspects of life in the United States. They are lawyers, doctors, journalists, social workers, businesspeople, and politicians. Italian Americans are also artists, writers, singers, and actors. It is hard to imagine the **premiere** (19) of a major motion picture without famous Italian American actors and directors pulling up in limousines to watch the first showing. It is not an **exaggeration** (20) to say that Italian Americans have enriched the United States beyond measure. Their contribution to American society cannot be overstated.

EXERCISE *Reading Strategically* ☞

Directions. Answer each of the following items by circling the letter of the correct answer. You may need to refer to the selection as you answer the items. The numbers of the items are the same as the numbers of the boldface Vocabulary Words in the selection.

1. According to the article, southern Italians **immigrated** to the U.S. by way of New York Harbor. Here, **immigrated** means
   (A) left the United States
   (B) resembled most people
   (C) moved to a country
   (D) visited another country

2. In order to give a clue to the meaning of **transit,** the writer
   (A) refers to a familiar picture
   (B) uses the phrase "across the Atlantic Ocean"
   (C) tells us that men and women gaze
   (D) hints that the New York skyline is impressive

3. In order to let us know that **jubilation** means gladness, the writer
   (A) tells us that the ships drew near the city
   (B) makes it clear that the streets were not paved with gold
   (C) uses the phrase "almost magical"
   (D) tells us that too often joy became frustration

4. Which of the following is a reason mentioned in the article that the Italian immigrants sometimes **grieved** over their decision to leave Italy?
   (A) Jobs were difficult to find.
   (B) They were overjoyed as they drew near Ellis Island.
   (C) The streets were paved with gold.
   (D) They were impressed by the New York skyline.

5. All of the following are good definitions for **accessible** *except*
   (A) obtainable
   (B) understandable
   (C) approachable
   (D) expensive

6. In order to give a clue to the meaning of **hospitable,** the writer
   (A) tells us that the Italians were immigrants
   (B) tells us that some people did not welcome the Italians
   (C) hints that people should not be quick-tempered
   (D) hints that **hospitable** means unwelcoming

7. The writer says that some people believed that Italian immigrants were too **impulsive**. Here, **impulsive** means
   (A) unwilling to make a commitment
   (B) very intelligent and thoughtful
   (C) likely to act on sudden feelings
   (D) easily discouraged

8. The writer states, "Such prejudice against Italians varied in **intensity**." Here, **intensity** means
   (A) kindness
   (B) degree
   (C) stupidity
   (D) cruelty

9. All of the following are good definitions of **fraudulent** *except*
   (A) dishonest
   (B) deceitful
   (C) crooked
   (D) business

10. In order to let us know that **bankrupt** means lacking in some quality, the writer
    (A) tells us that some people were involved in schemes
    (B) implies that employers can be dishonest
    (C) tells us that employers had no feelings for the innocent people they hurt
    (D) says some immigrants could not get out of debt no matter how hard they tried

11. You can tell from the article that **prosecuted** means
    (A) accused
    (B) tried in the courts
    (C) judged
    (D) thought to be illegal

12. You can tell from the article that **dilapidated** means
(A) run-down
(B) deserted
(C) large
(D) expensive

13. The writer indicates that the culture of southern Italy was allowed to **thrive**. Here, **thrive** means
(A) to preserve
(B) to disappear
(C) to grow
(D) to cook

14. The writer states, "On warm days, people opened what windows they had to allow the air to **circulate** through the building." Here, **circulate** means
(A) to heat
(B) to trap
(C) to flow
(D) to escape

15. The writer mentions the noisy laughter of **boisterous** children. Here, **boisterous** means
(A) rude and hateful
(B) gentle and kind
(C) faint and far away
(D) lively and loud

16. The writer states, "There was also **riotous** laughter from the adults as they exchanged jokes and gossip." Here, **riotous** means
(A) insincere
(B) loud
(C) cruel
(D) quiet

17. In the article, **acceptance** most nearly means
(A) threat
(B) enthusiasm
(C) importance
(D) approval

18. Which of the following is the most likely reason that Italian Americans began to see school as a **privilege**?
(A) The children enjoyed school.
(B) Education helped them escape poverty.
(C) The schools were seen as a threat.
(D) Everyone seemed trapped by poverty.

19. All of the following are good definitions of **premiere** *except*
(A) awards ceremony
(B) opening
(C) first showing
(D) first exhibition

20. The writer claims "It is not an **exaggeration** to say that Italian Americans have enriched the United States." Here, **exaggeration** means
(A) possibility
(B) enrichment
(C) advantage
(D) overstatement

READING NEW WORDS IN CONTEXT

Lesson 8 | **CONTEXT: Coming to the United States**

Introduction. The Statue of Liberty is associated undeniably with the new beginning sought by many immigrants to the United States. This monument to freedom, however, was not always in the New York Harbor and did not always mean the end of a traveler's journey.

The following article gives you an opportunity to expand your vocabulary. Below are twenty Vocabulary Words that are used in the article and in the exercise that follows it.

dedicate	exertion	imperative	liable	recuperate
depose	hamper	impose	memento	restrain
dispense	haven	inconsiderate	negligent	spacious
dissect	humidity	intercept	presume	tumult

The Statue of Liberty and Ellis Island

The image that most people have of immigrants arriving in the United States from Europe includes a picture of the Statue of Liberty. However, the statue was not a part of New York Harbor until 1886. The towering monument was the work of French sculptor Frédéric Auguste Bartholdi (1834–1904). It was a gift of the French people, who **dedicated** (1) it to—that is, presented it in honor of—the people of the United States.

Actually, the statue almost did not make it into the harbor. Completion was **hampered** (2) by a lack of funds, but publisher Joseph Pulitzer launched a campaign to raise the needed money and to speed up the process. The nation's people responded with enough pennies, nickels, and dimes to make the dream a reality.

Today, it is almost impossible to imagine the harbor without the statue. It has become a symbol of the United States as a **haven** (3) for the poor and burdened, as a place where people could be safe and have a chance at a better life. More than 100 million immigrants have sailed past the statue on their way into the United States.

When the descendants of those immigrants visit New York City, they usually feel it is **imperative** (4) to visit the monument. They feel that the visit is necessary out of respect to their families. Many come away with some sort of souvenir, or **memento** (5), such as a snapshot or a postcard, of their visit. However, most will need nothing to remind them of such a moving experience. The sight of the statue makes a lasting impression on people's minds. The inside of the huge monument is also remarkable. It is large and **spacious** (6), and it houses the American Museum of Immigration. The museum's exhibits tell the story of immigration to the United States. Climbing the stairs to the statue's crown requires great **exertion** (7); visitors must climb 142 steps to reach it, but the wonderful view from the observation windows is worth the effort.

Liberty After All?

When we imagine immigrants seeing the Statue of Liberty for the first time, we **presume** (8) that it was a joyous event. We may suppose that some people could barely **restrain** (9) their joy and relief, especially after a long, hard sea voyage. On the other hand, some immigrants probably held back their emotions because they feared that their escape to the U.S. was not final. Some of those immigrants whom the statue welcomed might not be allowed into the country after all.

From 1892 to 1954, immigrants who passed the Statue of Liberty went straight to Ellis Island, where they were "processed." There, they waited on the second floor of the reception center, referred to as the Tower of Babel. It is easy to imagine the noise and **tumult** (10) of thousands of people speaking many different languages as they awaited their fates. Incoming immigrants were met by officials whose duty was to **intercept** (11), or stop, and turn back those who were in less than perfect health. The immigrants received a complete but very brief physical. The officials **dispensed** (12), or dealt out, white chalk marks that indicated whether the new arrivals could stay or had to go. Some of the examiners were careless and **negligent** (13) at best. Others were downright dangerous. Imagine an official lifting eyelid after eyelid with a buttonhook to check for signs of disease!

It is also easy to imagine the fear of a young couple who have fled their country after taking part in a failed attempt to **depose** (14) a tyrant. Would they pass inspection, or would they be returned to face punishment for the attempted overthrow? The stress caused by being processed at Ellis Island was great. Moreover, immigrants faced this ordeal before they had a chance to **recuperate** (15) after their hard journey aboard a crowded ship. The facilities on Ellis Island made recovery from the hard trip difficult. In the winter, the building was cold and damp. In the muggy days of summer, the heat and **humidity** (16) could be unbearable. Decent sleeping arrangements were nonexistent, and processing could take days.

Once the immigrants passed inspection, they were **liable** (17) —in fact, almost certain—to encounter officials who were rude and **inconsiderate** (18). If their names were difficult for an official to pronounce or to spell, they were likely to come away with a new name **imposed** (19) on them by an official who changed it without a second thought.

Hopes for a Better Life

Despite this treatment, immigrants held on to their dreams of a better life in the United States. More than 100 million of them—the grandparents and great-grandparents and great-great grandparents of more than 40 percent of the citizens of the United States—came through Ellis Island.

Now, when their descendants come to New York for a glimpse of the statue that welcomed them, the descendants can also visit the museum that opened on Ellis Island in 1990 to honor the immigrants. Those who visit say that there is something awesome about simply being there. They also report feeling overwhelmed by emotion. Later, when they **dissect** (20) the feeling and examine its parts, they find that it is part joy, part hope, and part sorrow—but mostly it is love and pride.

EXERCISE   *Reading Strategically* ☞

Directions. Answer each of the following items by circling the letter of the correct answer. You may need to refer to the selection as you answer the items. The numbers of the items are the same as the numbers of the boldface Vocabulary Words in the selection.

1. The writer indicates that the French **dedicated** the statue. Here, **dedicated** means
   (A) made a sculpture of
   (B) presented in honor of
   (C) withheld from
   (D) worked hard on

2. In the second paragraph of the article, **hampered** means
   (A) held up   (C) finished
   (B) in a basket   (D) caused

3. In order to give a clue to the meaning of **haven,** the writer
   (A) points out that the statue is a symbol
   (B) notes that the United States is a place where people could be safe
   (C) says that the poor and oppressed saw the statue
   (D) mentions that more than 100 million immigrants came into New York Harbor

4. To let us know that **imperative** means essential or really important, the writer
   (A) tells us that the descendants come to New York
   (B) says that the descendants feel that the visit is necessary
   (C) notes that the ancestors were welcomed
   (D) believes that one should respect one's family

5. _____ is an example mentioned in the article of a **memento** that a visitor might take away from the monument.
   (A) A museum   (C) An experience
   (B) Respect   (D) A postcard

6. You can tell from the article that **spacious** means
   (A) roomy
   (B) historical
   (C) empty
   (D) dramatic

7. Which of the following is the most likely reason that it takes great **exertion** to reach the statue's crown?
   (A) The museum's exhibit tells the story of the immigrants.
   (B) The view from the observation windows is wonderful.
   (C) Visitors must climb 142 steps.
   (D) It is worth the effort.

8. You can tell from the article that **presume** means
   (A) to imagine feelings
   (B) to forget the past
   (C) to remember carefully
   (D) to suppose

9. To give a clue to the meaning of **restrain,** the writer
   (A) suggests that we imagine the joy of seeing the statue for the first time
   (B) tells us that seeing the statue was a joyous event for immigrants
   (C) contrasts immigrants who could not **restrain** their emotions with those who held back their emotions
   (D) says that some immigrants might not be allowed into the United States

10. The writer says that it is easy to imagine the noise and **tumult** at Ellis Island. Here, **tumult** means
    (A) unhappiness
    (B) boredom
    (C) commotion
    (D) language

11. The writer states, "Incoming immigrants were met by officials whose duty was to **intercept** . . . and turn back those who were in less than perfect health." Here, **intercept** means
    (A) to congratulate
    (B) to stop
    (C) to welcome
    (D) to prepare

12. The author writes, "The officials **dispensed**, or dealt out, white chalk marks that indicated whether the new arrivals could stay or go." Here, **dispensed** means
    (A) received
    (B) gave out
    (C) preferred
    (D) ignored

13. You can tell from the article that **negligent** means
    (A) nervous
    (B) professional
    (C) rude
    (D) careless

14. All of the following are good definitions of **depose** *except*
    (A) to create
    (B) to overthrow
    (C) to remove
    (D) to unseat

15. You can tell from the article that to **recuperate** means
    (A) to repeat
    (B) to recover
    (C) to remember
    (D) to relate

16. To let us know that **humidity** means the degree of dampness in the air, the writer
    (A) comments on the terrible conditions at Ellis Island
    (B) mentions the immigrants' hard journey
    (C) links **humidity** to the word *muggy*
    (D) tells us that decent sleeping arrangements were impossible to find

17. To give a clue to the meaning of **liable,** the writer
    (A) tells us that immigrants were almost certain to meet rude officials
    (B) tells us that names could be difficult to spell
    (C) says that processing could take days
    (D) says that officials were encountered

18. Another word that has nearly the same meaning as **inconsiderate** is
    (A) thoughtless
    (B) likely
    (C) difficult
    (D) vicious

19. The writer says that officials sometimes **imposed** a new name on an immigrant. Here, **imposed** means
    (A) called
    (B) repeated
    (C) forced
    (D) created

20. You can tell from the article that **dissect** means
    (A) to examine
    (B) to experience
    (C) to report
    (D) to recall

READING NEW WORDS IN CONTEXT

Lesson 9 **CONTEXT: Coming to the United States**

Introduction. In most cases, people came to the United States, bringing with them their culture. But in a few cases, as with American Indians and many Mexican Americans, the United States came to the people.

The following article tells how the United States came to the Mexicans living in Texas. The article gives you an opportunity to expand your vocabulary. Below are twenty Vocabulary Words that are used in the article and in the exercise that follows it.

aroma	dismantle	gracious	occupant	remote
baste	elegant	haughty	populate	rigid
capital	embarrass	manageable	prearrange	saturate
diminish	frequency	monopoly	probation	sedate

When the Country Came to the People: Mexican Americans

People whose ancestors came with John Smith to Virginia or with the Pilgrims to Massachusetts rightfully take pride in their roots. However, those that become **haughty** (1) about their colonial heritage should remember that another group of Europeans settled in the Americas first—the Spanish.

The Spanish frequently intermarried with the American Indian population. The children of Spanish and American Indian parents were called *mestizos*. The settlers in Mexico established forts, missions, and ranches and **populated** (2) villages in what is now the southwestern United States. They settled there long before other settlers pushed westward across the Mississippi River.

Life in the Southwest

Many of these settlements were isolated from one another, and the sprawling ranches could be very **remote** (3) indeed. However, in southern Texas and southern California, there were **elegant** (4) houses with luxurious furnishings and **gracious** (5), welcoming courtyards. The **occupants** (6) of these houses were wealthy families who had **capital** (7) to invest in the new territory, and they became the aristocrats of the Southwest.

In small villages, people lived by certain social rules. These rules may seem **rigid** (8) by today's standards, but the people who lived by them did not seem to find them too restrictive. For example, **sedate** (9) behavior was expected from young people, and being swept away by emotion was frowned upon. A young woman would not **embarrass** (10) her family by paying obvious attention to a young man. Similarly, no polite young man would make a young woman feel uncomfortable by being overly friendly. That could damage a girl's reputation and **diminish** (11), or lessen, her family's standing in the community.

Ranch life was much more rugged. On the ranches, the vaqueros, or cowboys, herded sturdy, rangy cattle. Such was life in the country, first under Spanish rule and later, after Mexico won its independence from Spain, under Mexican rule.

Settlers from the United States

The United States was pushing westward, and change was coming. In the early 1800s, Mexico began to encourage settlement in one of its northern provinces—what is now Texas. At first, no one group had a **monopoly** (12) on settling the region; people came from everywhere. However, more and more settlers came from the southern United States. Soon these people became anxious to mold the territory in their own image. It seems unlikely that they had **prearranged** (13) a revolution. They did not plan to revolt against Mexican rule. However, it is clear that they never truly thought of themselves as citizens of Mexico.

Settlers arrived from the United States with increasing **frequency** (14). More and more of them moved West, and they soon outnumbered the Mexican population five to one. The government of Mexico found it increasingly difficult to control the large number of people moving to Texas, and they decided to prohibit further immigration in an attempt to make the northern province more **manageable** (15). Their action was too late. The settlers were determined to achieve independence.

The settlers' decision to declare independence presented a problem for the Mexican community in Texas. Most were loyal to the Mexican government. After all, Mexico had only just succeeded in establishing its independence from Spain. Others, however, saw an advantage in establishing a new form of government, so some Mexicans sided with the U.S. citizens in the Texas Revolution.

When the war was over, the Mexicans in Texas had two choices. They could stay in their homes and accept their roles in a new country, or they could abandon their homes and move back across the new border to Mexico, Many Mexicans decided not to make a hasty decision. They wanted to avoid having to **dismantle** (16) their homes, to take apart everything they had worked for. They decided on a period of **probation** (17). They took a wait-and-see attitude. Many eventually decided to accept the change. It was in this manner that many people of Mexican descent became citizens of the United States.

Appreciating the American Southwest

Visitors to the Southwest are often entranced with the harsh beauty of the region. They soak up its culture so that later, back home, they can still see the sweeping plains, the rugged mountains, and the deep canyons. They can still smell the clean, fresh **aroma** (19) of the piñon tree. Their tongues remember the bite of jalapeño peppers and the rich flavor of ears of corn lightly **basted** (20), or moistened, with oil that had been **saturated** (18), or thoroughly soaked, with red pepper, and roasted on the grill. They fall in love with the architecture, with adobe and red tile, with the statues and the cathedrals. Most come away with a new appreciation of Mexican American culture and long to return.

EXERCISE *Reading Strategically*

Directions. Answer each of the following items by circling the letter of the correct answer. You may need to refer to the selection as you answer the items. The numbers of the items are the same as the numbers of the Vocabulary Words in the selection.

1. Another way to say **haughty** is
    (A) overly proud
    (B) thickly settled
    (C) colonial
    (D) forgetful

2. You can tell from the article that **populated** means
    (A) inhabited
    (B) destroyed
    (C) abandoned
    (D) conquered

3. The writer states, "Sprawling ranches could be very **remote** indeed." Here, **remote** means
   (A) old
   (B) large
   (C) isolated
   (D) rough

4. The writer states, "However, in southern Texas and southern California, there were **elegant** houses with luxurious furnishings. . . ." Here, **elegant** means
   (A) old-fashioned
   (B) luxurious
   (C) small
   (D) ranch style

5. In the article, an example of something **gracious** is a
   (A) wealthy family
   (B) southern Californian
   (C) welcoming courtyard
   (D) sprawling ranch

6. The writer uses the term **occupants** when talking about the houses. Here, **occupants** means
   (A) the furnishings of the houses
   (B) the people who lived in the houses
   (C) the visitors to the houses
   (D) the houses themselves

7. The writer gives a clue to the meaning of **capital**. What is the clue?
   (A) The writer notes that settlements were isolated from one another.
   (B) The writer implies that the wealthy families founded their own states.
   (C) The writer comments on the beautiful homes of the wealthy families.
   (D) The writer indicates that **capital** is what people invest.

8. The writer gives a clue to the meaning of **rigid**. What is the clue?
   (A) Young people went for strolls.
   (B) People lived in small villages.
   (C) Boys did not make girls feel uncomfortable.
   (D) People didn't find the rules too restrictive.

9. The writer states, "For example, **sedate** behavior was expected from young people. . . ." Here, **sedate** means
   (A) uncomfortable
   (B) rapid
   (C) calm
   (D) frowning

10. The writer says that a young woman would not **embarrass** her family. Here, **embarrass** means
    (A) to ignore
    (B) to ridicule
    (C) to make uncomfortable
    (D) to lie to

11. All of the following are good definitions of **diminish** except
    (A) improve
    (B) lessen
    (C) reduce
    (D) decrease

12. Which of the following is mentioned in the article to explain why, at first, no one group had a **monopoly** on the settlement of Texas?
    (A) Most Texas settlers were U.S. citizens.
    (B) Settlers from all over came to Texas.
    (C) Settlers came from the United States.
    (D) Mexico tried to discourage U.S. citizens from settling Texas.

13. You can tell from the article that **prearranged** means
   - (A) planned
   - (B) spontaneous
   - (C) loyal
   - (D) revolutionary

14. To let us know that **frequency** means the rate of occurrence, the writer
   - (A) mentions that more and more colonists moved to the West
   - (B) suggests that the government regretted its decision
   - (C) notes that white settlers never truly thought of themselves as citizens of Mexico
   - (D) reminds us that the province was in the northern part of Mexico

15. In this article, **manageable** means
   - (A) original
   - (B) controllable
   - (C) small
   - (D) similar

16. The writer states that the Mexicans didn't want to **dismantle** their homes. Here, **dismantle** means to
   - (A) build a fire in a fireplace
   - (B) construct
   - (C) take apart
   - (D) sell to the highest bidder

17. The writer states, "They decided on a period of **probation**." Here, **probation** means
   - (A) punishment
   - (B) forgiveness
   - (C) problem
   - (D) trial

18. To let you know that **saturate** means to soak, the writer
   - (A) refers to delicious southwestern food
   - (B) indicates that visiting the South-west is a strange experience
   - (C) refers to canyons
   - (D) notes that the oil had been soaked with red pepper.

19. The writer uses the word **aroma** when describing the piñion tree. Here, **aroma** means
   - (A) sweeping
   - (B) freshness
   - (C) smell
   - (D) cleanliness

20. You can tell from the article that **basted** means
   - (A) salted
   - (B) moistened
   - (C) soaked
   - (D) stitched

READING NEW WORDS IN CONTEXT

Lesson 10 | CONTEXT: Coming to the United States

Introduction. People immigrate to the United States for a number of reasons. Unhappily, one of the most common reasons for leaving one's country behind is war. In the 1970s and 1980s, many people left their homes and loved ones behind in the war-torn country of Vietnam to make a new home in the United States.

The following article tells you about Vietnamese immigration to the United States and gives you an opportunity to expand your vocabulary. Below are twenty Vocabulary Words that are used in the article and in the exercise that follows it.

access	dingy	jeopardize	persistent	remorse
accommodations	disagreeable	liberate	pleasantry	thrifty
adept	evacuate	maroon	provision	titanic
circumnavigate	humiliate	notify	regime	verify

Leaving Saigon

The country of Vietnam was torn by civil war for years. The United States military played a role in that war for many of those years, but by the early 1970s most U.S. troops had returned home. However, a few Americans remained. It was to these Americans that many Vietnamese turned in 1975 when the North Vietnamese entered Saigon, the capital of South Vietnam.

The North Vietnamese claimed they were freeing the city from a corrupt government, but many South Vietnamese did not feel that they were being **liberated** (1). They were afraid of the actions the new government might take. Many were certain to be imprisoned or executed by the new **regime** (2). The men and women who had worked for the U.S. felt particularly **jeopardized** (3) by the change in power. They knew they were in danger of being marked as traitors.

As the North Vietnamese troops approached Saigon, many South Vietnamese citizens made the decision to flee the city. U.S. citizens were also preparing to **evacuate** (4) their embassy. For

many Vietnamese, the embassy seemed to be the only escape. Crowds of people began to make their way there, hoping to be picked up and taken to safety by helicopters. It soon was clear that there would be too many people and not enough helicopters.

There was much confusion in the city. Family members were separated and could not find each other. Some who were leaving did not have time to **notify** (5) their families. They left without having the opportunity to say goodbye. Some felt guilty, as though they were abandoning their families, and this sense of **remorse** (6) would cause them much pain for many years. Eventually, many of these people made homes in the United States. They were the first of several waves of Vietnamese immigrants to this country.

The Boat People

In the late 1970s and early 1980s, many other Vietnamese fled turmoil in their homeland. Most escaped in small fishing boats. These boat people, as they were called, had to be careful, for they would be sent to prison if they were caught. They had to begin gathering their supplies and **provisions** (7) weeks in advance. They might hide cans of gasoline, jars of water, and extra bags of rice in the jungle. It was a **titanic** (8) undertaking, and it took all their strength and courage.

It was also a dangerous journey, for the fishing boats were never intended to sail the high seas. Still, the boat people were willing to **circumnavigate** (9), or sail around, the globe in these boats for a chance for a new life in a free country. However, their goal was the safety of a refugee camp in Thailand, Hong Kong, or the Philippines.

Today, we cannot **verify** (10) the exact number of Vietnamese who left in this way, nor can we confirm how many of them died at sea. We do know that thousands of Vietnamese people, desperate to escape Vietnam, began their journey to the United States in small boats.

The Camps

Those who survived the sea voyage ended up in refugee camps in other Southeast Asian countries. The **accommodations** (11) were terrible; people lived in small tents and flimsy lean-tos. Life in the camps was **disagreeable** (12) at best. For most, it was miserable. The refugees often had to wait long months in the dirty and dangerous camps before they could continue their journey to their new homelands.

In a New Country

Starting life in a new country is always difficult.

Sadly, many U.S. citizens made it even more difficult for Vietnamese immigrants. They demonstrated their prejudice in many ways. They often made rude remarks that caused the immigrants to feel embarrassed and **humiliated** (13).

A dark, **dingy** (14) apartment in a huge city is quite an adjustment for someone used to the rich, tropical lushness of Vietnamese village life. Sometimes refugees would be placed in apartments far from other Vietnamese people. Without telephones, transportation, or any other means of easy **access** (15) to other Vietnamese immigrants, they felt stranded, **marooned** (16). As soon as they could, they moved into one of the city's Vietnamese neighborhoods. There at least life was a bit more familiar. Grocery stores sold the vegetables and ingredients necessary to make Vietnamese food. The pharmacies carried familiar ointments and herbs. In the Vietnamese neighborhoods, immigrants could exchange gossip and **pleasantries** (17).

Life was hard. Yet, the Vietnamese people were **adept** (18) at survival. Years of hardship had made them strong and capable. They were also **persistent** (19). They did not give up in the face of difficulties. Many immigrants coped with their lack of resources by being **thrifty** (20). They lived as cheaply as possible and saved their money. They opened their own businesses and sent their children to college. Today, they have found a place in the United States, the country that they sometimes refer to as the Freedom Land.

© Houghton Mifflin Harcourt Publishing Company

EXERCISE *Reading Strategically* ☝

Directions. Answer each of the following items by circling the letter of the correct answer. You may need to refer to the selection as you answer the items. The numbers of the items are the same as the numbers of the boldface Vocabulary Words in the selection.

1. The writer of this article gives a clue to the meaning of **liberated**. What is the clue?
   (A) The South Vietnamese were afraid.
   (B) The new government would take action.
   (C) The North Vietnamese claimed they were freeing the city.
   (D) The South Vietnamese turned to the Americans for help.

2. You can tell from the article that **regime** means
   (A) government
   (B) workers
   (C) action
   (D) prison

3. The writer states, "The men and women who had worked for the U.S. felt particularly **jeopardized** by the change in power." Here, **jeopardized** means
   (A) excited
   (B) threatened
   (C) angered
   (D) criticized

4. In the third paragraph, **evacuate** means
   (A) to destroy
   (B) to overrun
   (C) to withdraw from
   (D) to go to an embassy

5. The writer states, "Some who were leaving did not have time to **notify** their families." Here, **notify** means
   (A) to remember
   (B) to abandon
   (C) to take
   (D) to tell

6. The writer indicates that some who left South Vietnam felt guilty and that the **remorse** caused them pain for many years. Here, **remorse** means
   (A) suffering
   (B) escape
   (C) guilt
   (D) impossibility

7. Which of the following is a way that some South Vietnamese people gathered **provisions** for their departure?
   (A) They knew it was important to be careful.
   (B) Those who were caught would go to prison.
   (C) They stored gasoline, water, and food for their trip.
   (D) They knew that the journey would be dangerous.

8. In this article, **titanic** means
   (A) enormous
   (B) courageous
   (C) important
   (D) special

9. The writer indicates that the Vietnamese were willing to **circumnavigate** the globe to find freedom. Here, **circumnavigate** means
   (A) to go fishing
   (B) to hide from
   (C) to begin again
   (D) to sail around

10. The writer says that we can't **verify** the exact number of Vietnamese who left. Here, **verify** means
    (A) to improve upon
    (B) to argue with
    (C) to confirm
    (D) to imagine

11. You can tell that **accommodations** means
(A) workload
(B) camping trip
(C) housing
(D) sea voyage

12. The writer states, "Life in the camps was **disagreeable** at best." Here, **disagreeable** means
(A) tending to argue
(B) unpleasant
(C) dull
(D) eventful

13. Which of the following is a reason mentioned in the article that some Vietnamese immigrants felt **humiliated**?
(A) Starting life in a new country is a challenging task.
(B) Some Vietnamese immigrants had never lived in a city.
(C) Some U.S. citizens made rude comments about them.
(D) Some Vietnamese immigrants lived far from other Vietnamese communities.

14. All of the following are good definitions of **dingy** *except*
(A) dirty
(B) dry
(C) grimy
(D) shabby

15. To suggest that **access** means a way to contact, the writer
(A) says that the Vietnamese did not have telephones or transportation
(B) mentions that many Vietnamese immigrants did not speak English
(C) refers to Vietnamese village life
(D) explains that there were Vietnamese neighborhoods

16. You can tell from the article that **marooned** means
(A) stranded
(B) unhappy
(C) unfriendly
(D) adventurous

17. The writer indicates that the Vietnamese exchange **pleasantries**. Here, **pleasantries** means
(A) recipes
(B) neighborhoods
(C) small talk
(D) businesses

18. All of the following are good definitions of **adept** *except*
(A) skilled
(B) very able
(C) expert
(D) clumsy

19. You can tell from the article that people who are **persistent**
(A) face hardship
(B) keep trying
(C) are immigrants
(D) live cheaply

20. The writer of this article gives a clue to the meaning of **thrifty**. What is the clue?
(A) Years of hardship had made Vietnamese immigrants strong.
(B) Vietnamese immigrants lived as cheaply as possible.
(C) Vietnamese immigrants did not give up in the face of difficulties.
(D) Vietnamese immigrants opened their own businesses.

READING NEW WORDS IN CONTEXT

Lesson 11 | CONTEXT: Voices of the United States

Introduction. History is not just the memorization of names and dates. The study of history can help us understand who we are, where we come from, and where we are going.

In the following story, a social studies teacher talks about what U.S. history means to him. The story also gives you an opportunity to expand your vocabulary. Below are twenty Vocabulary Words that are used in the story and in the exercise that follows it.

aspiration	foreword	obituary	pun	salutation
blockade	generate	obscure	quaint	satire
confiscate	indelible	pewter	quench	tariff
diplomat	neutral	premier	sable	urgent

A Teacher Speaks

James Matsamura teaches social studies at Washington Middle School. Today he is talking with some of his students about the political heritage of the United States.

"There are many things that I love about this country," he says, "but what moves me the most may be the Constitution of the United States. It reflects the **aspirations** (1), the ambitions, of the nation's people, both when it was written and today. Sometimes I feel as though the words 'We, the people' are a part of me, as if they are permanently written on my heart in **indelible** (2) ink."

Alan raises his hand. "Mr. Matsamura, why should we have to remember all this historical stuff? It happened a long time ago. Why should we remember that guy who made silver trays and **pewter** (3) candlesticks or whatever?"

Mr. Matsamura's tone is **urgent** (4) because he wants his students to mark his words. "The person you refer to, Paul Revere, might have been an **obscure** (5) silversmith, remembered by almost no one. After he died, there would have been nothing much to write in his **obituary** (6) other than the fact that he made nice tea services—if he

hadn't played such an important role in founding this country. The story of his ride is not just a **quaint** (7) little tale—a pleasant, old-fashioned story. It's part of our heritage. What other stories have you heard about the country's founders?"

A Student Discussion

Mr. Matsamura's remarks seem to **generate** (8) some enthusiasm. For a few minutes, the students in the class engage in a noisy discussion of stories. Then they focus on the Boston Tea Party. They discuss the colonists' decision to **confiscate** (9) British tea, to seize it and dump it into the harbor. They talk about the British **blockade** (10) of Boston Harbor following the incident, and they offer ideas about why the British wanted to cut Boston off from the rest of the world. They debate why the colonists resented the taxes, or **tariffs** (11), on imports and exports. It's a lively discussion.

An Explanation

After a while, Mr. Matsamura begins an explanation of why **diplomats** (12) were unable to resolve the differences between the colonists and England.

"Actually," he says, "I suppose **diplomat** is the wrong word, since **diplomacy** usually involves discussions between separate countries. Ben Franklin wasn't an official **diplomat** when he went to England in 1757, but he did represent the colonists. For him, it was of **premier** (13) importance that the British government understand the colonists' concerns. In fact, it was his first and only goal. Some British officials were **neutral** (14), but most were firm in their belief that the colonies should remain colonies. It's fascinating to imagine what the world would be like today if they had listened to the colonists' demands."

"I was wondering," Suni asks, "if you take all this stuff so seriously, why do you let us joke around about it?"

The Importance of Humor

"Remember that almost every one of the founders had a sense of humor," Mr. Matsamura says. "**Satire** (15), a form of writing that attacks faults, was one of their favorite weapons. Most of them loved a good **pun** (16), or play on words, too."

"Actually, this country has almost always had a sense of humor. I once read—I think it was in the

foreword (17) to a history of New England—that the Puritans believed that a certain element of fun and playfulness was important to even the most serious issues. I guess not many people have read that introduction because most people believe that the Puritans were a humorless bunch. Anyway, I also believe a sense of humor is very important. Anyone who wants to silence laughter is likely to be a person who wants to **quench** (18) the flame of liberty itself."

A Land of Freedom

Mr. Matsamura adds, "Let me share with you a couple of other things that I admire about this country. I like it when the President addresses us as 'My fellow Americans.' It's a little corny, but that **salutation** (19) says to me that in some way the President is like any other citizen."

"And I like to see people out demonstrating for various causes—people protesting the manufacturing of fur coats from animals like minks and **sables** (20), people protesting the dumping of sewage in our rivers, people protesting the closing of libraries. I don't always agree with their causes, but I love seeing people out there, exercising their constitutional rights. It reminds me that we live in a country that is truly free."

EXERCISE *Reading Strategically* ☞

Directions. Answer each of the following items by circling the letter of the correct answer. You may need to refer to the selection as you answer the items. The numbers of the items are the same as the numbers of the boldface Vocabulary Words in the selection.

1. The writer says the Constitution reflects the **aspirations** of the citizens of the United States. Here, **aspirations** means
   (A) frustrations
   (B) independence
   (C) ambitions
   (D) reflections

2. You can tell from the story that **indelible** means
   (A) permanent
   (B) black
   (C) unforgivable
   (D) interesting

© Houghton Mifflin Harcourt Publishing Company

3. You can tell by the story that **pewter** means
(A) very large
(B) a kind of metal
(C) beautiful
(D) very old

4. Which of the following is a reason mentioned in the story that Mr. Matsamura speaks with an **urgent** tone?
(A) He wants his students to know that he is joking.
(B) He wants his students to pay attention to what he says.
(C) He does not want his students to dwell on Paul Revere.
(D) He is annoyed by Alan's question.

5. The writer provides a clue to the meaning of **obscure**. What is the clue?
(A) Paul Revere was a talented silversmith.
(B) Mr. Matsamura's tone is **urgent**.
(C) Paul Revere played an important role in the founding of the United States.
(D) Paul Revere might not have been remembered by anyone.

6. The writer provides a clue to the meaning of **obituary**. What is the clue?
(A) Paul Revere played an important role in founding the country.
(B) The writer remembers the story of Revere's ride.
(C) The writer associates the word with something written after someone dies.
(D) The writer uses the word *heritage*.

7. You can tell from the story that **quaint** means
(A) pleasantly old-fashioned
(B) inherited
(C) American
(D) important but subtle

8. How does the writer let us know that **generate** means to cause or create?
(A) The discussion is over.
(B) Mr. Matsamura asks a question.
(C) There's not much enthusiasm over Mr. Matsamura's remarks.
(D) Mr. Matsamura's remarks start a discussion.

9. The writer states, "They discuss the colonists' decision to **confiscate** British tea, to seize it and dump it into the harbor." Here, **confiscate** means to
(A) drink
(B) borrow temporarily
(C) take away by force
(D) destroy senselessly

10. The writer of the story gives a clue to the meaning of **blockade**. What is the clue?
(A) The colonists resented taxes.
(B) The colonists destroyed British property.
(C) The British wanted to cut off Boston.
(D) The British taxed the colonists heavily.

11. The writer uses the word **tariffs** when writing about the colonists. Here, **tariffs** means
(A) taxes
(B) trade
(C) resentments
(D) punishments

12. You can tell from the article that **diplomats** are
(A) people from the colonies who went to England
(B) persons who represent the interests of one country to another
(C) any members of government
(D) people who are not from a particular country

© Houghton Mifflin Harcourt Publishing Company

13. The writer states, "For him, it was of **premier** importance that the British government understand the colonists' concerns." Here, **premier** means
    (A) major
    (B) understandable
    (C) general
    (D) some

14. The writer indicates that some British officials were **neutral**. Here, **neutral** means
    (A) not taking sides
    (B) patriots
    (C) uninterested
    (D) not serious

15. The writer indicates that **satire** was a favorite weapon of the country's founders. Here, **satire** means
    (A) physical attacks
    (B) writing that attacks faults
    (C) writing that resists humor
    (D) humor that makes a play on words

16. The writer states, "Most of them loved a good **pun**." Here, **pun** means
    (A) a word puzzle
    (B) writing that attacks faults
    (C) a play on words
    (D) jokes in a foreign language

17. All of the following are good definitions of **foreword** *except*
    (A) introduction
    (B) preface
    (C) opening remarks
    (D) conclusion

18. In the story, Mr. Matsamura compares a person who wants to **quench** the flame of liberty to someone who
    (A) drinks water
    (B) silences laughter
    (C) encourages laughter
    (D) writes humorous political sketches

19. An example of a **salutation** that appears in the story is
    (A) the President of the United States
    (B) a demonstrator
    (C) "My fellow Americans"
    (D) a corny or trite phrase

20. In the last paragraph, **sable** means
    (A) a protestor
    (B) an animal
    (C) a dark color
    (D) a fake fur coat

READING NEW WORDS IN CONTEXT

Lesson 12 CONTEXT: Voices of the United States

Introduction. One of the greatest compliments we can give someone is to say that he or she has a great sense of humor. It's not much fun being around someone who has lost his or her sense of humor—or who never had one at all.

The following selection gives you an opportunity to read about the role of humor in society. The selection also enables you to expand your vocabulary. Below are twenty Vocabulary Words that are used in the selection and in the exercise that follows it.

activate	colossal	essay	petty	successor
apt	confide	intolerance	pious	summit
charitable	deduction	invariable	proposal	tarnish
clarify	eccentric	irk	sarcasm	temperament

The Sound of Laughter

Most of us find it impossible to believe that someone really doesn't have a sense of humor. We assume that it's in there somewhere, and if we can only push the right button we'll be able to **activate** (1) it, to set it into motion.

Humor: No Laughing Matter

Since we all know that a sense of humor is important, why is it that we refuse to take it seriously? Okay, don't answer that. But think about this. If you started talking about what a great sense of humor people like George Washington and Abigail Adams had, some people might think you were attempting to **tarnish** (2) their reputation. Some people have an **intolerance** (3) for seeing famous people in this light. They would see it as an insult, not as a compliment. In fact, some people act as though our society would fall apart if we laughed at ourselves or our traditions. However, a more likely cause for a society to fall apart would be its inability to laugh at itself.

Cultural Diversity

The truth is that a sense of humor has always been an important part of the **temperament** (4) of the people of the United States. It's part of our national personality. Every group that has contributed to the cultural variety of the United States has contributed to our heritage of humor. American Indian cultures enjoy jokes and pranks. The British are famous for their **eccentric** (5) approach to humor: Few cultures have produced as many odd and offbeat humorists. Of course, the Irish are famous for laughter, and so are Jamaicans. Laughter seems to cut across religious lines, too. Even the most **pious** (6) nun or the most dedicated rabbi can enjoy a good laugh. The point is that laughter is universal and cuts across cultural boundaries.

© Houghton Mifflin Harcourt Publishing Company

Types of Humor

Humor in the United States comes in a variety of styles. There is a heritage of humor that is cutting and bitter, like the **sarcasm** (7) of H. L. Mencken (1880–1956). There is also humor that takes a more **charitable** (8) form, like the kindly humor of E. B. White (1899–1985). Some humor is lively and loud; some is quiet and easy to miss.

Another form is the humorous **essay** (9). For example, Benjamin Franklin (1706–1790) wrote short compositions designed not only to make a point but also to make the audience laugh. Today, humorous **essays** still appeal to us. For example, look at the success of newspaper columnist Dave Barry.

Now, humor also takes another form—the stand-up comic. Comedians who are **apt** Twain (10) in this particular style, such as Jerry Seinfeld, are **successors** (11) to Mark (1835–1910), Will Rogers (1879–1935), and numerous others who were famous for their ability to make an audience laugh. People like Seinfeld are following a long tradition. Some of these comics make jokes about politics, fads, and current events. Others seem to **confide** (12) the details of their personal lives. They treat audiences as trusted friends who will laugh with them at their foolish mistakes.

Traditionally, many humorists have focused on everyday things that **irk** (13), irritate, and annoy us, the small, even **petty** (14) details of everyday life. Sometimes they make us laugh by describing the ridiculous series of events that turned a minor mistake, such as wearing mismatched shoes, into a **colossal** (15) disaster, such as a herd of cattle stampeding through the White House Rose Garden during the annual Easter egg hunt.

Many people have tried to create humor by using some sort of logical process, but we can't be funny by using the process of **deduction** (16). It's hard to figure out logically what will make an audience laugh. Humor always seems to lose something when we try to make it clear by asking, "Why exactly is that funny?" When we try to **clarify** (17) the humor of something, the **invariable** (18) result of our attempt is confusion. It seems always to be true that we can't explain why something is funny—we just know humor when we see it or hear it.

As long as humor is not mean-spirited and hateful, it's good for us—as important as vegetables, exercise, rest, and fresh air. In fact, it's a wonder that no one has suggested that world leaders call a **summit** (19), or meeting of the heads of government, to discuss humor on a global scale. Here's my **proposal** (20)—lock them all in a room and don't let them out until they are all laughing.

EXERCISE — *Reading Strategically*

Directions. Answer each of the following items by circling the letter of the correct answer. You may need to refer to the selection as you answer the items. The numbers of the items are the same as the numbers of the Vocabulary Words in the selection.

1. You can tell from the selection that **activate** means
   (A) to push
   (B) to start
   (C) tpend
   (D) to avoid

2. The clue to the meaning of **tarnish** is
   (A) George Washington and Abigail Adams are famous citizens
   (B) We refuse to enjoy humor
   (C) Some would see it as an insult to say great people had a sense of humor
   (D) Great people have a sense of humor

3. The writer states, "Some people have an **intolerance** for seeing famous people in this light." Here, **intolerance** means
   (A) absence of a sense of humor
   (B) quality of seriousness
   (C) closed mind
   (D) inability

4. The writer of this selection gives a clue to the meaning of **temperament**. What is the clue?
   (A) Humor is part of the personality of the U.S.
   (B) A sense of humor has always been important.
   (C) People should be humorous.
   (D) The U.S. has cultural variety.

5. All of the following are good definitions of **eccentric** *except*
   (A) odd
   (B) offbeat
   (C) forgettable
   (D) unusual

6. You can tell from the selection that **pious** means
   (A) poor and humble
   (B) good-natured and humorous
   (C) humorless and serious
   (D) religiously devoted

7. The writer indicates that **sarcasm** plays a role in our heritage of laughter. Here, **sarcasm** means
   (A) cutting and bitter humor
   (B) old-fashioned, gentle humor
   (C) inherited humor
   (D) a variety of humor

8. In this selection, **charitable** means
   (A) loud
   (B) kind
   (C) famous
   (D) funny

9. The writer gives us a clue to the meaning of **essay**. What is the clue?
   (A) **Essays** are a part of the country's heritage.
   (B) **Essays** are written to make audiences laugh.
   (C) Some humor is quiet and easy to miss, and some is loud and lively.
   (D) Ben Franklin wrote short compositions designed to make a point.

10. In this selection, **apt** means
    (A) able
    (B) funny
    (C) unusual
    (D) talkative

11. The writer gives a clue to the meaning of **successors**. What is the clue?
    (A) Stand-up comedy is a form of humor.
    (B) Stand-up comics are following a long tradition.
    (C) Audiences laugh at stand-up comics.
    (D) Stand-up comics make jokes about politics.

12. The writer gives us a clue to the meaning of **confide**. What is the clue?
    (A) Stand-up comics treat the audience as trusted friends.
    (B) Stand-up comics' mistakes are foolish.
    (C) Stand-up comics are following a long tradition.
    (D) Stand-up comics make jokes about current events.

13. In this selection, **irk** means all of the following *except*
    (A) irritate
    (B) annoy
    (C) threaten
    (D) bother

14. The writer states, "Traditionally, many humorists have focused on small, even **petty** details of everyday life." Here, **petty** means
(A) lovely
(B) forgotten
(C) humorous
(D) unimportant

15. The writer indicates that a minor mistake might lead to a **colossal** blunder. Here, **colossal** means
(A) interesting
(B) enormous
(C) public
(D) everyday

16. Which of the following is the most likely reason that, in the writer's words, "We can't be funny by using the process of **deduction**"?
(A) Humor can't be created through a logical process.
(B) The writer is making a bad joke.
(C) Stand-up comics can make humor out of unimportant events.
(D) Some people try to analyze humor through a logical process.

17. The writer indicates that it's difficult to **clarify** our answers to questions about humor. Here, **clarify** means
(A) to laugh during
(B) to confuse
(C) to make clear
(D) to understand

18. In this selection, **invariable** means
(A) constant
(B) important
(C) likely
(D) occasional

19. In the last paragraph, **summit** means
(A) meeting of world leaders
(B) comedy
(C) humor on a global scale
(D) mountain top

20. Which of the following is an example of a **proposal** made by the writer?
(A) Humor is as important to us as vegetables, exercise, and rest.
(B) Lock all the world's leaders in a room until they are all laughing.
(C) Most people know humor when they see it, even if they can't explain it.
(D) Humor that is mean-spirited or hateful is not healthy.

READING NEW WORDS IN CONTEXT

Lesson 13 **CONTEXT:** Voices of the United States

Introduction. For Chinese Americans, the entryway to the United States between 1910 and 1940 was not New York Harbor and Ellis Island, but San Francisco Bay and Angel Island.

The following article gives you an opportunity to read about Chinese emigrants, people who left China in search of a better life. The article also enables you to expand your vocabulary. Below are twenty Vocabulary Words that are used in the article and in the exercise that follows it.

anonymous	contemporary	emphasize	fictitious	literal
casual	dictate	endorse	fragment	modify
climax	dilute	falter	improvise	occurrence
condemn	dispatch	famished	intrigue	therapy

Poems on the Wall: The Voices of Chinese Americans

When the United States Congress passed the Chinese Exclusion Act of 1882, it became nearly impossible for Chinese emigrants to enter the United States. Congress continued to **endorse** (1) the restrictions in this act or support similar ones for sixty years. The laws did allow for a few exceptions, and some Chinese people entered each year under special circumstances. The laws **dictated** (2) guidelines for entrance and also set the rules for determining who would be admitted to the country. The officials on Angel Island decided who met the requirements and would be allowed to stay.

Waiting on Angel Island
Most Chinese who arrived at Angel Island believed that they would be admitted to the United States right away. They were bitterly disappointed to discover that the **climax** (3) of their long journey was to await their fate for several nerve-wracking weeks on Angel Island. During this time, they were locked up as if they were criminals in prison. During their weeks of imprisonment, it is

not surprising that the hope of the would-be immigrants began to **falter** (4) as they realized that they might be turned away. For some, the weeks dragged to months, and they gave in to despair. Some would be **condemned** (5) by circumstances to spend two years on Angel Island.

The Writing on the Wall
With nothing to do but wait, many of the Chinese turned to writing. Perhaps writing served as a kind of emotional **therapy** (6) by helping to heal their frustration and stress. The form they chose was poetry, and they wrote it where they could—on the walls of their prison. These poems were not **fragments** (7) and they were not the **casual** (8) scribblings of graffiti. They were complete and formal works of art.

Not all the poems survived. Some were written in pencil and were eventually painted over, but others were carved into the walls. The poets are **anonymous** (9). They did not sign their work, so no one knows their names. People who read the poems are **intrigued** (10) by the power and the beauty of the poetry, and they become curious about the fates of individuals who wrote them. We don't know for sure, however, which poets were allowed to stay and which were turned away.

Powerful Voices

Translation of poetry can be difficult. Sometimes the translator has to **modify** (11) the poem, making changes that will help the readers understand its meaning. However, translation has not **diluted** (12) the emotional impact of the Angel Island poems. These are words of pain, and they are powerful enough to retain their full effect even in translation.

The poets were **famished** (13) in more ways than one. The food was inedible, but they were also starving for freedom, for respect, and for dignity. Some of their poems read like **dispatches** (14) from a battle front. They are messages from people struggling to survive.

It should be pointed out, and perhaps even **emphasized** (15), that some of the poems are better than others. Some of the poets had clearly been educated in the art of Chinese poetry. Others had to **improvise** (16), to make do with sheer imagination, in the absence of formal training.

The language of the wall poems is the language of poetry. It is often not **literal** (17). The poets used many figures of speech. For example, one poet wrote about his or her willingness to become an ox, just to have the chance to work hard for a living. It is easy to imagine the frustration this poet must have felt as he or she sat idle in the cell.

The poems can also serve as a brief introduction to Chinese history and culture. Some mention historical figures. Others mention **fictitious** (18) characters from Chinese literature and myth. Some poems are about **occurrences** (19) in the daily lives of the poets. For example, a poet might mention the breakfast that day or a conversation with another prisoner.

A Timeless Message

Angel Island was closed in 1940, and the wall poems were lost for almost thirty years until they were rediscovered in 1970. Even though the most recent of these poems was written long ago, they speak to **contemporary** (20) audiences. They remind us today of those the world over who are camped along borders and who are knocking on the doors of free nations asking to be admitted. However, they speak most strongly to the children and grandchildren of the Chinese wall poets. The poems express the voices of people of courage and vision, of people who contributed to the song of liberty and diversity in the United States.

EXERCISE *Reading Strategically*

Directions. Answer each of the following items by circling the letter of the correct answer. You may need to refer to the selection as you answer the items. The numbers of the items are the same as the numbers of the boldface Vocabulary Words in the selection.

1. The writer states, "Congress continued to **endorse** the restrictions in this act or support similar ones for sixty years." Here, **endorse** means
   (A) discourage
   (B) approve
   (C) leave off
   (D) throw out

2. In the article, a clue to the meaning of **dictated** is
   (A) that the laws also set the rules for determining entry
   (B) that some Chinese were admitted under special circumstances
   (C) that there were officials at Angel Island
   (D) that the rules were seldom followed

© Houghton Mifflin Harcourt Publishing Company

3. The writer uses **climax** when referring to a part of the journey. Here, **climax** means
(A) a sudden return to the beginning
(B) the most intense part
(C) an unlawful imprisonment
(D) an unplanned detour

4. Which of the following most likely caused the Chinese emigrants' hopes to **falter** when they arrived at Angel Island?
(A) Some managed to gain entry without much of a wait.
(B) They realized that they might be turned way.
(C) They believed that they would gain entry right away.
(D) They had successfully completed a long journey.

5. You can tell from the article that **condemned** means
(A) prevented
(B) encouraged
(C) bothered
(D) doomed

6. You can tell from the article that **therapy** means
(A) treatment for stress or illness
(B) feelings of anger and frustration
(C) the tendency to display emotion
(D) a special form of writing

7. The writer of the article gives a clue to the meaning of **fragments**. What is the clue?
(A) The writer contrasts **fragments** with complete works.
(B) The writer associates **fragments** with walls.
(C) The writer implies that most poems are **fragments**.
(D) The Chinese chose to write poetry.

8. The writer indicates that the poems were not **casual** scribblings. Here, **casual** means
(A) confused
(B) printed
(C) informal
(D) bad

9. To show that **anonymous** means unknown, the writer
(A) tells us that some poems did not survive
(B) tells us that the surviving poems were carved
(C) tells us that the poets did not sign their works
(D) hints that there were many poets

10. The writer states, "People who read the poems are **intrigued** by the power and the beauty of the poetry. . . ." Here, **intrigued** means
(A) fascinated
(B) frightened
(C) confused
(D) unimpressed

11. The writer says that the translators had to **modify** the poems so that readers would understand them. Here, **modify** means to
(A) borrow
(B) change
(C) destroy
(D) translate

12. All of the following are good definitions of **diluted** *except*
(A) lessened
(B) weakened
(C) destroyed by
(D) watered down

13. The writer gives a clue to the meaning of **famished**. What is the clue?

(A) The poems are messages.
(B) The Chinese were not allowed to enter the country.
(C) The poems have a strong impact.
(D) The poets were starving.

14. The writer states, "Some of their poems read like **dispatches** from a battle front." Here, **dispatches** means

(A) messages
(B) bullets
(C) struggles
(D) riddles

15. You can tell from the article that **emphasized** means

(A) noticed
(B) stressed
(C) ignored
(D) encouraged

16. The writer says that some poets had to **improvise**. Here, **improvise** means

(A) to borrow from
(B) to study
(C) to make do
(D) to forget about

17. The writer states, "The language of the wall poems is the language of poetry. It is often not **literal**." Here, **literal** means

(A) complex and confusing
(B) unbelievable, ridiculous
(C) full of unspoken meaning
(D) limited to exact meaning

18. The writer states, "Others mention **fictitious** characters from Chinese literature and myth." Here, **fictitious** means

(A) famous
(B) realistic
(C) imaginary
(D) borrowed

19. An example mentioned in the article of **occurrences** in the daily lives of the Angel Island poets is

(A) a brief introduction to Chinese history and literature
(B) a mention of a historical figure
(C) a mention of a character from Chinese myth
(D) a conversation with another prisoner

20. Another way to say **contemporary** is

(A) old-fashioned
(B) of the present day
(C) poet
(D) immigrant

READING NEW WORDS IN CONTEXT

Lesson 14 | CONTEXT: Voices of the United States

Introduction. Storytelling can be used to entertain or simply to pass the time. However, in the hands of people who have been denied the means of directly expressing their feelings, storytelling takes on a much more important role. For enslaved African Americans, whose every action and every word were closely watched, storytelling was a tool for survival.

In the following article, you will learn how African Americans turned to stories for hope and made important contributions to American literature. The article also gives you an opportunity to expand your vocabulary. Below are twenty Vocabulary Words that are used in the article and in the exercise that follows it.

articulate	denial	eligible	inclination	tangible
braggart	derive	extensive	miscellaneous	testify
category	detach	illuminate	secluded	unique
demolish	distraction	imply	superficial	upbraid

African American Folk Tales and Storytellers

The African American experience is **unique** (1) in at least one important way. Almost every other group of immigrants came to the United States by choice. African Americans, however, were forced to make the trip across the ocean in chains.

Unlike other immigrants, they did not have the chance to pack their goods, and, once they landed, they were not allowed to settle in family groups. They arrived in a frightening new world with nothing but their memories and their stories.

It is important to realize that the position of storyteller among most African peoples was an important one. The storyteller was not a **braggart** (2), or know-it-all, but was highly respected in the community. Perhaps that explains why the literature of African Americans is so **extensive** (3). African American culture has produced a vast number of writers and storytellers who work in a wide variety of forms. Many of the stories have roots in African folk tales.

A Word About Folk Tales

Some people don't understand the importance of folk tales. They think of them only as stories that people tell to children. However, folk tales are a very special **category** (4) of literature, a type that is important in itself.

If a folk tale is not read carefully, it may seem to be a **superficial** (5) story, one that lacks depth. A serious look at folk tales will **demolish** (6) that false belief and replace it with a new insight. Folk tales are more than the expression of fantastic events; they actually **articulate** (7) the deepest beliefs of a people.

Hidden Meanings

For the enslaved African Americans, the stories they told were a way of keeping their different cultures alive. They could tell their stories without inviting slaveholders' suspicion, in part because the slaveholders thought the stories were just entertainment, a kind of **distraction** (8). Certainly, they missed the folklore's significance. At any rate, the slaveholders, and whites in general, showed no tendency to take part in the oral literature of the African Americans, nor did they have an **inclination** (9) to examine it closely. If they had looked beyond what the stories said outright to what the stories **implied** (10), they might have been surprised and angered. Very likely, they would have felt the need to **upbraid** (11), or take the African Americans to task, and tried to stamp the stories out.

Anyone who was familiar with the stories could **testify** (12) that they were not just harmless tales told to amuse the children. Such people could also have borne witness to the fact that the stories played an important role in the African American culture, but no one was about to give the secret away.

Storytelling

The African Americans lived separately from the white masters. In the evenings, **secluded** (13) in the slave quarters, they told their stories. Some of the stories were **derived** (14) from African folk tales. For example, many of the animal stories, such as the stories of Brer Fox and Brer Bear, have their source in older, eastern African folk tales.

The stories allowed the African Americans to **detach** (15), or disconnect, themselves from their suffering, and to look at their experiences from a different perspective. The stories that seemed so innocent to the white masters were in fact powerful messages of hope for enslaved people.

Later Folk Tales

It is not true that only stories told long ago are **eligible** (16) to be included in a collection of folk tales. Stories being invented in the streets, homes, and schools today qualify as folk tales, too; people share these stories with each other in a meaningful way just as they have always shared folk tales.

Any collection of **miscellaneous** (17) African American folk tales will include in the assortment stories that were created after the enslaved people were freed. These tales are likely to show an awareness that they were not yet truly free. Such stories often reflect the African Americans' attitudes toward the continued **denial** (18) of their rights. Like a light in the darkness, the stories **illuminate** (19) the feelings of a people who were free and yet still chained.

The folk tales are **tangible** (20) proof of the courage and wisdom of African Americans. Concrete evidence of their influence can be observed in the works of many African American writers, including Zora Neale Hurston (1891–1960), Langston Hughes (1902–1967), Toni Morrison (b. 1931), Alice Walker (b. 1944), Toni Cade Bambara (1939–1995), and Ralph Ellison (1914–1994). African American stories continue to give shape and voice to one more version of the American experience.

EXERCISE *Reading Strategically*

Directions. Answer each of the following items by circling the letter of the correct answer. You may need to refer to the selection as you answer the items. The numbers of the items are the same as the numbers of the boldface Vocabulary Words in the selection.

1. The writer states, "The African American experience is **unique**. . . ." Here, **unique** means
   (A) one of a kind
   (B) similar to others
   (C) an interesting story
   (D) frequently considered

2. You can tell from the article that **braggart** means
   (A) boastful person
   (B) intelligent person
   (C) respected person
   (D) important person

3. According to the article, African American literature is **extensive.** Here, **extensive** means
   - (A) important
   - (B) vast
   - (C) original
   - (D) unusual

4. The writer states, "However, folk tales are a very special **category** of literature. . . ." Here, **category** means
   - (A) organization
   - (B) type
   - (C) version
   - (D) folk tale

5. You can tell from the article that **superficial** means
   - (A) very serious
   - (B) out of the ordinary
   - (C) confusing
   - (D) lacking depth

6. All of the following are good definitions of **demolish** *except*
   - (A) to destroy
   - (B) to tear down
   - (C) to replace
   - (D) to smash

7. To give a clue to the meaning of **articulate,** the writer
   - (A) lets us know that new insights are possible
   - (B) associates **articulate** with the word *depth*
   - (C) associates **articulate** with the word *expression*
   - (D) lets us know that folk tales are important

8. The writer explains that slaveholders "thought the stories were just entertainment, a kind of **distraction**." Here, **distraction** means
   - (A) stories
   - (B) culture
   - (C) amusement
   - (D) confusion

9. The writer says that the whites had no **inclination** to examine the literature. Here, **inclination** means
   - (A) tendency
   - (B) understanding
   - (C) examination
   - (D) time

10. To give a clue to the meaning of **implied,** the writer
    - (A) says the slaveholders were not interested in African American stories
    - (B) hints that the stories were not just entertainment
    - (C) hints that an **implied** meaning is not stated outright
    - (D) says that slaveholders did not try to stamp out oral literature

11. All of the following are good definitions for **upbraid** *except*
    - (A) criticize
    - (B) harm
    - (C) scold
    - (D) blame

12. You can tell from the article that **testify** means to
    - (A) completely understand
    - (B) bear witness
    - (C) pretend
    - (D) fully deny

13. The writer gives us a clue to the meaning of **secluded.** What is the clue?
    - (A) African Americans told stories.
    - (B) African Americans lived separately.
    - (C) Stories were told in the evenings.
    - (D) African American storytellers used African folk tales as sources for stories.

14. To let us know that **derived** means taken from, the writer

(A) gives an example of an African American folk tale that comes from an African source

(B) says the African Americans were taken from their homes without their consent

(C) associates **derived** with the term *folk tales*

(D) tells us that the stories of Brer Fox and Brer Bear are part of America's folklore

15. The writer indicates that the stories allowed African Americans to **detach** themselves from their suffering. Here, **detach** means to

(A) review

(B) separate

(C) reconnect

(D) understand

16. To let us know that **eligible** means qualified or suitable, the writer

(A) hints that most folk tales are passed down from generation to generation

(B) uses the phrase "long ago"

(C) says that new stories can qualify as folk tales

(D) uses the word *collection*

17. To let us know that **miscellaneous** means "various kinds of," the writer

(A) hints that stories are constantly being created

(B) mentions memories

(C) refers to the time after the enslavened people were freed

(D) refers to an assortment of stories

18. The writer states, "Such stories often reflect the African Americans' attitudes toward the continued **denial** of their rights." Here, **denial** means

(A) extension of

(B) eventual acceptance of

(C) decision to advance

(D) refusal of a request

19. Which of the following items is an example of how folk tales **illuminate** the feelings of African Americans?

(A) The stories reflect African American values and culture.

(B) The stories are proof of the courage and wisdom of African Americans.

(C) The stories continue to give shape and voice to one version of the American experience.

(D) The stories reveal, like a light in darkness, the feelings of a people.

20. To let us know that **tangible** means "capable of being felt," the writer

(A) says the old stories are proof of African American courage and wisdom

(B) restates **tangible** proof as concrete evidence

(C) mentions several famous authors

(D) associates **tangible** with the phrase "continue to give shape and voice to"

READING NEW WORDS IN CONTEXT

Lesson 15 CONTEXT: Voices of the United States

Introduction. Many people think of a job as something they do to make money for themselves or their families. However, a job is more than that. Each person's work, whether it is in a science laboratory, on the farm, or in the home, contributes to the country as a whole.

In the following story, an eighth-grade class is talking about the jobs the members of their families do. The story gives you an opportunity to expand your vocabulary. Below are twenty Vocabulary Words that are used in the passage and in the exercise that follows it.

aeronautics	automaton	erosion	parasitic	respiration
agenda	commute	hydraulic	photogenic	synthetic
antibiotics	congest	hypothesis	planetarium	technology
arrogant	considerate	malfunction	rebate	warranty

Building the United States

Mr. Nguyen's students at Quannah Parker Middle School are discussing how members of their families are contributing to today's world.

"My grandfather was always interested in flying," says Mohammed. "That's why he's very pleased that my father is doing research in the field of **aeronautics** (1)."

"My mom does research, too," says Mariante. "She's working on developing a new **antibiotic** (2). It's for people who are allergic to most other **antibiotics**. If she can develop it, it will really help them when they get infections. At least that's her **hypothesis** (3)."

"Excuse me," says Arnold, "but what's a **hypothesis**?"

"An unproven theory," says Mariante. "She thinks that's what will happen, but she hasn't proved it yet."

"That's interesting," Juan Carlos responds. "You know, my brother is thinking about going into research. He's interested in applying scien-

tific knowledge to farming, in the **technology** (4) of farming. He may become a soil scientist. He's especially interested in learning how to prevent soil **erosion** (5)—you know, to prevent the soil from wearing away. He's also interested in plant diseases, especially in **parasitic** (6) ones—the kind that are caused by an organism that draws its life from the plant it lives on."

Silvia remarks, "My grandparents were farmers. They used to grow cotton, but then people started wearing **synthetic** (7) fabrics like polyester, so they tried some other crops. Finally, they decided to just farm part time and to take other jobs."

"There are still farmers in my family," says Kenneth. "I've always loved the farm machinery. When I was a little kid, it seemed enormous. Today I can operate some of that equipment, and someday I'm going to be a farmer."

"Not me," says Meigumi. "I like living in the city. There's always something to do. Last week, one of the things on our **agenda** (8) was to go to the **planetarium** (9). We made sure that it was included in our schedule because there was a special show. On the ceiling was a kind of movie of the planets and stars, projected up there like a film."

"That's interesting, Meigumi, but let's try to stay on the topic of careers," says Mr. Nguyen.

Tasha raises her hand. "My sister is a sociologist, and she studies urban life. She says the crime rate in cities is always higher. Of course, there is crime in the country, but not as often."

"What other jobs do your family members have?" asks Mr. Nguyen.

"Well, my sister is very **photogenic** (10). That's why she decided to be a model. I don't mean to sound **arrogant** (11), or conceited, but she's been on the cover of three magazines," Leroi says.

Camilla says, "My mom gives this special kind of treatment at the hospital. The treatment she gives helps people with **respiration** (12), or breathing, problems. She is a **respiratory** specialist. Sometimes a person's lungs will become **congested** (13) because they're filling up with fluid, and my mom works to prevent that from happening."

"My sister works at the electronics factory out in Redbud," say Tanika. "She checks to make sure that a **warranty** (14) is packed in the box with every microwave oven. That's the little piece of paper that guarantees that the microwave will work for at least twelve months. During that time, if it starts overcooking your food or

malfunctions (15) in some other way, you can get it replaced. Sometimes her duties change. Last week, she was checking to make sure there was a **rebate** (16) coupon packed in with every VCR. If you bought a certain brand of videotape, you could get two dollars off with the coupon."

"My dad isn't working right now," says Chris. "He finds ways to stay busy, though. He's a really **considerate** (17) person. One of the nice things he does is to help some of the elderly people in our neighborhood do their shopping and stuff. He says he'd like to get a job doing that."

"You know," adds Estelle, "both my dad and mom were out of work for a while last year. It was pretty tough. Now Mom works at home doing day care, and Dad **commutes** (18) back and forth between here and the auto plant out in Green Springs. His job has something to do with **hydraulic** (19) brakes."

"Hywhatics?"

"**Hydraulic**. You know. Brakes that are operated by the pressure of a liquid forced through the brake lines. The new plant there is really cool— it's totally modern. They have—what do you call them?—**automatons** (20) working on the assembly line. Can you imagine working with a robot?"

"Let's save that question for science. What other jobs have members of your families done?" Mr. Nguyen looks out at the class. Six more hands go up.

EXERCISE *Reading Strategically* ✍

Directions. Answer each of the following items by circling the letter of the correct answer. You may need to refer to the selection as you answer the items. The numbers of the items are the same as the numbers of the Vocabulary Words in the selection.

1. You can tell from the story that **aeronautics** means
   (A) a contribution to today's world
   (B) an occupation
   (C) a field that needs research
   (D) the science of aircraft

2. The writer provides a clue to the meaning of **antibiotics**. What is the clue?
   (A) Many people are allergic to **antibiotics**.
   (B) Mariante's mother does research on **antibiotics**.
   (C) **Antibiotics** are new.
   (D) **Antibiotics** help people who get infections.

3. You can tell from the story that
hypothesis means
(A) interesting research
(B) unproven theory
(C) scientific research
(D) scientific proof

4. The writer tells us that Juan Carlos's
brother is interested in the scientific
aspects, or **technology,** of farming.
Here, **technology** means
(A) farm equipment
(B) applied science
(C) soil
(D) information

5. Juan Carlos says, "He's especially in-
terested in learning how to prevent
soil **erosion.**" Here, **erosion** means
(A) wearing away
(B) disease
(C) technology
(D) a kind of science

6. The writer indicates that Juan Carlos's
brother is interested in studying **para-
sitic** diseases. Here, **parasitic** means
(A) like or of any disease
(B) farming equipment
(C) living off a living thing
(D) the research of plant life and plant
diseases

7. The writer indicates that people wear
synthetic fabrics. Here, **synthetic**
means
(A) expensive
(B) cotton or other natural fibers
(C) not of natural origin
(D) anything raised on a farm

8. The writer states, "Last week, one of
the things on our **agenda** was to go to
the planetarium." Here, **agenda** means
(A) serious thoughts
(B) errands to run
(C) leisure time
(D) list of things to do

9. Meigumi tells us that they went to the
planetarium last week. **Planetarium**
means
(A) something to do
(B) special show
(C) a place that shows a kind of film
of the stars
(D) a movie theater that shows science
fiction films only

10. The writer gives us a clue to the meaning of **photogenic.** What is the clue?
(A) Leroi has a sister.
(B) Leroi's sister made a decision con-
cerning her career path.
(C) Leroi's sister has a successful
career.
(D) Leroi's sister has been on the
cover of three magazines.

11. All of the following are good
definitions of **arrogant** *except*
(A) haughty
(B) vain
(C) conceited
(D) meek

12. Camilla says that her mother helps
people who have **respiration** prob-
lems. Here, **respiration** means
(A) having to do with the emotions
(B) having to do with breathing
(C) having to do with hospitals
(D) special

13. Which of the following is the most
likely reason that lungs become
congested?
(A) Camilla's mother helps them.
(B) People have breathing problems.
(C) People are in the hospital.
(D) Lungs fill up with fluid.

14. You can tell from the story that
warranty means
  (A) a package
  (B) a guarantee
  (C) a little
  (D) a microwave oven

15. An example the story mentions of one
way a microwave oven **malfunctions**
is that
  (A) it may come with a little piece of
      paper
  (B) it will work for at least twelve
      months
  (C) it may overcook food
  (D) it may be replaced

16. To let us know that a **rebate** is a reduc-
tion or discount, the writer
  (A) lets us know that the coupon was
      good for two dollars off
  (B) hints that the job is a new one
  (C) suggests that a **rebate** should be
      included in every box
  (D) hints that the VCR would not
      work without a **rebate**

17. In this story, **considerate** means
  (A) thoughtful
  (B) busy
  (C) unemployed
  (D) interested only in the elderly

18. Estelle says that her dad **commutes**
back and forth between home and a
job at an auto plant. Here, **commutes**
means
  (A) runs a day-care center
  (B) runs
  (C) travels back and forth
  (D) works

19. The writer of the story gives us a clue
to the meaning of **hydraulic**. What is
the clue?
  (A) The brakes are installed at an
      automobile assembly plant in
      Green Springs.
  (B) Brakes are operated by the pres-
      sure of a liquid forced through the
      brake lines.
  (C) The brakes are in automobiles.
  (D) Mr. Nguyen doesn't approve
      of lengthy discussions about
      hydraulics.

20. The writer of this story gives us a clue
to the meaning of **automatons**. What is
the clue?
  (A) The writer mentions the pressure
      created by a liquid.
  (B) The writer links **automatons** to
      brake lines.
  (C) The writer links **automatons** to the
      word robot.
  (D) Mr. Nguyen seems reluctant to
      spend class time talking about
      automatons.

Vocabulary Words

abuse
acceptance
access
accessible
accessory
accommodations
activate
adapt
adept
adequate
adjacent
advantageous
advent
aeronautics
agenda
aggressive
alliance
anonymous
anthology
antibiotics
anxiety
appalling
apt
aristocrat
aroma
arrogant
articulate
artisan
aspiration
assumption
attain
automaton

badger
baffle
bankrupt
barbarism
basis
baste
bewilder
blockade
boisterous
boycott

braggart
burly

calamity
calculation
capital
casual
catastrophe
category
censorship
charitable
circulate
circumnavigate
clarify
climax
colossal
commute
complement
condemn
confederation
confide
confiscate
congest
consecutive
considerate
contagious
contemporary
controversy
convert
creative
customary

decade
deceased
deceive
dedicate
deduction
defy
delegate
demolish
denial
deport
depose

derive
descend
detach
dictate
diction
dilapidated
dilute
diminish
dingy
diplomat
disagreeable
discord
dismantle
dispatch
dispense
dissect
distraction
durable

eccentric
ecology
elegant
eligible
embarrass
emigrate
eminent
emphasize
endorse
enhance
epidemic
erosion
essay
evacuate
exaggeration
exertion
extensive

falter
famine
famished
feasible
feline
ferocious

fictitious
folklore
foresight
foreword
fragile
fragment
fraudulent
frequency

gallery
generate
glorify
gnarled
gracious
grieve

hamper
harmonious
haughty
haven
hilarious
hospitable
humidity
humiliate
hydraulic
hypothesis

illuminate
immense
immigrate
impel
imperative
imply
impose
improvise
impulsive
incite
inclination
incomparable
inconsiderate
indelible
inevitable
inflexible

Vocabulary Words, *(continued)*

ingenious
inherit
insoluble
integrity
intelligible
intensity
intentional
intercept
intervene
intolerance
intrigue
invariable
irk
isolation

jeopardize
jubilation

knoll

liable
liberate
literal

malfunction
malnutrition
manageable
maroon
memento
menace
menagerie
miscellaneous
misdeed
modify
monopoly
morale
motivate
multicolored
multitude

mutual
myriad
mystical

nationality
naturalization
negligent
neutral
notify
nourish
novelty

obituary
obscure
occupant
occurrence
omission
optimism
ordeal

pacify
parasitic
persistent
petition
petty
pewter
phenomenon
photogenic
picturesque
pious
planetarium
pleasantry
populate
posterity
potential
prearrange
predicament
premier
premiere

presume
primitive
privilege
probable
probation
propaganda
proposal
prosecute
provision
pulverize
pun

quaint
quench

rebate
recuperate
refuge
regime
remorse
remote
resolute
respiration
restore
restrain
revelation
rigid
riotous
romantic
ruthless

sable
salutation
sanctuary
sarcasm
satire
saturate
secluded
sedate

sincerity
spacious
strategy
successor
summit
superficial
sustain
synthetic

tangible
tariff
tarnish
technology
temperament
testify
therapy
thrifty
thrive
titanic
transit
tumult

unique
upbraid
urban
urgent

valid
valor
verify
vitality

warranty

Vocabulary Tests

CONTENTS

(Summative Assessment continues)

NOTE TO THE TEACHER

This section contains formative assessments for ongoing evaluation. It also contains summative assessments for testing mastery. The formative assessments include one test for each of the thirty lessons included in the Making New Words Your Own phase of *Vocabulary Practice*.

The summative assessments consist of three tests. Each summative test corresponds to ten of the lessons in Making New Words Your Own, five of the lessons in Understanding New Words and Their Uses, five of the lessons in Connecting New Words and Patterns, and five of the lessons in Reading New Words in Context.

Because each summative test covers more material than can be tested easily in one class period, every test is divided into two major parts. Each part is designed to be tested in one class period.

The answers for each test are included in a separate answer key booklet. The point scoring for each test follows the directions for each part of that test. The total score for each test is 100 points.

FORMATIVE ASSESSMENT

Tests 1–30

USING NEW WORDS ON TESTS

Test 1

Directions. In the space provided, write the letter of the word or phrase closest in meaning to the boldface word. *(10 points each)*

_____ **1.** the **appalling** tale
(A) humorous
(B) horrifying
(C) brief
(D) surprising

_____ **2.** a **contagious** disease
(A) tropical
(B) minor
(C) fatal
(D) catching

_____ **3.** the **eminent** judge
(A) mild
(B) harsh
(C) distinguished
(D) qualified

_____ **4.** the **epidemic** of smallpox
(A) cause
(B) outbreak
(C) infection
(D) cure

_____ **5.** **intentional** insults
(A) personal
(B) angry
(C) serious
(D) deliberate

_____ **6.** a **myriad** of problems
(A) careful study
(B) small number
(C) large study
(D) large number

_____ **7.** **picturesque** landscapes
(A) unusual
(B) charming
(C) common
(D) ugly

_____ **8.** **probable** causes
(A) likely
(B) unreasonable
(C) good
(D) unpopular

_____ **9.** **romantic** tales
(A) moral and believable
(B) fanciful and unrealistic
(C) realistic and enchanting
(D) horrifying and gruesome

_____ **10.** the **ruthless** tyrant
(A) pitiless
(B) foreign
(C) unreasonable
(D) homeless

© Houghton Mifflin Harcourt Publishing Company

Using New Words on Tests

Test 2

Directions. In the space provided, write the letter of the word or phrase closest in meaning to the boldface word. *(10 points each)*

_____ **1.** to **abuse** a privilege
(A) ignore
(B) misuse
(C) respect
(D) withhold

_____ **2.** to **baffle** the police
(A) puzzle
(B) recognize
(C) battle
(D) respect

_____ **3.** the **barbarism** of the colonists
(A) cruelty
(B) superstitions
(C) diet
(D) appearance

_____ **4.** to **bewilder** me
(A) answer
(B) confuse
(C) help
(D) believe

_____ **5.** to suffer a **calamity**
(A) disaster
(B) mistake
(C) failure
(D) setback

_____ **6.** to **deceive** a buyer
(A) encourage
(B) attract
(C) mislead
(D) find

_____ **7.** to study **folklore**
(A) all humankind
(B) ancient history
(C) the animal kingdom
(D) unwritten customs

_____ **8.** to climb the **knoll**
(A) mountain peak
(B) cliff face
(C) small hill
(D) tall ladder

_____ **9.** to be a **novelty**
(A) something expensive
(B) something new
(C) something frail
(D) something old

_____ **10.** to speak with **sincerity**
(A) skill
(B) vigor
(C) confidence
(D) honesty

USING NEW WORDS ON TESTS

Test 3

Directions. In the space provided, write the letter of the word or phrase closest in meaning to the boldface word. *(10 points each)*

_____ **1. aggressive** players
   (A) assertive
   (B) victorious
   (C) fresh
   (D) exhausted

_____ **2.** a natural **catastrophe**
   (A) situation
   (B) disaster
   (C) talent
   (D) cause

_____ **3.** to study **ecology**
   (A) living things and water
   (B) living things and food
   (C) living things and weather
   (D) living things and environments

_____ **4.** a **ferocious** beast
   (A) loud
   (B) strange
   (C) caged
   (D) fierce

_____ **5.** an **inevitable** result
   (A) unexpected
   (B) avoidable
   (C) unavoidable
   (D) unsatisfactory

_____ **6.** his **intelligible** answer
   (A) clear
   (B) confused
   (C) lengthy
   (D) short

_____ **7.** to **motivate** the team
   (A) encourage
   (B) equip
   (C) follow
   (D) exercise

_____ **8.** to seek **sanctuary**
   (A) a place of shelter
   (B) good fortune
   (C) new lands
   (D) a leader

_____ **9.** the **strategy** of the game
   (A) plan
   (B) length
   (C) score
   (D) rules

_____ **10.** a **valid** argument
   (A) pointless
   (B) reasonable
   (C) loud
   (D) weak

USING NEW WORDS ON TESTS

Test 4

Directions. In the space provided, write the letter of the word or phrase closest in meaning to the boldface word. *(10 points each)*

_____ **1.** the **advent** of war
   (A) tragedy
   (B) glamour
   (C) coming
   (D) equipment

_____ **2.** a strong **alliance**
   (A) argument
   (B) agreement
   (C) odor
   (D) rivalry

_____ **3.** an **anthology** of songs
   (A) collection
   (B) composer
   (C) performance
   (D) review

_____ **4.** to **defy** the police
   (A) flee from
   (B) resist openly
   (C) call for
   (D) show respect for

_____ **5.** a reputation for **integrity**
   (A) uprightness
   (B) dishonesty
   (C) skill
   (D) bravery

_____ **6.** committed a **misdeed**
   (A) unpleasant job
   (B) clever trick
   (C) good deed
   (D) bad act

_____ **7.** a **mystical** symbol
   (A) special
   (B) treasured
   (C) secret
   (D) strange

_____ **8.** to **nourish** hope
   (A) reject
   (B) starve
   (C) lose
   (D) promote

_____ **9.** to **pacify** a child
   (A) feed
   (B) discipline
   (C) soothe
   (D) frighten

_____ **10.** to **sustain** peace
   (A) withhold
   (B) support
   (C) relinquish
   (D) promise

USING NEW WORDS ON TESTS

Test 5

Directions. In the space provided, write the letter of the word or phrase closest in meaning to the boldface word. *(10 points each)*

_____ 1. colorful **accessory**
(A) suit
(B) assistant
(C) story
(D) adornment

_____ 2. to **badger** someone
(A) pester
(B) love
(C) dislike
(D) ignore

_____ 3. a careful **calculation**
(A) movement
(B) description
(C) estimation
(D) purchase

_____ 4. a perfect **complement**
(A) tribute
(B) moment
(C) completion
(D) joke

_____ 5. to **convert** the Model T
(A) change
(B) drive
(C) wreck
(D) treasure

_____ 6. her **customary** smile
(A) kindly
(B) shy
(C) usual
(D) helpless

_____ 7. to visit a **gallery**
(A) famous historical site
(B) place filled with paintings
(C) local carnival
(D) government building

_____ 8. afraid to **intervene**
(A) attempt
(B) interfere
(C) audition
(D) refuse

_____ 9. the hero's **valor**
(A) strength
(B) appearance
(C) bravery
(D) deeds

_____ 10. a person's **vitality**
(A) personality
(B) energy
(C) ability
(D) laziness

USING NEW WORDS ON TESTS

Test 6

Directions. In the space provided, write the letter of the word or phrase closest in meaning to the boldface word. *(10 points each)*

_____ **1. adjacent** buildings
   (A) adjoining
   (B) larger
   (C) ancient
   (D) distant

_____ **2.** the work of an **artisan**
   (A) druggist
   (B) student
   (C) psychologist
   (D) craftsperson

_____ **3.** to **attain** success
   (A) desire
   (B) lack
   (C) crave
   (D) achieve

_____ **4.** property of the **deceased**
   (A) wealthy landlord
   (B) dead person
   (C) deathly ill person
   (D) one named in a lawsuit

_____ **5. fragile** dishes
   (A) antique
   (B) expensive
   (C) delicate
   (D) ornamented

_____ **6.** to **glorify** a name
   (A) choose
   (B) forget
   (C) erase
   (D) honor

_____ **7. harmonious** sounds
   (A) agreeable
   (B) bothersome
   (C) frightening
   (D) familiar

_____ **8. incomparable** strength
   (A) matchless
   (B) uncharacteristic
   (C) inferior
   (D) questionable

_____ **9.** a **multicolored** dress
   (A) dark-colored
   (B) snow-white
   (C) many-colored
   (D) light-colored

_____ **10.** to **pulverize** a rock
   (A) push
   (B) remove
   (C) crack
   (D) crush

© Houghton Mifflin Harcourt Publishing Company

USING NEW WORDS ON TESTS

Test 7

Directions. In the space provided, write the letter of the word or phrase closest in meaning to the boldface word. *(10 points each)*

_____ **1.** the **confederation** of states
   (A) honor
   (B) league
   (C) enemy
   (D) equality

_____ **2.** a qualified **delegate**
   (A) attorney
   (B) officer
   (C) teacher
   (D) representative

_____ **3.** **discord** among the members
   (A) loud discussion
   (B) extreme secrecy
   (C) disagreement
   (D) quiet agreement

_____ **4.** a **feline** movement
   (A) rare
   (B) familiar
   (C) catlike
   (D) simple

_____ **5.** to have **foresight**
   (A) a looking forward
   (B) a visual problem
   (C) a moving forward
   (D) poor business sense

_____ **6.** the hermit's **isolation**
   (A) aloneness
   (B) lifestyle
   (C) attitude
   (D) habitat

_____ **7.** to keep a **menagerie**
   (A) collection of animals
   (B) wild beast
   (C) group of assistants
   (D) special souvenir

_____ **8.** an unexplained **phenomenon**
   (A) beautiful scene
   (B) rare occurrence
   (C) strange feeling
   (D) distant star

_____ **9.** to save for **posterity**
   (A) future goals
   (B) an emergency
   (C) next year
   (D) future generations

_____ **10.** an important **revelation**
   (A) reconsideration
   (B) change
   (C) fact
   (D) disclosure

USING NEW WORDS ON TESTS

Test 8

Directions. In the space provided, write the letter of the word or phrase closest in meaning to the boldface word. (*10 points each*)

_____ 1. **adequate** supplies
    (A) outdated
    (B) useful
    (C) sufficient
    (D) unnecessary

_____ 2. **advantageous** positions
    (A) defensive
    (B) thrilling
    (C) unlikely
    (D) favorable

_____ 3. to **descend** the wall
    (A) move down
    (B) climb up
    (C) lean against
    (D) go around

_____ 4. to **enhance** the flavor
    (A) like
    (B) dislike
    (C) increase
    (D) decrease

_____ 5. **gnarled** branches
    (A) slender
    (B) willowy
    (C) knotty
    (D) dead

_____ 6. to **incite** a crowd
    (A) contain
    (B) arouse
    (C) calm
    (D) arrest

_____ 7. **inflexible** views
    (A) odd
    (B) modern
    (C) unknown
    (D) unyielding

_____ 8. to **inherit** a fortune
    (A) find suddenly
    (B) receive by will
    (C) spend freely
    (D) give to a relative

_____ 9. a sense of **menace**
    (A) unhappiness
    (B) threat
    (C) guilt
    (D) happiness

_____ 10. **mutual** mistrust
    (A) unusual
    (B) shared
    (C) earned
    (D) strong

USING NEW WORDS ON TESTS

Test 9

Directions. In the space provided, write the letter of the word or phrase closest in meaning to the boldface word. *(10 points each)*

_____ 1. to **adapt** to change
   (A) adjust
   (B) protest
   (C) refuse
   (D) dislike

_____ 2. based on that **assumption**
   (A) reliable information
   (B) something taken for granted
   (C) scientific guess
   (D) careless error

_____ 3. **basis** for a decision
   (A) foundation
   (B) suggestion
   (C) forethought
   (D) order

_____ 4. a great **controversy**
   (A) party
   (B) agreement
   (C) dispute
   (D) change

_____ 5. to **impel** someone
   (A) reject
   (B) anger
   (C) cure
   (D) urge

_____ 6. a careless **omission**
   (A) something left out
   (B) use of the facts
   (C) plan of action
   (D) person assigned to a task

_____ 7. to write a **petition**
   (A) play
   (B) request
   (C) novel
   (D) refusal

_____ 8. **potential** savings
   (A) great
   (B) small
   (C) impossible
   (D) possible

_____ 9. **primitive** cultures
   (A) foreign
   (B) modern
   (C) earlier
   (D) uninteresting

_____ 10. to **restore** an antique
   (A) return to a former condition
   (B) put away in a safe place
   (C) discard immediately
   (D) sell at a profit

USING NEW WORDS ON TESTS

Test 10

Directions. In the space provided, write the letter of the word or phrase closest in meaning to the boldface word. *(10 points each)*

_____ 1. for five **consecutive** days
   (A) busy
   (B) long
   (C) interrupted
   (D) successive

_____ 2. **creative** ideas
   (A) silly
   (B) reasonable
   (C) original
   (D) forgotten

_____ 3. a singer's **diction**
   (A) music
   (B) pronunciation
   (C) voice
   (D) performance

_____ 4. **durable** merchandise
   (A) easy-to-use
   (B) unreliable
   (C) long-lasting
   (D) well-known

_____ 5. her **feasible** plan
   (A) unusual
   (B) possible
   (C) foolish
   (D) impossible

_____ 6. a **hilarious** play
   (A) boring
   (B) popular
   (C) funny
   (D) sad

_____ 7. an **immense** task
   (A) easy
   (B) difficult
   (C) limited
   (D) enormous

_____ 8. **ingenious** plans
   (A) outdated
   (B) clever
   (C) foolish
   (D) impossible

_____ 9. an **insoluble** mystery
   (A) unsolvable
   (B) exciting
   (C) uninteresting
   (D) imaginative

_____ 10. a frightening **ordeal**
   (A) memory
   (B) novel
   (C) experience
   (D) message

USING NEW WORDS ON TESTS

Test 11

Directions. In the space provided, write the letter of the word or phrase closest in meaning to the boldface word. *(10 points each)*

_____ 1. a wealthy **aristocrat**
   (A) member of a secret society
   (B) citizen of a foreign country
   (C) member of Parliament
   (D) member of the nobility

_____ 2. to fight **censorship**
   (A) judging and sentencing
   (B) removing and destroying
   (C) examining and removing
   (D) copying and editing

_____ 3. to wait a **decade**
   (A) long time
   (B) ten-year period
   (C) ten-minute period
   (D) short time

_____ 4. to **deport** a felon
   (A) rescue from death row
   (B) send to another country
   (C) give shelter to
   (D) sentence to prison time

_____ 5. forced to **emigrate**
   (A) remain
   (B) return
   (C) relocate
   (D) release

_____ 6. tragedy of **famine**
   (A) widespread shortage of food
   (B) widespread fatal disease
   (C) widespread shortage of water
   (D) widespread annual flooding

_____ 7. to suffer from **malnutrition**
   (A) severe dizziness
   (B) poor nourishment
   (C) extreme neglect
   (D) nervous disease

_____ 8. good **morale**
   (A) main idea
   (B) course of action
   (C) level of energy
   (D) state of mind

_____ 9. heartening **optimism**
   (A) total agreement
   (B) sunny weather
   (C) good news
   (D) expectation of the best

_____ 10. a place of **refuge**
   (A) punishment
   (B) beauty
   (C) shelter
   (D) danger

USING NEW WORDS ON TESTS

Test 12

Directions. In the space provided, write the letter of the word or phrase closest in meaning to the boldface word. *(10 points each)*

____ **1.** feelings of **anxiety**
   (A) worry
   (B) anger
   (C) great joy
   (D) tenderness

____ **2.** to **boycott** a product
   (A) purchase in quantity
   (B) refuse to buy
   (C) order in advance
   (D) use wisely

____ **3.** a **burly** athlete
   (A) good-looking
   (B) highly skilled
   (C) well-known
   (D) big and strong

____ **4.** to address a **multitude**
   (A) great crowd
   (B) few people
   (C) loyal following
   (D) single individual

____ **5.** to reveal your **nationality**
   (A) choice of candidates
   (B) patriotic song
   (C) nation of origin
   (D) military strength

____ **6.** his **naturalization** papers
   (A) business
   (B) immigration
   (C) government
   (D) citizenship

____ **7.** one **predicament** after another
   (A) run of good luck
   (B) distressing situation
   (C) good-natured joke
   (D) false tale

____ **8.** to spread **propaganda**
   (A) large amounts of information
   (B) good cheer
   (C) bad feelings
   (D) ideas to help a cause

____ **9.** to remain **resolute**
   (A) important
   (B) determined
   (C) unhappy
   (D) silly

____ **10.** the **urban** landscape
   (A) city
   (B) country
   (C) peaceful
   (D) foreign

USING NEW WORDS ON TESTS

Test 13

Directions. In the space provided, write the letter of the word or phrase closest in meaning to the boldface word. *(10 points each)*

_____ 1. an **accessible** neighbor
    (A) approachable
    (B) nosy
    (C) familiar
    (D) wise

_____ 2. the **bankrupt** business
    (A) illegal
    (B) established
    (C) impoverished
    (D) successful

_____ 3. the **boisterous** crowd
    (A) rowdy
    (B) young
    (C) large
    (D) small

_____ 4. **dilapidated** buildings
    (A) falling to pieces
    (B) out-of-date
    (C) sturdily built
    (D) old-fashioned

_____ 5. **fraudulent** schemes
    (A) original
    (B) dishonest
    (C) failed
    (D) odd

_____ 6. **hospitable** treatment
    (A) cruel and unjust
    (B) unfair and unequal
    (C) open and receptive
    (D) medically superior

_____ 7. her **impulsive** decision
    (A) spontaneous
    (B) thoughtful
    (C) final
    (D) important

_____ 8. to attend the **premiere**
    (A) gala event
    (B) celebrity party
    (C) first act
    (D) first performance

_____ 9. the **riotous** crowd
    (A) large
    (B) disorderly
    (C) angry
    (D) calm

_____ 10. merchandise in **transit**
    (A) storage
    (B) stores
    (C) passage
    (D) warehouse

USING NEW WORDS ON TESTS

Test 14

Directions. In the space provided, write the letter of the word or phrase closest in meaning to the boldface word. *(10 points each)*

____ 1. **acceptance** of a belief
   (A) approval
   (B) disapproval
   (C) statement
   (D) explanation

____ 2. to **circulate** a rumor
   (A) hear
   (B) create
   (C) spread
   (D) ignore

____ 3. tendency toward **exaggeration**
   (A) error
   (B) identification
   (C) excuse
   (D) overstatement

____ 4. to **grieve** for a loss
   (A) have disregard
   (B) feel sorrow
   (C) take into account
   (D) make up

____ 5. to decide to **immigrate**
   (A) enter and settle
   (B) move away from
   (C) move around
   (D) enter a contest

____ 6. the **intensity** of a storm
   (A) winds
   (B) rainfall
   (C) fear
   (D) strength

____ 7. a scene of **jubilation**
   (A) confusion
   (B) sadness
   (C) celebration
   (D) interest

____ 8. the **privilege** of voting
   (A) civil right
   (B) punishment by confinement
   (C) legal requirement
   (D) peculiar custom

____ 9. to **prosecute** in court
   (A) make a plan of action
   (B) take legal action against
   (C) to bring a judgment against
   (D) receive a verdict

____ 10. plants that **thrive**
   (A) require care
   (B) produce food
   (C) grow vigorously
   (D) do poorly

USING NEW WORDS ON TESTS

Test 15

Directions. In the space provided, write the letter of the word or phrase closest in meaning to the boldface word. *(10 points each)*

_____ 1. to **dedicate** a lifetime
   (A) waste
   (B) devote
   (C) treasure
   (D) live fully

_____ 2. to **depose** someone
   (A) remove from office
   (B) gain respect for
   (C) elect to office
   (D) support in office

_____ 3. to **dispense** forms
   (A) create
   (B) distribute
   (C) complete
   (D) withhold

_____ 4. to **dissect** the problem
   (A) cause
   (B) ignore
   (C) analyze
   (D) recognize

_____ 5. requiring tremendous **exertion**
   (A) ability
   (B) dislike
   (C) enjoyment
   (D) effort

_____ 6. a **haven** for a ship
   (A) payment
   (B) course
   (C) harbor
   (D) cargo

_____ 7. the degree of **humidity**
   (A) cold
   (B) moisture
   (C) heat
   (D) dryness

_____ 8. the child's **memento**
   (A) plaything
   (B) souvenir
   (C) memory
   (D) friend

_____ 9. to **restrain** the horse
   (A) control
   (B) overwork
   (C) race
   (D) walk

_____ 10. the crowd's **tumult**
   (A) size
   (B) demand
   (C) commotion
   (D) orderliness

USING NEW WORDS ON TESTS

Test 16

Directions. In the space provided, write the letter of the word or phrase closest in meaning to the boldface word. *(10 points each)*

_____ 1. a **hamper** of food
   (A) lack
   (B) variety
   (C) lot
   (D) basket

_____ 2. an **imperative** request
   (A) demanding
   (B) unreasonable
   (C) unnecessary
   (D) usual

_____ 3. to **impose** a tax
   (A) remove
   (B) pay
   (C) inflict
   (D) increase

_____ 4. **inconsiderate** remarks
   (A) impatient
   (B) thoughtless
   (C) written
   (D) unrehearsed

_____ 5. to **intercept** a messenger
   (A) hire
   (B) stop
   (C) send
   (D) assist

_____ 6. **liable** for damages
   (A) legally responsible
   (B) regularly critized
   (C) not responsible
   (D) legally prepared

_____ 7. **negligent** about details
   (A) careless
   (B) responsible
   (C) exact
   (D) interested

_____ 8. to **presume** something
   (A) do without
   (B) examine and remove
   (C) take for granted
   (D) need immediately

_____ 9. to **recuperate** slowly
   (A) resolve
   (B) recover
   (C) rebound
   (D) remove

_____ 10. a **spacious** apartment
   (A) roomy
   (B) decorated
   (C) small
   (D) modern

USING NEW WORDS ON TESTS

Test 17

Directions. In the space provided, write the letter of the word or phrase closest in meaning to the boldface word. *(10 points each)*

_____ **1.** a tantalizing **aroma**
   (A) sight
   (B) fragrance
   (C) offer
   (D) wish

_____ **2.** business **capital**
   (A) executive decision
   (B) annual plan
   (C) total wealth
   (D) money borrowed

_____ **3.** **elegant** furnishings
   (A) cheap and showy
   (B) unusual and expensive
   (C) modest and refined
   (D) tasteful and luxurious

_____ **4.** the **frequency** of occurrence
   (A) number of times
   (B) surprising fact
   (C) constant expectation
   (D) unusual possibility

_____ **5.** her **gracious** act
   (A) courteous
   (B) wicked
   (C) unfriendly
   (D) thankless

_____ **6.** a **haughty** person
   (A) friendly
   (B) well-qualified
   (C) conceited
   (D) well-known

_____ **7.** the **manageable** class
   (A) unsupervised
   (B) high-level
   (C) enjoyable
   (D) controllable

_____ **8.** to have a powerful **monopoly**
   (A) exclusive control
   (B) industrial machine
   (C) business leader
   (D) ability to succeed

_____ **9.** a former **occupant**
   (A) one who lives in
   (B) one who rents
   (C) one who sells
   (D) one who sues

_____ **10.** a period of **probation**
   (A) rain
   (B) trial
   (C) thought
   (D) peace

USING NEW WORDS ON TESTS

Test 18

Directions. In the space provided, write the letter of the word or phrase closest in meaning to the boldface word. *(10 points each)*

_____ 1. to **baste** a chicken
   (A) pluck
   (B) feed
   (C) moisten
   (D) raise

_____ 2. to **diminish** in number
   (A) increase
   (B) decrease
   (C) vary
   (D) peak

_____ 3. to **dismantle** something
   (A) completely repair
   (B) make unfit
   (C) resist openly
   (D) tear down

_____ 4. to **embarrass** a friend
   (A) embrace fondly
   (B) ask a favor of
   (C) apologize to
   (D) cause to feel awkward

_____ 5. to **populate** a colony
   (A) begin
   (B) attack
   (C) inhabit
   (D) surrender

_____ 6. to **prearrange** it
   (A) arrange in advance
   (B) forget to arrange
   (C) arrange well
   (D) arrange poorly

_____ 7. some **remote** cabin
   (A) out-of-the-way
   (B) comfortable
   (C) primitive
   (D) run-down

_____ 8. a **rigid** pole
   (A) flexible
   (B) wooden
   (C) stiff
   (D) short

_____ 9. to **saturate** the sponge
   (A) squeeze
   (B) soak
   (C) clean
   (D) discard

_____ 10. a **sedate** group of people
   (A) quiet
   (B) irritable
   (C) well-known
   (D) well-informed

USING NEW WORDS ON TESTS

Test 19

Directions. In the space provided, write the letter of the word or phrase closest in meaning to the boldface word. *(10 points each)*

_____ 1. to have **access**
   (A) too much
   (B) not enough
   (C) entrance
   (D) an excuse

_____ 2. comfortable **accommodations**
   (A) seats
   (B) income
   (C) lodgings
   (D) clothing

_____ 3. to **circumnavigate** the world
   (A) travel across
   (B) be the first to explore
   (C) study the cultures of
   (D) travel around

_____ 4. to **evacuate** the building
   (A) vacate
   (B) invade
   (C) rebulid
   (D) repair

_____ 5. to **liberate** the prisoners
   (A) capture
   (B) hold
   (C) lecture
   (D) release

_____ 6. to **notify** of a change
   (A) inform
   (B) disapprove
   (C) feel the effect
   (D) notice the result

_____ 7. to exchange a **pleasantry**
   (A) friendly smile
   (B) special gift
   (C) rude comment
   (D) polite remark

_____ 8. a **provision** of food
   (A) purchase
   (B) barrel
   (C) dislike
   (D) supply

_____ 9. a harsh **regime**
   (A) opponent
   (B) government
   (C) law
   (D) climate

_____ 10. to feel **remorse**
   (A) reliance
   (B) regret
   (C) relief
   (D) restless

USING NEW WORDS ON TESTS

Test 20

Directions. In the space provided, write the letter of the word or phrase closest in meaning to the boldface word. *(10 points each)*

_____ 1. **adept** at writing
 (A) unfair
 (B) unskilled
 (C) skilled
 (D) experienced

_____ 2. **dingy** clothes
 (A) snow-white
 (B) secondhand
 (C) old-fashioned
 (D) dirty-looking

_____ 3. a **disagreeable** mood
 (A) bubbly
 (B) despairing
 (C) unpleasant
 (D) thoughtful

_____ 4. to **humiliate** an enemy
 (A) defeat
 (B) release
 (C) capture
 (D) embarrass

_____ 5. to **jeopardize** the plan
 (A) make
 (B) threaten
 (C) finance
 (D) improve

_____ 6. **maroon** socks
 (A) navy blue
 (B) blue-green
 (C) dark brown
 (D) purplish red

_____ 7. **persistent** coughing
 (A) bothersome
 (B) harmful
 (C) occasional
 (D) continuing

_____ 8. **thrifty** homeowners
 (A) proud
 (B) hardworking
 (C) frugal
 (D) careful

_____ 9. the **titanic** spaceship
 (A) atomic
 (B) imaginary
 (C) enormous
 (D) large

_____ 10. to **verify** the fact
 (A) check
 (B) believe
 (C) ignore
 (D) state

USING NEW WORDS ON TESTS

Test 21

Directions. In the space provided, write the letter of the word or phrase closest in meaning to the boldface word. (10 points each)

_____ **1.** a great **aspiration**
(A) ambition
(B) joy
(C) plan
(D) failure

_____ **2.** a skilled **diplomat**
(A) worker
(B) boss
(C) representative
(D) student

_____ **3.** the **foreword** to the book
(A) illustrations
(B) copyright
(C) index
(D) introduction

_____ **4.** to read the **obituary**
(A) poem in praise
(B) local news article
(C) public notice of death
(D) feature article

_____ **5.** to meet the **premier**
(A) local celebrity
(B) prime minister
(C) movie producer
(D) supreme court judge

_____ **6.** to make a **pun**
(A) dinner roll
(B) silly joke
(C) play on words
(D) lengthy speech

_____ **7.** **sable** cloth
(A) black
(B) white
(C) yellow
(D) blue

_____ **8.** offered a **salutation**
(A) sample
(B) suggestion
(C) greeting
(D) meal

_____ **9.** the novel's **satire**
(A) well-developed plot
(B) sarcastic wit
(C) main theme
(D) critical acceptance

_____ **10.** eliminate a **tariff**
(A) new law
(B) strict code
(C) tax on an import
(D) tax on luxuries

USING NEW WORDS ON TESTS

Test 22

Directions. In the space provided, write the letter of the word or phrase closest in meaning to the boldface word. *(10 points each)*

_____ **1.** to **blockade** the harbor
 (A) obstruct
 (B) enter
 (C) build
 (D) admire

_____ **2.** to **confiscate** the goods
 (A) seize
 (B) purchase
 (C) examine
 (D) want

_____ **3.** to **generate** enthusiasm
 (A) maintain
 (B) lose
 (C) recognize
 (D) produce

_____ **4.** the **indelible** impression
 (A) favorable
 (B) permanent
 (C) sudden
 (D) false

_____ **5.** a **neutral** opinion
 (A) attempting to understand
 (B) lacking concern
 (C) taking no sides
 (D) showing agreement

_____ **6.** **obscure** places
 (A) hidden
 (B) strange
 (C) uninteresting
 (D) different

_____ **7.** **pewter** dishes
 (A) leaded glass
 (B) very expensive
 (C) tin alloy
 (D) silver-plated

_____ **8.** **quaint** houses
 (A) flimsy and run-down
 (B) unusual and charming
 (C) remodeled and refurnished
 (D) modern and split-level

_____ **9.** to **quench** her thirst
 (A) remember
 (B) satisfy
 (C) ignore
 (D) intensify

_____ **10.** the **urgent** request
 (A) insistent
 (B) unimportant
 (C) ridiculous
 (D) unreasonable

USING NEW WORDS ON TESTS

T est 23

Directions. In the space provided, write the letter of the word or phrase closest in meaning to the boldface word. *(10 points each)*

_____ 1. to **activate** the machine
(A) design
(B) start
(C) repair
(D) break

_____ 2. **charitable** contributions
(A) highly unusual
(B) very expensive
(C) given by the rich
(D) generous to the needy

_____ 3. **colossal** mistakes
(A) careless
(B) unimportant
(C) gigantic
(D) financial

_____ 4. to **confide** a secret
(A) learn of
(B) listen carefully to
(C) repeat to another
(D) entrust with

_____ 5. **eccentric** behavior
(A) brave
(B) good
(C) odd
(D) terrible

_____ 6. an **intolerance** of weakness
(A) prejudice
(B) understanding
(C) ignorance
(D) investigation

_____ 7. **invariable** truths
(A) typical
(B) unchanging
(C) confusing
(D) ordinary

_____ 8. a **petty** remark
(A) spiteful
(B) pleasant
(C) humorous
(D) loud

_____ 9. **pious** people
(A) devout
(B) angry
(C) fearful
(D) awkward

_____ 10. to **tarnish** the family honor
(A) disgrace
(B) defend
(C) ignore
(D) prove

USING NEW WORDS ON TESTS

Test 24

Directions. In the space provided, write the letter of the word or phrase closest in meaning to the boldface word. *(10 points each)*

_____ **1.** **apt** to cause blindness
(A) likely
(B) certain
(C) unlikely
(D) quick

_____ **2.** to **clarify** the statement
(A) make understandable
(B) make confusing
(C) make important
(D) make memorable

_____ **3.** to solve by **deduction**
(A) reasoned conclusion
(B) sheer luck
(C) questioning witnesses
(D) stating the problem

_____ **4.** to write the **essay**
(A) long poem
(B) interesting story
(C) business letter
(D) prose composition

_____ **5.** to **irk** the leader
(A) ignore
(B) assist
(C) annoy
(D) hurry

_____ **6.** to support the **proposal**
(A) problem
(B) plan
(C) result
(D) treatment

_____ **7.** disliked his **sarcasm**
(A) rude behavior
(B) sharp remark
(C) unpleasant expression
(D) thoughtless remark

_____ **8.** the president's **successor**
(A) one who opposes
(B) one who assists
(C) one who follows
(D) one who precedes

_____ **9.** the **summit** of her career
(A) beginning
(B) peak
(C) conclusion
(D) challenge

_____ **10.** an uncertain **temperament**
(A) disposition
(B) result
(C) schedule
(D) storm

USING NEW WORDS ON TESTS

Test 25

Directions. In the space provided, write the letter of the word or phrase closest in meaning to the boldface word. (*10 points each*)

_____ 1. to be **anonymous**
   (A) healthy
   (B) angry
   (C) nameless
   (D) happy

_____ 2. their **casual** meeting
   (A) fortunate
   (B) planned
   (C) informal
   (D) regular

_____ 3. the story's **climax**
   (A) hidden meaning
   (B) point of greatest intensity
   (C) complicated plot
   (D) colorful descriptions

_____ 4. a **contemporary** writer
   (A) good
   (B) famous
   (C) living
   (D) popular

_____ 5. the **famished** birds
   (A) noisy
   (B) starving
   (C) hunted
   (D) crowding

_____ 6. his **fictitious** account
   (A) newspaper
   (B) endless
   (C) published
   (D) imaginary

_____ 7. to **fragment** the glass
   (A) break into pieces
   (B) look through
   (C) cut to size
   (D) look behind

_____ 8. the **literal** interpretation
   (A) lengthy
   (B) likely
   (C) mysterious
   (D) exact

_____ 9. an unusual **occurrence**
   (A) test
   (B) trial
   (C) sale
   (D) happening

_____ 10. to get **therapy** for his back
   (A) support
   (B) bedrest
   (C) medicine
   (D) treatment

USING NEW WORDS ON TESTS

Test 26

Directions. In the space provided, write the letter of the word or phrase closest in meaning to the boldface word. *(10 points each)*

_____ **1.** to **condemn** a person
  (A) convict
  (B) defend
  (C) forgive
  (D) avoid

_____ **2.** to **dictate** to someone
  (A) give orders
  (B) be helpful
  (C) be rude
  (D) give trouble

_____ **3.** to **dilute** the soup
  (A) eat
  (B) discard
  (C) thicken
  (D) thin

_____ **4.** to **dispatch** a message
  (A) ignore
  (B) lose
  (C) send
  (D) dictate

_____ **5.** to **emphasize** the importance
  (A) stress
  (B) recognize
  (C) lessen
  (D) determine

_____ **6.** to **endorse** the candidate
  (A) elect
  (B) oppose
  (C) support
  (D) defeat

_____ **7.** to **falter** slightly
  (A) cough
  (B) smile
  (C) wave
  (D) hesitate

_____ **8.** to **improvise** a tune
  (A) rehearse several times
  (B) sing off-key
  (C) sing in a high pitch
  (D) compose without preparation

_____ **9.** involved in **intrigue**
  (A) strenuous exercise
  (B) a government mission
  (C) unusual work
  (D) secret planning

_____ **10.** to **modify** actions
  (A) observe
  (B) alter
  (C) criticize
  (D) explain

USING NEW WORDS ON TESTS

Test 27

Directions. In the space provided, write the letter of the word or phrase closest in meaning to the boldface word. *(10 points each)*

_____ **1.** the most **articulate** argument
(A) carefully studied
(B) carefully prepared
(C) clearly spoken
(D) long-lasting

_____ **2.** a **category** of books
(A) list
(B) library
(C) pile
(D) classification

_____ **3.** to **demolish** a house
(A) rent
(B) ruin
(C) repair
(D) beautify

_____ **4.** a **denial** of the request
(A) rephrasing
(B) rejection
(C) copy
(D) basis

_____ **5.** to **detach** from the rest
(A) differ
(B) separate
(C) unglue
(D) take

_____ **6.** to drive me to **distraction**
(A) a better location
(B) seek help
(C) mental distress
(D) a point of departure

_____ **7.** to **illuminate** a point
(A) clarify
(B) confuse
(C) eliminate
(D) accept

_____ **8.** a slight **inclination**
(A) dislike
(B) motion
(C) tendency
(D) wind

_____ **9.** to **testify** against
(A) listen to evidence
(B) give evidence
(C) argue evidence
(D) ignore evidence

_____ **10.** to **upbraid** the child
(A) be concerned about
(B) speak loudly to
(C) criticize sharply
(D) refuse to tell

USING NEW WORDS ON TESTS

Test 28

Directions. In the space provided, write the letter of the word or phrase closest in meaning to the boldface word. *(10 points each)*

_____ **1.** always the **braggart**
(A) generous person
(B) boastful person
(C) helpful person
(D) fussy person

_____ **2.** to **derive** enjoyment
(A) get
(B) lose
(C) desire
(D) neglect

_____ **3.** **eligible** to vote
(A) eager
(B) not fit
(C) too young
(D) qualified

_____ **4.** **extensive** knowledge
(A) limited
(B) vast
(C) average
(D) specific

_____ **5.** to **imply** guilt
(A) prove
(B) disprove
(C) suggest
(D) forgive

_____ **6.** **miscellaneous** tools
(A) useful
(B) useless
(C) assorted
(D) few

_____ **7.** a **secluded** spot
(A) crowded
(B) isolated
(C) familiar
(D) pleasant

_____ **8.** a **superficial** examination
(A) shallow
(B) careful
(C) lengthy
(D) scientific

_____ **9.** **tangible** evidence
(A) unimportant
(B) necessary
(C) concrete
(D) pleasing

_____ **10.** the **unique** jewel
(A) beautiful
(B) one-of-a-kind
(C) valuable
(D) many-colored

USING NEW WORDS ON TESTS

Test 29

Directions. In the space provided, write the letter of the word or phrase closest in meaning to the boldface word. *(10 points each)*

_____ 1. an **arrogant** person
   (A) meek
   (B) angry
   (C) overbearing
   (D) dangerous

_____ 2. to **commute** a sentence
   (A) change to less severe
   (B) analyze the parts of
   (C) review the details of
   (D) enforce the details of

_____ 3. to **congest** the exit
   (A) widen
   (B) clog
   (C) repair
   (D) close

_____ 4. a **considerate** father
   (A) proud
   (B) thoughtful
   (C) strict
   (D) puzzled

_____ 5. an interesting **hypothesis**
   (A) unproven theory
   (B) legal theory
   (C) strong wish
   (D) military maneuver

_____ 6. **malfunction** of the brakes
   (A) repair
   (B) failure
   (C) replacement
   (D) liner

_____ 7. receive a **rebate**
   (A) hint
   (B) chance
   (C) price
   (D) refund

_____ 8. **synthetic** fibers
   (A) artificial
   (B) very strong
   (C) natural
   (D) expensive

_____ 9. world-wide **technology**
   (A) applied science
   (B) ignorance of the future
   (C) changing lifestyles
   (D) plans for the future

_____ 10. a one-year **warranty**
   (A) vacation
   (B) trial
   (C) plan
   (D) guarantee

USING NEW WORDS ON TESTS

Test 30

Directions. In the space provided, write the letter of the word or phrase closest in meaning to the boldface word. *(10 points each)*

_____ 1. expert in **aeronautics**
    (A) ship design
    (B) aircraft design
    (C) study of language
    (D) study of disease

_____ 2. an **agenda** for the meeting
    (A) items of business
    (B) list of expenses
    (C) list of speakers
    (D) budget review

_____ 3. to take **antibiotics**
    (A) medicines
    (B) temperatures
    (C) vitamins
    (D) breaks

_____ 4. a useful **automaton**
    (A) appliance
    (B) vehicle
    (C) robot
    (D) helper

_____ 5. **erosion** of the hillside
    (A) gorgeous view
    (B) building up
    (C) gradual slope
    (D) wearing away

_____ 6. the **hydraulic** press
    (A) electric-operated
    (B) water-operated
    (C) hand-operated
    (D) run-down

_____ 7. a **parasitic** person
    (A) extremely funny
    (B) highly educated
    (C) free-spirited
    (D) living at others' expense

_____ 8. **photogenic** faces
    (A) very frightened
    (B) full of expression
    (C) suitable for photographing
    (D) never photographed

_____ 9. to visit a **planetarium**
    (A) health and exercise facility
    (B) general hospital
    (C) building for viewing stars
    (D) large, open greenhouse

_____ 10. checked his **respiration**
    (A) heartbeat
    (B) watch
    (C) breathing
    (D) schedule

Tests 1–3

USING NEW WORDS ON TESTS

Test 1 | CONTEXT: The American Indians

Making New Words Your Own   Lessons 1–10
Understanding New Words and Their Uses   Lessons 1–5
Connecting New Words and Patterns   Lessons 1–5
Reading New Words in Context   Lessons 1–5

PART A • Studying American Indian Cultures
Context Clues

Directions. From the list below, choose the word that best completes the sentence. Write the word in the blank. You will use each word only once. *(1 point each)*

assumption	calamity	ecology	fragile
attain	confederation	enhance	harmonious
badger	convert	feasible	inherit
baffle	customary	folklore	nourish
basis	deceased	foresight	posterity

1. "The unit we have just finished was designed to improve, or _____, your understanding of American Indian culture," says Mr. Henderson.

2. "It has become _____ in this class for me to give you a chance to discuss a unit when we've finished it. So, let's close this unit in the usual way. What did you like best?"

3. Latrice says, "I was interested in how Hiawatha was able to _____ the goal of having all the Five Nations form a league. Reaching that goal was really an amazing achievement."

4. Marshall adds, "That _____ of nations interested me, too. I thought it was especially interesting that their union was a sort of model for our nation."

5. "I thought it was interesting to hear how missionaries tried to _____ American Indians to Christianity," Timothy says.

6. "My _____ had been that all the American Indian nations were much the same," says Chico, "so I was really surprised to discover how different they were."

7. "I liked studying the _____ more than anything else," says Sunni. "I've always been fascinated by myth and legend."

8. Paula agrees, "I liked the stories about animals—especially the story about the bear and the one about the _____."

9. "I liked the story of White Buffalo Calf Woman who came to the Dakota people in a time of misery and _____ and showed them how to follow the Good Red Road," Liz adds.

10. "I am fascinated by the Cherokee story of Old Grandmother who became corn in order to _____ the starving people," says Sunni.

11. "I'm most impressed by the understanding the American Indians had of the relationships between living things and their environment. They had a good understanding of _____," Kim remarks.

12. "Most American Indians seemed to have a _____ relationship with the natural world. They knew they were one of many parts of the natural order, where everything had a place," Paula offers.

13. "Yes, and they recognized that because the balance in nature was _____, it was easy to destroy. They worked to preserve it," adds Mike.

14. "I was impressed with the _____ American Indians showed by planning for the future," says Latrice.

15. "Clearly, they intended for future generations to _____ a world that was undamaged," Latrice continues.

16. "Is it really true that some nations made many decisions based on how they would affect the next seven generations?" asks Ashley. "Did they really plan for _____?"

17. "Yes," says Mr. Henderson. "Concern for the future was often the _____ on which decisions were made."

18. "You can see why European ways would _____ the American Indians. They must have thought that Europeans were very strange," says Eric.

19. "Do you realize that we have been discussing only the people who lived in the past, people who are now _____?" asks Liz.

20. "I'm glad it's possible for us to learn about American Indians in the past," says Latrice. "Would it also be _____ for us to study American Indians of today?"

Like Meanings

Directions. For each item below, circle the letter of the choice that means the same, or about the same, as the boldface word. *(1 point each)*

21. a permanent **alliance**
    - (A) location
    - (B) agreement
    - (C) condition
    - (D) position

22. a **contagious** disease
    - (A) common
    - (B) harmless
    - (C) fatal
    - (D) catching

23. to **deceive** the enemy
    - (A) trick
    - (B) avoid
    - (C) fight
    - (D) stop

24. a grassy **knoll**
    - (A) small hill
    - (B) fertile plain
    - (C) large field
    - (D) large hill

25. the **advent** of the season
    - (A) middle
    - (B) trip
    - (C) arrival
    - (D) highlight

26. a major **catastrophe**
    - (A) holiday
    - (B) disaster
    - (C) talent
    - (D) adventure

27. **intelligible** directions
    - (A) confusing
    - (B) unspoken
    - (C) understandable
    - (D) brilliant

28. a woman of **integrity**
    - (A) intelligence
    - (B) honesty
    - (C) friendship
    - (D) talent

29. an interesting **accessory**
    - (A) useful
    - (B) crime
    - (C) loss
    - (D) attachment

30. the **adjacent** land
    - (A) adjoining
    - (B) expensive
    - (C) distant
    - (D) beautiful

Opposite Meanings

Directions. For each item below, circle the letter of the choice that means the opposite, or about the opposite, of the boldface word. *(1 point each)*

31. an **eminent** author
- (A) distinguished
- (B) dead
- (C) retired
- (D) unimportant

32. an **intentional** act
- (A) unplanned
- (B) purposeful
- (C) worldwide
- (D) local

33. an unbelievable **ordeal**
- (A) enjoyable experience
- (B) painful experience
- (C) difficult experience
- (D) distressing experience

34. having a **mystical** meaning
- (A) mysterious
- (B) special
- (C) ordinary
- (D) sacred

35. a **ferocious** animal
- (A) gentle
- (B) foreign
- (C) rare
- (D) dangerous

36. to **glorify** the event
- (A) praise
- (B) understand
- (C) ridicule
- (D) attend

37. a woman of **valor**
- (A) courage
- (B) strength
- (C) money
- (D) cowardice

38. a man of **vitality**
- (A) faith
- (B) energy
- (C) idleness
- (D) honesty

39. an **adequate** defense
- (A) insufficient
- (B) suitable
- (C) complicated
- (D) unusual

40. an **advantageous** position
- (A) useless
- (B) small
- (C) large
- (D) helpful

Word Analysis

Directions. Read each numbered pair of words below. Then, circle the letter of the choice that best describes the meaning of the underlined prefix or suffix as it is used in each pair. *(1 point each)*

41. hilari<u>ous</u>　courage<u>ous</u>
   (A) opposite of
   (B) filled with
   (C) study of
   (D) result of

42. <u>mis</u>deed　<u>mis</u>match
   (A) many
   (B) bad
   (C) partly
   (D before

43. barbar<u>ism</u>　hero<u>ism</u>
   (A) somewhat
   (B) like
   (C) in the direction of
   (D) belief or practice of

Directions. For each of the following items, circle the letter of the word that correctly completes the sentence. *(1 point each)*

44. The Latin word *sanctus*, meaning "sacred," will help you understand the meaning of
   (A) posterity
   (B) sincerity
   (C) sanctuary
   (D) isolation

45. The Latin word *pulvis*, meaning "powder," will help you understand the meaning of
   (A) posterity
   (B) pulverize
   (C) provision
   (D) pun

46. The Greek word *myrios*, meaning "countless," will help you understand the meaning of
   (A) mutual
   (B) mystical
   (C) myriad
   (D) nourish

Multimeaning

Directions. Read each numbered sentence below. Then, circle the letter of the choice that uses the boldface word in the same way it is used in the numbered sentence. *(1 point each)*

47. The Plains Indians found it difficult to **sustain** themselves after the bison were destroyed.
- (A) Today, most people would **sustain** the Indians' objection to the slaughter of the bison.
- (B) A single herd of buffalo could **sustain** hundreds of Indians by serving as a source of food, clothing, shelter, and fuel.
- (C) This would not be the only hardship that the Plains Indians would **sustain**.
- (D) The disappearance of the buffalo herds forced the Indians to **sustain** a major loss.

48. We can never be sure what the first, or **primitive,** culture in North America was.
- (A) By today's standards, the traditional dwellings of American Indians may seem **primitive,** but they were actually very ingenious.
- (B) The Navajo artist painted in the **primitive** style.
- (C) Because of this, art critics referred to him as a **primitive**.
- (D) Perhaps a single group of **primitive** myths influenced the later myths of different American Indian groups.

49. Mr. Henderson explains, "The position taken by the U.S. government at one time seemed to be to **abuse** the rights of American Indians."
- (A) "One prime example of the **abuse** of power by the U.S. government was the Trail of Tears."
- (B) "As the Cherokee traveled the miles from the southeast United States to Oklahoma, they were subjected to much **abuse** by the soldiers and the harsh conditions."
- (C) "Soldiers who cursed at and struck the Cherokee considered such **abuse** acceptable."
- (D) A student asks, "What was the point? I mean, why was it acceptable to **abuse** these people? It doesn't make sense."

50. Studying about reservation life will **complement** the unit on American cultures.
- (A) We now have a **complement** of books and films we can use to study American Indian life. We won't need any more research materials.
- (B) Unfortunately, we don't have time to study the entire **complement** of American Indian cultures.
- (C) This book will **complement** our study of Plains Indians better than that other one.
- (D) That film we saw was the perfect **complement** to our reading about the Trail of Tears.

PART B • More About American Indians
Context Clues

Directions. From the list below, choose the word that best completes the sentence. Write the word in the blank. You will use each word only once. *(1 point each)*

adapt	defy	inevitable	probable
appalling	discord	inflexible	restore
bewilder	epidemic	menace	romantic
controversy	immense	pacify	sincerity
creative	impel	potential	strategy

51. I have an idea for a novel that I think has _____—it might develop into something good.

52. In the book, a Navajo woman returns to her reservation after medical school. Life on the reservation is very different from what she has been used to, but she does her best to _____ to it.

53. She finds herself involved in a family _____, a debate with her grandfather, a healer, about how to treat patients.

54. In addition to _____, or strife, in the family, she discovers some problems on the reservation. The novel's plot will involve a company that has spilled toxic waste in the reservation's water supply.

55. Most of the people she knows find this act horrifying, or _____.

56. They see the company's action not only as a threat to the environment but also as a(n) _____ to the community.

57. They want to do something before the problems become _____ and spread too quickly to manage.

58. As a doctor, the main character works hard to _____ the good health of her patients who were made ill by the incident.

59. The reservation is _____—thousands of square miles—and I'd have to make her a character who is always curious about what is going on so it's not surprising that she would be driving all over the reservation.

60. I want the reader of my book to believe that it is _____, or likely, that she would get involved in a campaign to end the threat to the reservation.

61. There is ample reason to _____ her to get involved, to motivate her to help save the reservation.

62. As a doctor, the main character does not have a very _____ view of the world. She is realistic and does not have high hopes for changing the state of the reservation's water supply.

63. Still, she believes her people have the right to clean water, and she plots her _____ for exposing the company's illegal dumping of waste.

64. The main character's actions will _____ her grandfather, who loves his granddaughter but can't understand her.

65. The grandfather is not totally _____, but he is somewhat set in his ways.

66. The main character will try to _____, or calm, her upset grandfather.

67. She doesn't want to _____ her grandfather because she believes in respecting her elders.

68. However, they have views that clash, so conflict is going to occur sooner or later: It's _____.

69. The reader will be aware of the honesty, the _____, of the main character.

70. My friends agree that this idea is very _____, that it shows I have talent. One of them recommends that I read a novel by Tony Hillerman, who also uses a Navajo reservation as his setting.

Like Meanings

Directions. For each item below, circle the letter of the choice that means the same, or about the same, as the boldface word. *(1 point each)*

71. careful **diction**
- (A) choices
- (B) language
- (C) handwriting
- (D) plans

72. to make a **calculation**
- (A) estimate
- (B) discovery of wrongdoing
- (C) list
- (D) costly mistake

73. a **gnarled** hand
- (A) broken
- (B) dirty
- (C) friendly
- (D) twisted

74. a large **menagerie**
- (A) circus tent
- (B) variety of vegetables
- (C) collection of animals
- (D) ethnic restaurant

75. **mutual** interests
- (A) financial
- (B) individual
- (C) shared
- (D) demanding

76. a strange **phenomenon**
- (A) happening
- (B) disaster
- (C) opening
- (D) individual

77. three **consecutive** terms
- (A) following in order
- (B) with time between
- (C) very difficult
- (D) completely unexpected

78. an **insoluble** problem
- (A) mathematical
- (B) difficult
- (C) preventable
- (D) unsolvable

79. the visiting **artisan**
- (A) talented speaker
- (B) famous astronomer
- (C) artistic person
- (D) gifted athlete

80. an **anthology** of modern poetry
- (A) bound volume
- (B) analysis
- (C) collection
- (D) lively discussion

Opposite Meanings

Directions. For each item below, circle the letter of the choice that means the opposite, or about the opposite, of the boldface word. *(1 point each)*

81. to **descend** the stairs
    (A) jump off
    (B) build
    (C) walk down
    (D) climb

82. to **motivate** the class
    (A) discourage
    (B) inspire
    (C) move
    (D) prompt

83. the person's **isolation**
    (A) complete separation
    (B) hospital ward
    (C) nearness to others
    (D) required silence

84. an interesting **revelation**
    (A) information
    (B) coverup
    (C) demonstration
    (D) party

85. a **durable** fabric
    (A) attractive
    (B) strong
    (C) ugly
    (D) weak

86. an **ingenious** approach
    (A) extraordinary
    (B) difficult
    (C) unoriginal
    (D) easy

87. the **omission** of information
    (A) avoidance
    (B) inclusion
    (C) loss
    (D) intention

88. a **valid** complaint
    (A) well-founded
    (B) typical
    (C) false
    (D) well-balanced

89. to **intervene** carefully
    (A) attempt to prevent
    (B) come between
    (C) stay out of
    (D) make clear

90. the **novelty** of the idea
    (A) difference
    (B) newness
    (C) availability
    (D) commonness

Word Analysis

Directions. Read each numbered pair of words below. Then, circle the letter of the choice that best describes the meaning of the underlined prefix or suffix as it is used in each pair. *(1 point each)*

91. <u>multi</u>colored   <u>multi</u>talented
- (A) bright
- (B) against
- (C) many
- (D) before

92. pictur<u>esque</u>   statu<u>esque</u>
- (A) against
- (B) study of
- (C) one who
- (D) like

93. <u>in</u>comparable   <u>in</u>correct
- (A) under
- (B) before
- (C) not
- (D) like

Directions. For each of the following items, circle the letter of the word that correctly completes the sentence. *(1 point each)*

94. The Middle English word *reutheles,* meaning "pitiless," will help you understand the meaning of
- (A) romantic
- (B) ruthless
- (C) restless
- (D) revelation

95. The Latin words *in* for "on" and *citare* for "to urge" will help you understand the meaning of
- (A) inclination
- (B) incite
- (C) inconsiderate
- (D) incident

96. The Latin word *feles,* meaning "cat," will help you understand the meaning of
- (A) catastrophe
- (B) ferocious
- (C) feline
- (D) feasible

Multimeaning

Directions. Read each numbered sentence below. Then, circle the letter of the choice that uses the boldface word in the same way it is used in the numbered sentence. *(1 point each)*

97. Within the Iroquois Confederacy, a group of people would elect a **delegate** to represent them at meetings.
  (A) Leaders of the Confederacy would sometimes **delegate** their authority to younger individuals.
  (B) Occasionally, the Confederacy would **delegate** a person to make contact with a neighboring nation.
  (C) This individual would function as a **delegate** for the entire Confederacy.
  (D) This person would not be allowed to **delegate** to others this important responsibility.

98. I saw the works of several Hopi artists in a **gallery** in Santa Fe, New Mexico.
  (A) That **gallery** specializes in American Indian art.
  (B) The old house has many long, narrow hallways. You never know what you'll find at the end of one of these **galleries**.
  (C) The **gallery** applauded when Maria Tallchief finished her dance.
  (D) I watched the play about Hopi life from the **gallery**.

99. One of our local artists is **descended** from both the Cherokee and the Iroquois people.
  (A) The stairs **descended** in a spiral.
  (B) As she **descended** the stairs of the concert hall, all eyes followed her movements.
  (C) The crowd **descended** on her as she entered the room. Everyone wanted to greet her.
  (D) She is **descended** from a long line of strong female ancestors.

100. Many students at our school have signed a **petition** that urges the school board to purchase more books about American Indians for the library.
  (A) It is unusual for students at our school to **petition** the school board.
  (B) The **petition** is certainly for a good cause.
  (C) I think that students should have the right to **petition** a school board to spend money in a certain way.
  (D) We all read about our right to **petition** the government in civics class.

USING NEW WORDS ON TESTS

Test 2 ☐ **CONTEXT: Coming to the United States**

Making New Words Your Own   Lessons 11–20
Understanding New Words and Their Uses   Lessons 6–10
Connecting New Words and Patterns   Lessons 6–10
Reading New Words in Context   Lessons 6–10

PART A • My Family Tree
Context Clues

Directions. From the list below, choose the word that best completes the sentence. Write the word in the blank. You will use each word only once. (*1 point each*)

acceptance	fraudulent	morale	refuge
accommodations	haven	multitude	resolute
anxiety	hospitable	nationalities	thrifty
aristocrat	immigrated	optimism	thrive
exaggeration	impulsive	persistent	urban

1. When I looked at my family tree, I realized I had a(n) _____ of cultures and heritages in my family. Like many U.S. citizens, I seem to have come from everywhere!

2. I can name at least twelve different _____—from English to Italian—that make up my heritage.

3. One of my ancestors on my mother's side, William Trent, was quite a(n) _____: He was the youngest son of an English duke. He came to North Carolina in the late 1600s.

4. There he met Catherine DuBois, who had left France to seek _____ from religious persecution.

5. Family legend has it that William Trent met Catherine DuBois just after her ship sailed into its _____. They fell in love at first sight, right there at the port.

6. William and Catherine had a son who fell in love with Mary Tenkiller. She finally agreed to marry this _____ young man who was steadfast in his love for her.

7. My father's great-grandfather Enzo _____ to the United States from Sicily with his parents. They came to Boston in the 1890s.

8. They traveled by ship from Italy. The _____ were terrible, and so my great-great-grandfather Enzo had to sleep on the deck.

9. It may be a(n) _____, but family legend has it that he was seasick every day and lost thirty pounds on the voyage!

10. You would think that after such a terrible experience, his _____ would have been low.

11. However, he began his new life with _____. He was sure that life in the United States would be wonderful.

12. In contrast, the woman whom he would marry, Anna, felt some _____ and fear when she first arrived in the United States.

13. She had grown up on a farm in Germany, and her move to the city of Boston, a big _____ center, made her uneasy. Still, she worked hard to adjust.

14. She was _____ in her decision to learn English. She stayed faithful to her goal by learning ten new words each day.

15. Eventually, she found the United States to be a _____ place, but at first she felt very isolated and lonely.

16. She was a rather _____ person. For example, according to family legend, she decided to marry Enzo the moment she saw him.

17. Anna wrote to her family in Germany to tell them that she had married. Then she went to meet her husband's family to ask for their blessing, or, at least, for their _____.

18. At first, his parents accused her of using _____ means to trick their son into marriage.

19. However, they soon grew to love her and to appreciate her hard work and _____ ways with money. Because of her savings plan, she and Enzo were eventually able to open a restaurant.

20. Thanks to Anna's business sense, the restaurant began to _____. In fact, you can still buy strudel and pizza at Enzo and Anna's restaurant downtown!

Like Meanings

Directions. For each item below, circle the letter of the choice that means the same, or about the same, as the boldface word. (*1 point each*)

21. to **boycott** the meeting
- (A) allow students to attend
- (B) refuse to go to
- (C) insist upon going to
- (D) be late for

22. to **deport** oneself properly
- (A) change
- (B) remove
- (C) treat
- (D) behave

23. suffering from **malnutrition**
- (A) poor nourishment
- (B) great sadness
- (C) a minor illness
- (D) poor health

24. to **prosecute** the goal
- (A) pursue
- (B) understand
- (C) support
- (D) ignore

25. political **propaganda**
- (A) continued attacks
- (B) dishonest politicians
- (C) information
- (D) people

26. a **bankrupt** business
- (A) well-known
- (B) unable to pay debts
- (C) qualified for a bank loan
- (D) well-off

27. to **circulate** the petition
- (A) refuse to sign
- (B) turn in
- (C) pass around
- (D) seriously consider

28. to **intercept** a message
- (A) read
- (B) block
- (C) leave
- (D) carry

29. **liable** for damages
- (A) free of responsibility
- (B) closely inspected
- (C) likely to cause
- (D) legally responsible

30. to **presume** to be true
- (A) accept
- (B) doubt
- (C) pretend
- (D) argue

Opposite Meanings

Directions. For each item below, circle the letter of the choice that means the opposite, or about the opposite, of the boldface word. (*1 point each*)

31. a **boisterous** child
(A) female
(B) male
(C) loud
(D) calm

32. a **dilapidated** building
(A) run-down
(B) very tall
(C) out-of-date
(D) well-kept

33. the **premiere** showing
(A) last
(B) first
(C) second
(D) famous

34. a **braggart** manner
(A) rude
(B) overbearing
(C) modest
(D) boastful

35. a worthwhile **exertion**
(A) relaxation
(B) exercise
(C) effort
(D) accomplishment

36. an **inconsiderate** remark
(A) thoughtless
(B) careless
(C) thoughtful
(D) smart

37. a **negligent** approach
(A) interesting
(B) difficult
(C) negative
(D) careful

38. a **spacious** home
(A) large
(B) unfriendly
(C) cramped
(D) expensive

39. to **dismantle** the bicycle
(A) fall off
(B) refuse to ride
(C) take apart
(D) put together

40. an **elegant** chair
(A) crude
(B) ornate
(C) small
(D) large

Word Analysis

Directions. Read each numbered pair of words below. Then, circle the letter of the choice that best describes the meaning of the underlined prefix or suffix as it is used in each pair. (*1 point each*)

41. acess<u>ible</u>   afford<u>able</u>
   (A) theory of
   (B) opposite of
   (C) capable of being
   (D) subject to

42. <u>circum</u>navigate   <u>circum</u>ference
   (A) two
   (B) around
   (C) with
   (D) through the middle

43. riot<u>ous</u>   miracul<u>ous</u>
   (A) away from
   (B) state of being
   (C) belonging to
   (D) characterized by

Directions. For each of the following items, circle the letter of the word that correctly completes the sentence. (*1 point each*)

44. The Latin word *sedare*, meaning "to settle," will help you understand the meaning of
   (A) saturate
   (B) censorship
   (C) sedate
   (D) pleasantry

45. The Greek word *deka*, meaning "ten," will help you understand the meaning of
   (A) delegate
   (B) decade
   (C) dispense
   (D) dedicate

46. The Latin word *regere*, meaning "to rule," will help you understand the meaning of
   (A) recuperate
   (B) aroma
   (C) regime
   (D) resolve

Multimeaning

Directions. Read each numbered sentence below. Then, circle the letter of the choice that uses the boldface word in the same way it is used in the numbered sentence. (*1 point each*)

47. Because they were married during the Great Depression, my father's grandparents had to **dispense** with a honeymoon.
    (A) My great-grandmother Carmen would always **dispense** advice to the customers when she worked in the restaurant.
    (B) Her grandson Henry, my father, never wanted to be in the restaurant business. He wanted to **dispense** the law, and so he became a police officer.
    (C) My aunt Elena became a pharmacist. Her job is to **dispense** prescriptions.
    (D) During World War II, the family had to **dispense** with their plans to remodel the restaurant. There were not enough building materials available.

48. Spanish was Carmen's first language, but she realized that it was **imperative** to learn to speak English well.
    (A) Carmen always had trouble with the **imperative** form in English.
    (B) Carmen's mother-in-law, Anna, was an **imperative** presence around the restaurant—no one questioned her authority.
    (C) Anna issued one **imperative** after another to her new daughter-in-law.
    (D) Carmen knew that it was **imperative** that the two of them get along well.

49. Carmen's father did not want Carmen to **impose** upon, or take advantage of, her new family.
    (A) Instead, her mother-in-law, Anna, worried that customers would **impose** upon Carmen's good nature.
    (B) Anna tended to **impose** quite a few rules regarding the business, and no one dared to break them.
    (C) Carmen, however, was able to **impose** some changes of her own.
    (D) Carmen once tried to **impose** salami on a customer who had asked for prosciutto. Anna was furious when she found out about it.

50. Germany seems a very **remote** place to me.
    (A) Many of my **remote** ancestors came from Germany.
    (B) Great-great-grandmother Anna always became **remote** and a little cool when she was asked about her father's family.
    (C) We have always thought there was a **remote** chance that they were horse thieves.
    (D) How did she ever find the courage to come to a country so **remote** from her family and friends?

PART B • Making It in a New World
Context Clues

Directions. From the list below, choose the word that best completes the sentence. Write the word in the blank. You will use each word only once. (*1 point each*)

adept	embarrassed	marooned	privilege
aroma	gracious	memento	provision
burly	grieve	naturalization	recuperate
diminish	humidity	notified	rigid
dingy	jubilation	predicament	saturated

51. When my great-grandmother Esther left the Polish city of Krakow, her family made a(n) _____, or arrangement, for her to live with her uncle's family in Pennsylvania.

52. However, her uncle lived on a farm, and my great-grandmother felt as if she were _____ in the isolated countryside.

53. Once, on a trip to Pittsburgh, she met a husky, or _____, steelworker named Karl, who gave her directions when she was lost.

54. They began to write letters to one another. Finally, Karl _____, or informed, Esther's uncle that he wanted to marry Esther.

55. Her uncle had some rather _____ ideas about the man his niece should marry, but his feelings softened after meeting Karl.

56. Esther's uncle soon realized that beneath Karl's rough exterior was a very _____ person, and he was pleased to welcome such a refined young man into the family.

57. There was great _____ when he gave his blessing to the young couple; everyone rejoiced.

58. Esther did _____ a little because her mother would not be able to travel from Poland to attend the wedding, but she kept her spirits up by making her own wedding dress.

59. Two of Esther's daughters and three of her granddaughters wore that dress at their weddings, but now all that is left is a piece of lace that my mother keeps as a(n) _____.

60. When my great-grandfather Karl first immigrated to Pittsburgh from Norway, he was bothered by the heat and _____. In Norway the weather was not so hot and sticky.

61. Karl would go out to look for work early in the mornings, and by noon his clothes were _____, or soaked, with sweat.

62. My great-grandfather had many skills, but he was especially _____ at carpentry.

63. He had come to the United States with enough money to last three months if nothing went wrong; unfortunately, he soon found himself in a terrible _____.

64. He became ill with a fever, and it took him several weeks to _____ and be well enough to return to his job.

65. Soon he was almost out of money, and he had to leave his bright, clean boarding-house, and move to a(n) _____ room on Ohio Street.

66. At first, he missed the _____ of his former landlady's good cooking. Soon things became even worse, for he had no money with which to buy food, and he began to miss the smell of any food at all!

67. Asking to work for food _____ him. He had never before felt such shame.

68. However, his situation didn't _____ his enthusiasm for life in his new country; he had as much good feeling as ever.

69. Soon he was making plans to acquire his _____. He now knew he could make it in the United States and wanted to do it as a citizen.

70. He felt lucky to have immigrated to the United States, and he told all his children and grandchildren what a great _____ it is to be born there.

Like Meanings

Directions. For each item below, circle the letter of the choice that means the same, or about the same, as the boldface word. (*1 point each*)

71. the **occupant** of the house
    - (A) location
    - (B) resident
    - (C) vacancy
    - (D) style

72. to **populate** the area
    - (A) to live in
    - (B) to argue with
    - (C) to leave
    - (D) to build a house in

73. to **restrain** one's anger
    - (A) worry about
    - (B) try to overcome
    - (C) feel deeply
    - (D) hold back

74. to place on **probation**
    - (A) an examining table
    - (B) a period of freedom
    - (C) a period of trial
    - (D) rigid restrictions

75. to **evacuate** the building
    - (A) enter
    - (B) destroy
    - (C) leave
    - (D) remodel

76. an **arrogant** attitude
    - (A) haughty
    - (B) insincere
    - (C) friendly
    - (D) unwilling

77. to engage in **pleasantries**
    - (A) polite remarks
    - (B) a pleasant activity
    - (C) baked goods
    - (D) gift giving

78. to **dissect** the speech
    - (A) ignore
    - (B) publish
    - (C) repeat
    - (D) analyze

79. pain of great **intensity**
    - (A) disaster
    - (B) darkness
    - (C) degree
    - (D) need

80. to **depose** the king
    - (A) resemble
    - (B) support
    - (C) remove
    - (D) flatter

Opposite Meanings

Directions. For each item below, circle the letter of the choice that means the opposite, or about the opposite, of the boldface word. *(1 point each)*

81. a **haughty** spirit

(A) proud
(B) ghostly
(C) tall
(D) humble

82. to feel **remorse**

(A) pride
(B) guilt
(C) deeply
(D) prepared

83. to **liberate** the birds

(A) feed
(B) escape
(C) capture
(D) free

84. to **humiliate** her opponent

(A) embarrass
(B) praise
(C) humble
(D) include

85. to **jeopardize** the friendship

(A) understand
(B) begin
(C) risk
(D) protect

86. **dedicated** to the cause

(A) pledged
(B) lost
(C) disloyal
(D) important

87. occurring with **frequency**

(A) excessive kindness
(B) not often
(C) great speed
(D) extreme boredom

88. a **manageable** amount

(A) unusual
(B) ordinary
(C) uncontrollable
(D) controllable

89. to **verify** the story

(A) confirm
(B) deny
(C) tell
(D) discuss

90. in the midst of the **tumult**

(A) calm
(B) storm
(C) pavement
(D) lawn

Word Analysis

Directions. Read each numbered pair of words below. Then, circle the letter of the choice that best describes the meaning of the underlined prefix or suffix as it is used in each pair. *(1 point each)*

91. <u>dis</u>agreeable   <u>dis</u>like
   (A) in
   (B) between
   (C) not
   (D) among

92. <u>pre</u>arrange   <u>pre</u>pay
   (A) between
   (B) under
   (C) against
   (D) before

93. censor<u>ship</u>   owner<u>ship</u>
   (A) one who
   (B) full of
   (C) state of being
   (D) like

Directions. For each of the following items, circle the letter of the word that correctly completes the sentence. *(1 point each)*

94. The Latin word *fames*, meaning "hunger," will help you understand the meaning of
   (A) nourish
   (B) famine
   (C) malnutrition
   (D) frequency

95. The Latin word *migrare*, meaning "to move," will help you understand the meaning of
   (A) circumnavigate
   (B) evacuate
   (C) imperative
   (D) emigrate

96. The Greek word *monos*, meaning "single," will help you understand the meaning of
   (A) maroon
   (B) manageable
   (C) monopoly
   (D) aroma

Multimeaning

Directions. Read each numbered sentence below. Then, circle the letter of the choice that uses the boldface word in the same way it is used in the numbered sentence. *(1 point each)*

97. My great-grandfather Karl's **capital** strength was his optimism.
    (A) He wished he had enough **capital** to open his own business.
    (B) In his eyes, giving up was the **capital** weakness.
    (C) Once he was mistaken for a man who had committed a **capital** crime.
    (D) Here's a picture taken of him in the state **capital**.

98. My great-grandmother Esther was a very talented person. She could cut, **baste,** and sew her own clothes.
    (A) She was also an excellent cook. Grandmother Marie told me how her mother would **baste** a turkey and cook it to perfection.
    (B) Once, my grandmother actually dropped a holiday turkey on the floor! But her mother did not **baste** her; she just sighed and rolled her eyes.
    (C) Great-grandmother Esther taught my grandmother all sorts of things—everything from how to **baste** a hem to how to fix a car!
    (D) My grandmother says the most important thing she learned from her mother was to be patient and kind, and to never **baste** anyone for his or her mistakes.

99. My great-grandparents weathered some hardships, but they never let tough times **hamper** them.
    (A) Daily chores occupied most of Esther's time. In the days before she had a washing machine, a **hamper** of clothes was a whole day's work for her.
    (B) Great-grandfather Karl valued education and often lectured his children not to let anything **hamper** their studies.
    (C) Occasionally, he and Esther would find time to enjoy themselves and take the children and a picnic **hamper** to the park.
    (D) Even when money was tight, the family always had warm clothes and plenty of potatoes in the **hamper**.

100. Esther had not had **access** to higher education in Poland; only wealthy families sent their children to the university.
    (A) She wanted to be sure that her children had **access** to all that public education in the United States offered.
    (B) As her ship made its **access** to New York harbor, she made a vow to the Statue of Liberty.
    (C) In an **access** of emotion, she swore that any children she bore would have a good life.
    (D) Now that information can be stored on computerized databases, it may be easier for people to **access** information about their own family histories at city halls and libraries.

USING NEW WORDS ON TESTS

Test 3 | CONTEXT: Voices of the United States

Making New Words Your Own   Lessons 21–30
Understanding New Words and Their Uses   Lessons 11–15
Connecting New Words and Patterns   Lessons 11–15
Reading New Words in Context   Lessons 11–15

PART A • Each Immigrant Has a Story
Context Clues

Directions. From the list below, choose the word that best completes the sentence. Write the word in the blank. You will use each word only once. *(1 point each)*

arrogant	contemporary	emphasize	literal
articulate	demolished	extensive	modify
category	dilute	fictitious	quaint
climax	distraction	indelible	superficial
condemn	eccentric	intrigued	unique

1. Many immigrants have written poems and short stories that _____ their experiences, while others have expressed themselves by painting.

2. Hollywood has explored immigrant issues from its earliest days to _____ times.

3. *Hester Street*, a 1975 film, tells the story of a young Jewish woman who makes the trip across the Atlantic Ocean in the early 1900s to join her husband. The woman's husband has become acclimated to life in the United States, and he sees his wife's ways as _____, or old-fashioned.

4. The story reaches its _____—the point of highest tension—when the woman feels she must choose between her husband and her heritage.

5. Many audiences have been _____ by the 1983 video *Ellis Island*, in which the ordeal of immigration is expressed in a fascinating dance.

6. Some films about immigrants and their experiences have been quite _____; they do not explore the issue in depth.

7. However, we shouldn't _____ these films completely, for many of them are very entertaining.

8. Still, such films do not usually make a(n) _____ impression on us; we are likely to forget them shortly after we see them.

9. Many Hollywood filmmakers are the children or grandchildren of immigrants. They have made _____ use of their background in their films. In fact, some filmmakers make reference to the immigrant experience in every one of their films.

10. It is not that they are _____ about their ancestors' experiences; they are deservedly proud of the sacrifices these people made for them and want to make the immigrant experience known.

11. Of course, the characters in their movies are often _____, but their experiences are drawn from real life.

12. Each immigrant's experience is _____; no one else's is exactly like it. But many people can identify with the experiences of the characters on the screen.

13. Even serious films about the immigrant experience are likely to have comic touches. For example, a character who is just learning English becomes confused because of a _____ interpretation of a figure of speech like "She kicked the bucket."

14. Sometimes a character's customs seem strange, or _____, to the grandchildren, who may poke fun at their grandparent.

15. One _____ of art that we have not mentioned is U.S. musical theater. This class of theater has been successful in dealing with the immigrant experience.

16. The musical *Flower Drum Song* explores how Chinese immigrants _____ their culture, changing it to fit in with life in San Francisco.

17. The songs and dances of the musical *West Side Story* do not _____ the impact of the story of Puerto Ricans in New York City; in fact, they strengthen it.

18. A movie about immigrants may include an elderly grandparent who considers U.S. popular culture to be a silly _____, one that causes young people to forget their own heritage.

19. Films may examine the reasons that immigrants leave their homeland; for example, people may leave when their village is _____ and their homes destroyed during a war.

20. Some directors have chosen to _____ the positive aspects of coming to the United States, while others focus on the negative.

Like Meanings

Directions. For each item below, circle the letter of the choice that means the same, or about the same, as the boldface word. *(1 point each)*

21. to **blockade** the port
    (A) search within
    (B) close off
    (C) move around
    (D) enter forcefully

22. the discovery of **antibiotics**
    (A) double agents in United States government
    (B) hidden treasures
    (C) serious illnesses
    (D) medicines that fight infection

23. an efficient **automaton**
    (A) robot
    (B) can opener
    (C) vending machine
    (D) dishwasher

24. to **commute** between towns
    (A) go back and forth
    (B) send mail
    (C) openly communicate
    (D) change jobs

25. to **derive** happiness from it
    (A) wish
    (B) encourage
    (C) get
    (D) remove

26. a professional **diplomat**
    (A) doer of good deeds
    (B) government representative
    (C) expert witness
    (D) legal representative

27. to **endorse** the position
    (A) disagree with
    (B) enter into
    (C) approve of
    (D) try to resolve

28. an interesting **hypothesis**
    (A) choice of solutions
    (B) unproven theory
    (C) large, furry animal
    (D) proven theory

29. to **confiscate** the plane
    (A) unload
    (B) purchase
    (C) borrow
    (D) seize

30. a strange **occurrence**
    (A) incident
    (B) adventure
    (C) person
    (D) tale

Opposite Meanings

Directions. For each item below, circle the letter of the choice that means the opposite, or about the opposite, of the boldface word. *(1 point each)*

31. the **intolerance** of the mob
   (A) prejudice
   (B) unacceptance
   (C) racism
   (D) understanding

32. to **activate** the machine
   (A) turn off
   (B) start repeatedly
   (C) put together
   (D) break down

33. **invariable** habits
   (A) ever-changing
   (B) well-formed
   (C) never-changing
   (D) good-natured

34. the **successor** to the presidency
   (A) the person who always succeeds
   (B) the person who always fails
   (C) the person who came before
   (D) the person who came after

35. at the **summit** of the mountain
   (A) foot
   (B) top
   (C) face
   (D) side

36. a **famished** person
   (A) famous
   (B) well-known
   (C) well-fed
   (D) starving

37. told in **fragments**
   (A) incomplete sentences
   (B) another language
   (C) small pieces
   (D) an unbroken unit

38. to **detach** the hose
   (A) use
   (B) ignore
   (C) unhook
   (D) attach

39. a friendly **salutation**
   (A) civilian
   (B) soldier
   (C) greeting
   (D) farewell

40. a **considerate** person
   (A) thoughtless
   (B) polite
   (C) silly
   (D) serious

Word Analysis

Directions. Read each numbered pair of words below. Then, circle the letter of the choice that best describes the meaning of the underlined prefix or suffix as it is used in each pair. *(1 point each)*

41. <u>fore</u>word   <u>fore</u>sight
  (A) against
  (B) before
  (C) from
  (D) with

42. tempera<u>ment</u>   judg<u>ment</u>
  (A) against
  (B) state of
  (C) like
  (D) result of

43. charit<u>able</u>   honor<u>able</u>
  (A) cause to be
  (B) like
  (C) becoming
  (D) capable of being

Directions. For each of the following items, circle the letter of the word that correctly completes the sentence. *(1 point each)*

44. The Latin word *clarus*, meaning "clear," will help you understand the meaning of
  (A) climax
  (B) colossal
  (C) clarify
  (D) transparent

45. The Latin word *obire*, meaning "die," will help you understand the meaning of
  (A) obsolete
  (B) obituary
  (C) descendant
  (D) fatal

46. The Greek word *sarkazein*, meaning "to tear flesh like dogs," or "to speak bitterly," will help you understand the meaning of
  (A) distraction
  (B) dispatch
  (C) sarcasm
  (D) satire

Multimeaning

Directions. Read each numbered sentence below. Then, circle the letter of the choice that uses the boldface word in the same way it is used in the numbered sentence. *(1 point each)*

47. Hannah had little money when she arrived in the United States, so she always bought clothing in **neutral** colors. That way everything would match with everything else.
    - (A) Her co-workers in the factory often quarreled, but she tried to remain **neutral**.
    - (B) She even spoke in a **neutral** way, always indefinite about her real feelings.
    - (C) One day, a heated argument broke out because a machine that was supposed to be running at full speed had been left in **neutral**.
    - (D) Her room in the boardinghouse was painted in the same **neutral** tones that she chose for her clothing.

48. She wished that the tree did not **obscure** the view from her window.
    - (A) She came from a village in an **obscure** part of Poland.
    - (B) Her father was an **obscure** poet.
    - (C) She spoke several **obscure** languages fluently.
    - (D) Her talent as a writer would soon **obscure** her poverty.

49. Poverty did not **quench** her enthusiasm for learning.
    - (A) Before going to bed on a winter's evening, she would **quench** the fire in the grate.
    - (B) She read until midnight every night, but this did not **quench** her appetite for reading.
    - (C) She would read so intently that she wouldn't put her book down even to **quench** her thirst.
    - (D) She often worried about her brother. He worked at a dangerous job at the steel factory where he would **quench** hot steel by plunging it into water.

50. She wrote with efficiency and **dispatch**.
    - (A) She sent a **dispatch** to her aunt in Poland, but her aunt never received the message.
    - (B) She was writing a novel about a woman who decides to **dispatch** her rival.
    - (C) The character handles the situation with **dispatch**, in spite of the fact that she is frightened and upset.
    - (D) The doctors **dispatch** an ambulance, but it is too late.

PART B • Telling My Family's Story
Context Clues

Directions. From the list below, choose the word that best completes the sentence. Write the word in the blank. You will use each word only once. *(1 point each)*

agenda	erosion	inclination	sable
colossal	essay	miscellaneous	satire
confide	falter	pewter	secluded
deduction	generated	pious	tangible
denial	imply	proposal	testify

51. I have many things on my _____ for the day, but first on the list is to do my English assignment.

52. I'm writing a(n) _____ for my English class. I'm supposed to consider my topic seriously and then write about it.

53. I need to narrow my topic because my prewriting activities have _____ too much material. It seems as if I've produced enough information to stock a library!

54. I have all sorts of varied, _____ details and information about many of my ancestors.

55. When I first suggested to my teacher that I write about my family history, she didn't like my _____.

56. Even when my teacher said the topic was too big, my enthusiasm didn't _____; I was determined to succeed.

57. I now have _____, concrete proof that my teacher was right—I have enough notes to write a book!

58. I can certainly _____ to the fact that my topic is too broad—my lack of a focused subject proves it.

59. I suppose I could write a complete family history, but I'd have to do years of research. I don't have any _____ to tackle such a big project. Instead, I'd prefer to focus on a branch of my family.

60. I started out with so much enthusiasm, but now I feel the process of _____ having its effect on my project; my excitement is rapidly wearing away.

61. I don't mean to _____ that I don't want to write the paper; I still intend to do it, but I don't know how to go about it.

62. I decided to _____ my problem to my mother; I always trust her to give good advice. She suggested that I narrow my topic by focusing on my grand-parents.

63. She suggested I write about when they took me on tour of the _____ statue that towers above New York Harbor, the Statue of Liberty.

64. I could also write about my ancestor who was a silversmith; she made candlesticks from silver and from _____, which is made up of many metals.

65. I could write about my great-great-grandmother. She was a _____ woman—a devout Christian—who fled her country to escape religious persecution.

66. My great-aunt is another interesting member of my family. She is an animal-rights activist who wears a fake _____ coat because she doesn't believe in killing animals for their fur.

67. Then there's my great-great-uncle who was falsely accused of a crime in the old country. He fled because no one believed his _____ of involvement in the crime.

68. He moved to an isolated, _____ farm in Washington where he felt he wouldn't be found.

69. Using a false name, he drew political cartoons and wrote political _____ to criticize governments that mistreat their citizens.

70. Maybe I'll write about all of these people! I wonder if there will be a _____ from my score if I turn the paper in late.

© Houghton Mifflin Harcourt Publishing Company

Like Meanings

Directions. For each item below, circle the letter of the choice that means the same, or about the same, as the boldface word. *(1 point each)*

71. a silly **pun**
  (A) childish prank
  (B) play on words
  (C) circus clown
  (D) mischievous child

72. to increase the **tariff**
  (A) tax
  (B) weight
  (C) amount
  (D) profits

73. with a five-year **warranty**
  (A) loan
  (B) degree
  (C) arrest
  (D) guarantee

74. a new **technology**
  (A) building technique
  (B) business know-how
  (C) application of science
  (D) kind of evidence

75. to become a **braggart**
  (A) helper
  (B) bully
  (C) show-off
  (D) do-gooder

76. a **photogenic** gorilla
  (A) suitable for photographing
  (B) unsuitable for photographing
  (C) shown in the photograph
  (D) not shown in the photograph

77. a visit to the **planetarium**
  (A) place for viewing celestial images
  (B) informal restaurant
  (C) government office building
  (D) state-owned opera house

78. a small **rebate**
  (A) tax
  (B) disagreement
  (C) price
  (D) refund

79. rate of **respiration**
  (A) blood pressure
  (B) heartbeat
  (C) breathing
  (D) calorie burning

80. to **tarnish** one's reputation
  (A) forget
  (B) make
  (C) polish
  (D) disgrace

Opposite Meanings

Directions. For each item below, circle the letter of the choice that means the opposite, or about the opposite, of the boldface word. *(1 point each)*

81. a **synthetic** fabric
   (A) expensive
   (B) inexpensive
   (C) artificial
   (D) natural

82. to **upbraid** the employee
   (A) praise
   (B) blame
   (C) scold
   (D) dismiss

83. to **congest** the halls
   (A) clean
   (B) soil
   (C) empty
   (D) overcrowd

84. a **parasitic** personality
   (A) dependent
   (B) irritating
   (C) interesting
   (D) independent

85. to **irk** the neighbor
   (A) harass
   (B) bother
   (C) annoy
   (D) please

86. an **apt** student
   (A) clever
   (B) intelligent
   (C) average
   (D) bright

87. a **petty** matter
   (A) inexpensive
   (B) important
   (C) expensive
   (D) unimportant

88. an **eligible** contestant
   (A) elderly
   (B) qualified
   (C) unqualified
   (D) young

89. to **improvise** a speech
   (A) deliver without preparation
   (B) carefully plan
   (C) improve upon
   (D) publicly disapprove of

90. an **urgent** message
   (A) unimportant
   (B) outdated
   (C) confusing
   (D) secret

Word Analysis

Directions. Read each numbered pair of words below. Then, circle the letter of the choice that best describes the meaning of the underlined prefix or suffix as it is used in each pair. *(1 point each)*

91. <u>aero</u>nautics   <u>aero</u>space
 (A) around
 (B) against
 (C) air
 (D) twice

92. <u>mal</u>function   <u>mal</u>formed
 (A) between
 (B) away
 (C) to
 (D) bad

93. hydraul<u>ic</u>   dramat<u>ic</u>
 (A) against
 (B) to do or make
 (C) pertaining to
 (D) belief

Directions. For each of the following items, circle the letter of the word that correctly completes the sentence. *(1 point each)*

94. The Greek word *onyma,* meaning "name," will help you understand the meaning of
 (A) obscure
 (B) anonymous
 (C) omission
 (D) erosion

95. The Greek word *therepeuein,* meaning "to nurse or cure," will help you understand the meaning of
 (A) respiration
 (B) technology
 (C) synthetic
 (D) therapy

96. The Latin word *primus,* meaning "first," will help you understand the meaning of
 (A) pious
 (B) parasitic
 (C) premier
 (D) respiration

Multimeaning

Directions. Read each numbered sentence below. Then, circle the letter of the choice that uses the boldface word in the same way it is used in the numbered sentence. *(1 point each)*

97. The woman from Ethiopia had an **aspiration** to be a great singer.
  (A) The **aspiration** of dust into her throat made her cough.
  (B) The doctor used **aspiration** to remove the foreign matter from her mouth.
  (C) Because of her throat injury, she started having trouble pronouncing some sounds that required **aspiration**.
  (D) Medical problems were preventing her from achieving her **aspiration**.

98. Many of her fellow immigrants were anxious about life in the United States, but she had a **casual** attitude.
  (A) She could only find **casual** work, but that suited her fine.
  (B) She had many **casual** acquaintances but only a few good friends.
  (C) Sometimes they paid her **casual** visits.
  (D) Overall, she was very **casual** in her approach to life. She felt the best strategy was to remain relaxed.

99. The lamp **illuminated** the room where the Herstowskis gathered for their first Christmas in the United States.
  (A) On the wall was a copy of a religious manuscript that had been **illuminated** with beautiful colors by monks.
  (B) Mr. Herstowski explained and **illuminated** the pictures on the borders of the pages.
  (C) A Christmas tree, **illuminated** with artificial candles, stood in the corner of the room.
  (D) Mr. Herstowski said that he had visited an expert and had been **illuminated** about the making of the manuscript.

100. The immigration official **dictated** a letter.
  (A) He said he would do what his conscience **dictated**.
  (B) He didn't care if the law **dictated** that the young man should be returned to his native country.
  (C) He took the message that the lawyer **dictated** over the phone.
  (D) He **dictated** that his staff should help the immigrant.

NOTES

NOTES

NOTES

NOTES

NOTES

NOTES